Carlo Terpolilli

UNBORN ARCHITECTU

Ipostudio projects 1983–2023

FORMA

INDEX

Jottings

Thoughts swarm the body
and move the hand;
a mark, a line,
black ink drenching the page,
overflowing like a river in flood.
A drawing;
suspensions, arabesques and fragments,
curved lines, broken lines,
dashes, unexplored geometries
and shapes appear,
meaningless words
and worlds, countries,
unexplored territories.
Then, suddenly, it evaporates,
the flow dries up!
And it is then, only then,
that a strange, unholy
personal hieroglyphic reveals itself.

Venice, September 10, 2002

Unborn architecture. An archive of projects that never saw the light. An inventory of architectural projects that will never see the light. Not projects drafted, not aborted works, that is, not unsuccessful or unfinished projects, not stillborn, but at least born in the sense of "being", though, for different reasons, not intentionally, locked away in drawers, in the obscurity of file cabinets, at times lost from memory. Some never had any chance whatsoever, from the outset, others were actually starting to be. Some were stopped, for various reasons, some known, some comprehensible, but for many, the reasons appear obscure and senseless.

Works that were never born, that would have wanted to be there where they were imagined. Now, years later, it becomes necessary to give them another chance. There is a desire to bring them up from the basements, to awaken them from sleep, to bring them out into light and make them public and, in some, certainly relative way, to restore them to a new life.

Works that never saw the light, but that are closely tied to particular cities: some experienced daily, others only visited and many more only imagined. The works and the cities, forever linked, to the point that, in our memory and in our archive, every project is identified, beyond its specific character, above all by the name of the city where it was meant to have been born. As for each of us, with our birthplace!

> "Architecture is the learned game, correct and magnificent, of forms assembled in the light."

For Le Corbusier, light seems to have been – and probably was – the essential and sufficient precondition to speak of Architecture. We are aware of this, but the love we have for our work, for those unborn children, makes us imagine and, above all, think that they really have come to light and live in the cities where we imagined them, at least in our mind. Many of our projects were completed, the project fully ready to be built; others, on the contrary, were just getting started; some were no more than ideas. Many of these projects, even now, could be built, could effectively be brought into the world in the very place where they were imagined. No! Sadly, this is not possible: an architectural project, even one that has achieved a certain stage of completion, is always born "here and now", unless it is a model for replication, perhaps at the initial stage of a bud or seedling.

A project is closely related to time and space, it is born intrinsically connected, it exists in that place and in that time. Sometimes, particular conditions of function or location bring a project to mind, and one thinks of resurrecting it and trying it again, in that other place. We may have started out with the desire to acknowledge the value of that project and give it another chance but, due to some strange mechanism, inexorably and naturally, we found that it was necessary to adapt it a little, to make some adjustment, and a slight rearrangement that, in effect, modified and even completely altered its very essence, its nature. It was not mimetic desire (guilt feeling) that was acting, nor was it simply intellectual honesty that effectively prevented the presentation of that project, no matter how beloved, just as it had been; there was something else.

The truth is that we are intimately bound to the project that our mind created at *that* time, which was *our* time, that time when we lived with the awareness and knowledge we had then: that singular state, made of moments of exaltation and disappointment, of frustration and excitement. When all this is calmed and we find a peaceful state, when we remove that product of our imagination that was a singular state of balance between desire and representation, that moment, that state of being, can never be repeated.

The truth is that, as in life, we move on, for better or for worse, whether we want to or not, always in a process of becoming; this is true more than ever when we take a project in hand. We are always already projected toward the next time, as toward an event, an opportunity to show that we have already gone beyond, ahead of where we were before. The conditions have changed because we have changed, we are not who we were yesterday and, though we remember, we bring to mind that which is past, and may also experience nostalgia for the time when we produced that work. The desire for other (for that which is not yet) is powerful, because we are convinced that what comes next will be better, more interesting, more fascinating.

Every project, every work, in addition to being a product of its time – that time in history of which every project expresses the prevailing movements and paradigms, acquires its characteristics but also, perhaps, rejects them –, every project, every work reflects a specific time of our existence as men and women. If for no other reason than the physical time that every project requires: hours, days, months and, in some cases, years! And yet, in the meantime, in that time, the life of each of us flows on, things happen and they overlap. For better or for worse, in joy and in sorrow, the singular and collective lives intersect with the events of the stages of production of the work, to the point that each of us, in our memories, makes moments and seasons of our existence coincide with *that* project in *that* time: births, deaths, marriages, christenings, trips, love affairs. Every project could tell or conceal our stories or, as often happens with memories, colour the memory of those moments with exaltation or regret.

We cannot escape the constant dialogue with history and with memory, if only because the products of history, the buildings, our models, are mostly all still there, in front of us, and we interrogate them constantly, trying to determine what they mean.

We never start from zero. There is, in our work, constant research and a critical reinterpretation of the theoretical bases of modern culture.

History – and the collective memory – are not like a wardrobe that we open to select the right outfit to wear for the occasion, but are the place in our mind where we store pictures, ideas, facts, models we are constantly renewing and recombining as we incessantly reread them.

We can say that, through the years, re-examining the work produced, we can trace a path of points and lines joined one to another but all circumscribed in a rather clearly defined domain. Putting them in order, imagining solutions to themes that often turn out to be incompatible with one another, never with a specific attitude but always open to discovery: this is the environment within which we can find the deeper meaning of those outlines, of those connections.

Every time is the first time; every beginning is a story that can only be told at the end. The architectural project moves through this intricate interaction between idealizations, the principle of reality, the pleasure principle and, at times, going even beyond the pleasure principle we could concretely say, between scientific, philosophical and technical knowledge, between technology and artistic sensitivity. All this, in a balance that from time to time is sought, constructed and stabilized without any of these elements prevailing. All this happens not a priori, but takes shape and is arrived at little by little over the process of time, a posteriori. A work of architecture is such only at the end, when it is built and occupied, when it becomes part of the landscape and life of the community. It is necessary, however, to be aware of the fact that this state of equilibrium is not always achieved. That this causes frustration and suffering.

The difference between the work of architecture built, that lives in the light, and the unborn work, is that the latter nonetheless exists, in its being in the way that it is part of its Author, who feels its pull. For the others, the difference is obvious, unquestionable, simple: for the mere fact that they live in the reality of the world, they are born and, like all things, can also die; the unborn, however, exist only in the archives of memory.

The built work opens its doors to receive those who will live in it; that is the moment, just as it should be for a child, when the work separates from its Author, takes flight, lives its live, exists, that is, it becomes *itself*, outside of the person who imagined and desired it. That is as it must be! We risk getting too attached to the thing, remaining blocked in that stage; we must, instead, try to work through the loss, to establish a new condition dominated by the pathos of the distance, that method necessary to enable us to grasp both the quality and the critical aspects of the work, to entrust it to the world and then, move on. Like when, one morning, still at work on the final stages of completion of a primary school, the Author is stunned when a flock of chattering children rush in with their backpacks and bookbags, and asks himself what the devil they are doing there: it was simply the First Day of School. From then on, that place, inhabited for months and months by the Author, that place, so thoroughly known, so lovingly attended to, no longer belongs to him. He had been evicted, while the work begins to really live, and thus to exist.

On the contrary, the unborn work remains forever attached to the person who longed for and conceived of it; we are never able to detach ourselves because we refuse to banish it to the darkness, to the shadow of what should have been and was not, because the unborn work does not live in reality. We want to keep it alive because this work was the result of an intense, exhausting labour, but mainly because it was the product of a desire. This condition removes the work from the daily routine, from the times of reality, projecting it into another world, that of memory and nostalgia, where the important and memorable things live.

One case, not the only one, alas, of a work of architecture meant to see the light, and that instead would never be brought into the world, never be built, swallowed by a sort of black hole, lost in time and space.

It happened in May! This was the slogan that designated the project, winner of the competition for the construction of the City of Education at Sarno. And it really was in May, in the year 2000, that we delivered our project. The competition was announced by what was then the provincial government of Salerno as a necessary gesture, a reparation, one could say, for the tragedy that had happened at Sarno when a terrible flood had killed 300 people. That disaster was what had happened in May, on May 5, 1998, to be exact. The slogan was clearly linked to the memory of that date, but was also inspired by a lovely piece of that great repertoire of Neapolitan love longs *Era de maggio*, full of pathos, of hope and love. May was also the month in 1983, when the adventure of Ipostudio began.

The competition was launched with the best of intentions and everything was proceeding smoothly, according to plan. The committee appointed to judge the works was first rate: among others, Mario Botta, Francesco Cellini, Alberto Ferlenga, Benedetto Gravagnuolo, Marino Folin, and the National President of the Architects and Engineers. The first stage of the competition was announced just a year after the disaster, followed by the second stage and, immediately after, the appointment to draft the outline of the project and draw up the executive plans.

From that point on, the timeline began to disintegrate, governments rose and fell, parties and platforms changed. Years went by. The reasons that had led people to think they could build a school complex, nothing less than a City of Education, that would contain all the high schools of the city of Sarno, freeing them, among other things, of the social and economic costs of the community, evaporated. Even the economic resources made available to build the work were swallowed up and detoured by the technical-bureaucratic and political machine and, in the end, had vanished. They had even obtained the building concession, and years later initiated the expropriations.

More time went by, many many years! But our hope of building that work did not die and we remained determinedly optimistic and confident. Indeed, how could our project be if not borne aloft by hope which, as they say, is the last to die.

This story, however, was hard on our morale and affected our attitude. In 2000, the partners of Ipostudio were between 45 and 47 years old. Then came 2005, and 2010 and finally 2013, and by that time we were close to 60! A new administration, after reflecting intently on the state of things and also thanks to our determination and our continuous urging and remembering, decided to resuscitate the work. At long last!

We started out with a first functional section, building just one of the three schools. What mattered, after such a long time, was to start. Before opening the contract bidding, however, it was necessary to revise the project, because in the meantime new technical regulations had been decreed. What happened after that in the contract bidding to select the building belongs to the history of this country-companies no longer qualified, maximum cost cutting, etc., by now deaf and blind to architecture, to what should absolutely be the physical representation of the Common Good, and in the very country that has given such a fundamental contribution to the history of architecture and the relationship between it and the civilization of a community. Let's just say it was a collective suicide!

Almost unnoticed, a ceremony was finally held to lay the cornerstone. It was held so quietly, as if in hopes that the gods wouldn't notice what we were doing, perhaps! It was May 18, 2018, once again May. That extraordinary month, full of hope and promise. Our project was 18 years old by then, all grown up and ready to take off. The project of the City of Education began to come to light, it could show itself to the world, for better or for worse!

But this story did not have a happy ending: that would be too easy. After that first stone the whole thing came to a halt yet again. Why? At this point, it doesn't matter. Knowing the reasons would make no difference. This time, the Author, despite our determination never to abandon the work to the darkness, was forced, perhaps like other times, to surrender and withdraw in as orderly a manner as possible. Against obscure powers one can do nothing! Obscure? Not really, quite well known actually!

One final consideration: aside from the fatigue and sorrow of the Author in not seeing a dream come true, as is the case whenever we develop a project that doesn't get built, there was the loss of a community. However, not building a work of that size and importance, a school, or rather a City of Education, with classrooms, laboratories, gymnasium, library, cafeteria, playing fields is a cruel thing, and shows a lack of sentiment, also as reparation for the tragedy of an entire community, because, if nothing else, the construction of that project could improve its life. The only positive character who comes out of this whole is the chief architect of the province of Salerno at the time, the person who wanted the project and defended it, as long as he could.

We live in pursuit of beauty; it is our mandate but also our obsession. Beauty in architecture is the result of a deception, an artifice! Because it is deceptive.

When we talk about beauty, we are certainly thinking of the shape, the structure, the colours, the physical material of which the thing is made. Beauty is not just harmony or proportion, but also tension, conflict; it is continuous equilibrium among forces that would tend to destroy it, to tear it apart.

The search for beauty is an obsession and a deception because as soon as we think we know what it is, it escapes our definition; because it has to do with the inexpressible. Probably, what we call beauty is an expectation, the wish for a lost balance, the result, indeed, of our own anguish.

Extraordinary things, wonderful things – these are absolute categories, but what is it, then, that we are searching so desperately to find? Something that satisfies us, or the rest of the world, the collectivity? We can acknowledge the question that Mies posed on the subject of the birth of form, that is, it should be understood not as an absolute but as the result of limitations and factors emerging internally or externally to it and which, in a developing process, can give rise, when subjected to unforeseen stresses, to a different form: and yet, after we have acknowledged this, here is the anguish, because we pursue something that is at the mercy of the events, whether desired or merely undergone.

Only someone who has known the anguish of beginning, of the blank page, that grips writer and the architect at the outset of a new project can fully appreciate the wild raving of Calvino in *If on a Winter's Night a Traveller*; or the wavering, and the feeling of identification between "the productive writer and the tormented one" who observe each other from a distance, and each feels envy and, at the same time, admiration for the other: in desperate search for the easier, or happier writing, that can charm the reader. Is that what we are looking for?

The structure of the book is conceived in such a way as to collect, in a few chapters, a number of architectural projects from different epochs, which share certain similarities, conceptual characteristics and common principles, in order to highlight their connections and interactions. Over the years, often, these projects have passed the torch from one to the next.

Building the city in what were its outskirts. It's not just a matter of repairing.

Freeing the land, rising above it. Trying, desperately, to touch the ground at little as possible. Aiming for elevation so that the earth can flow uninterrupted below.

Being part of the continuous movement of the city's growth. Replacement, expansion, addition, ways and shapes whereby the new becomes part of what already existed.

Architecture that reflects in water; those who live near it, on it, around it.

Architecture that is part of and in the earth. Architecture that measures itself against the vastness of the region. Landscape architecture.

Everything happens around a court, whether open or closed

A perennial torment and conflict Between sacred and profane: Churches.

Describing the genesis and development of the process of architectural design is our main intention in writing this book; even the names given to the individual works were rewritten to fit the conceptual framework of the book and evoke the profound, almost literary meaning attributed to them. What can these unborn projects tell us? They have one advantage: they will never be tested against reality, but will forever retain the potential of extraordinary ideas.

Each of them tells a story but, like all stories and historical events, these projects are like the tiles in a great historical mosaic that involves the story of a method, a mode of approaching reality, of a will that unfolds over time, in a lifetime, and over a space as large as that of a vast horizon. However, it is very likely, and we like to think of it so, that every project is a piece of a great puzzle. Each of them in some way should fit in with the others, though it may not be obvious at first glance. The match is not easy to see and sometimes great patience is necessary, as we must wait until part of the design takes shape.

Almost all the projects collected here participated in competitions of architecture at the national and international level. Some won, others were classified among the first, others only mentioned, but most of them received no notice at all, and went nowhere.

To us, however, they always appeared extremely interesting – as they say, every child looks beautiful to its mother –; these were interesting, at the very least, because they were the product of serious, joyful, painful, exhausting labour, but always labour done with passion and devotion to the profession. Each and every time, the effort that we put into framing and developing these projects was enormous, always with the idea that a positive outcome might allow them to see the light.

A somewhat rhetorical question arises, in the long run: just who is the author of these projects of architecture, these unborn works of architecture that never saw the light, that will never see the light? The answer could seem simple and immediate: Ipostudio, but who is Ipostudio? Who is hiding behind this name, this enterprise? Historically, the founding partners and those who later joined them and are still active; but Ipostudio is much more. It is a way of working, a way of being together! It has been, and is, a workshop of craftsmen, in the finest tradition of this city that welcomed us and where we still live and work, our home: Florence. Certainly, at the outset of Ipostudio there is just a beginning – as Massimo Montanari says in his *The Myth of Origins. Brief History of Spaghetti and Tomato Sauce* – but to know its true identity, one has to know the whole story. It is a story of meetings, chance encounters and interminglings.

In all these years, dozens and dozens of people have crossed paths and met, some briefly, some for longer periods. Every work described in this book, every project is indebted, more or less, to work contributed by all those who have come and gone at Ipostudio, working with us or as external consultants. The identity and character of Ipostudio, however, is in a state of constant becoming, never stopping; it is changeable and in constant flux, always in search of one more way to continue to tell stories: our own story.

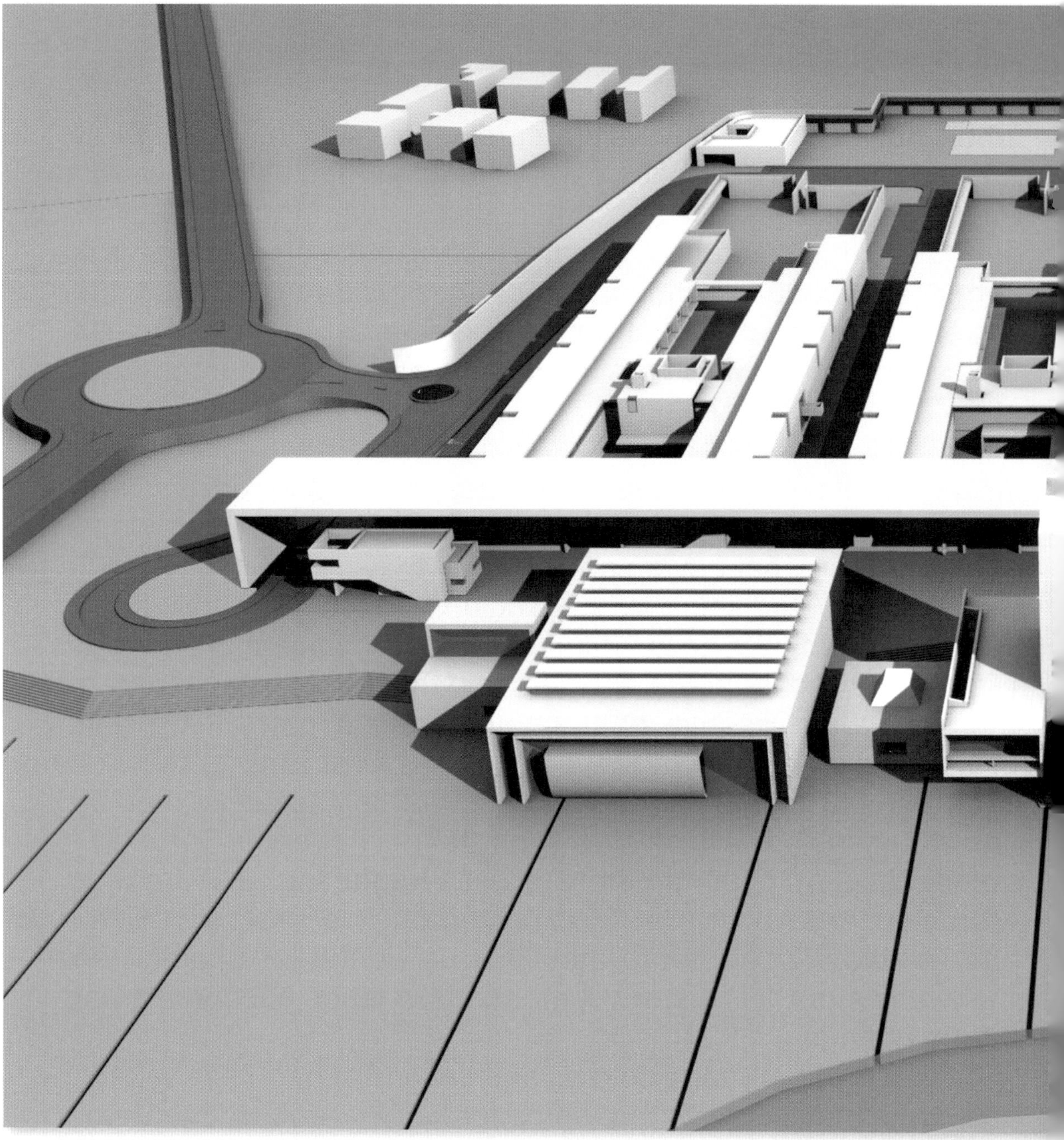

THE CITY OF EDUCATION
School Complex, Sarno (Salerno)
Slogan: *It happened in May*
International competition in two stages, 1st prize, 2000
Client and contracting body: Province of Salerno
Preliminary project, definitive executive 2001-2009
Structures: AEI Progetti srl, Gipieffe Architettura
Systems: Consilium srl
Economic and safety analyses: Michele Dota

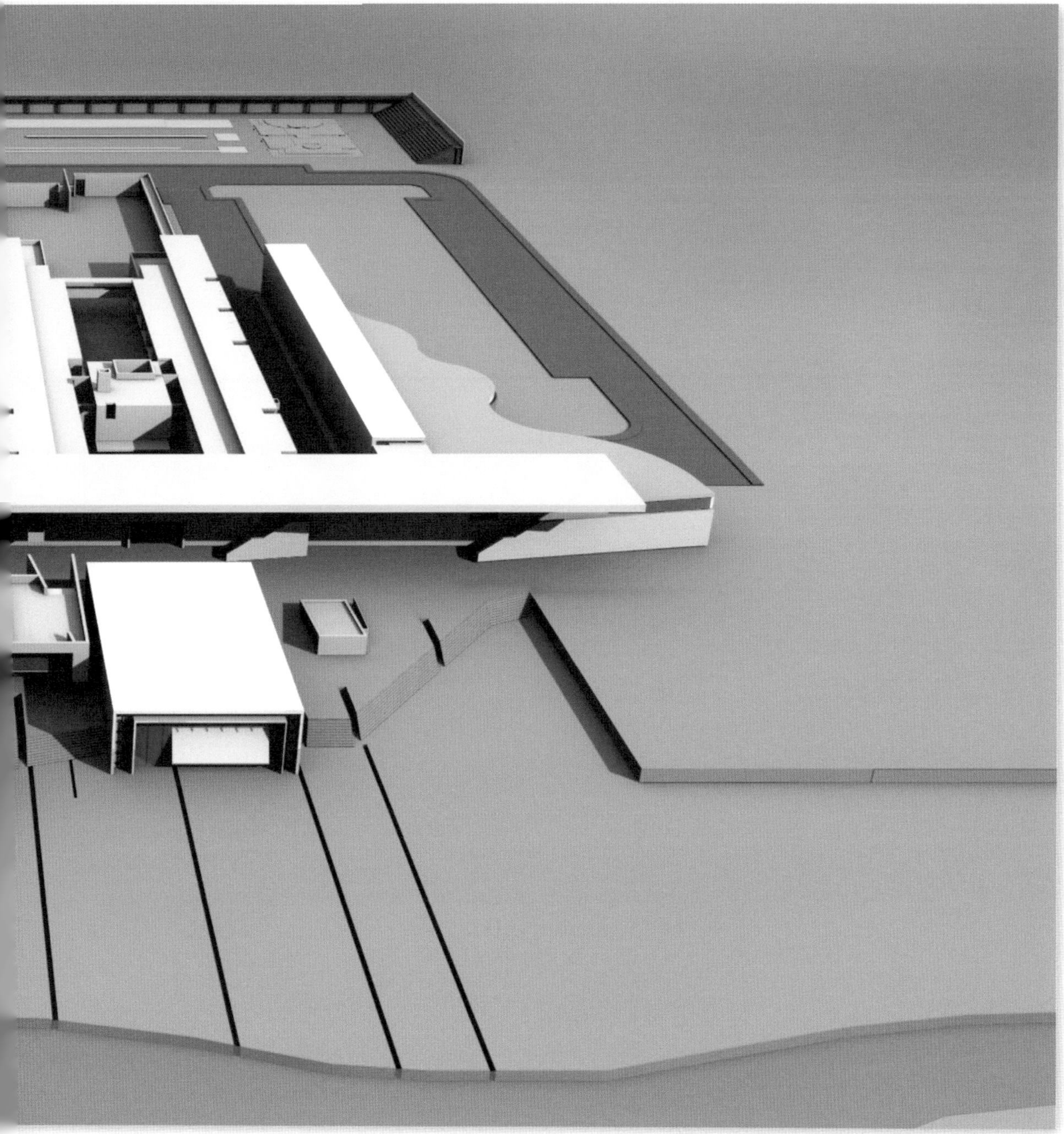

1. Building the city in what were its outskirts. It’s not just a matter of repairing.

Any work of urban redevelopment, of restructuring a building or construction of a new architectural project cannot fail to take account of the surrounding conditions, the morphology of the area, the environment, the types of existing structures. In other words, what Aldo Rossi called *"The Architecture of the City"*.

The parts of a city – or even just a building – live on relationships, internal to the nature of their structure and/or external, due to their position or their role. They are, they exist, in the measure to which they have value, because they are part of a whole and, as part, add value to the whole. Obviously, cities are made of "stone" of solid matter, but also of connections and interactions, of visible and invisible aspects, tangible and intangible elements.

The redevelopment of the urban outskirts is possible only if it has the function of expanding the general characteristics of the city outward toward the periphery. What does that mean? Generally speaking, it involves moving outward what is called a mixture of functions that make life on the outskirts complex and varied. It is not simply a matter, therefore, of providing to the outskirts those social services unavailable to it until now, but of bringing to the area the complexity of all the economic, social and cultural activities typical of a consolidated urban structure. What we are doing, in other words, is creating urban structures where none existed. But this is not enough, if it does not serve to create an urban identity from the architectural standpoint, without which we would never achieve that urban attractiveness that makes the space of human relations so interesting.

Lately, the term most widely used in connection with works on the outskirts is "mending"; an intriguing word, but one that does not clarify what really has to be done to turn the outskirts into a city. Mending is done when there is a fabric; the technical art of mending is to pick up the broken threads of the weave and reconstruct it exactly as it was.

The condition of the urban outskirts, in most cases, is that of structures without a design, without a weave.

Mending, repairing a torn fabric, stitching up a laceration, closing a broken seam, are images that bring to mind caretaking. The affectionate care we have for the things that matter to us. The gesture, the action, the good and right thing, in many urban sites nowadays, hardly seems sufficient. Demolition and replacement are often necessary to restore order to the development of the city.

1.1 EXTENDING THE CITY ALL THE WAY TO THE WATERFRONT
Redevelopment of the waterfront, Messina, 2011

The city block and the structure of the urban fabric are the materials on which this project is based: the continuation of the foundational layout of the city of Messina, extended all the way to the waterfront, an absolute antithesis with the idea of constructing a seafront road or boardwalk. The urban design, while maintaining the graduated height of the gutter line as it approaches the sea, is raised above the soil to leave space for the park and gardens of the coast, and at the same time, mindful of a tragedy, the tidal wave that devastated Messina, it leaves open space, when it happens, if it happens again, for the wave to pass under the houses, without offering more than the slightest resistance.

Making sense, once again, of the coast line free of obstacles, so that this place of transition between land and sea is multiform and changing but otherwise free to acquire the configurations that the changes that time and the conditions of the sea will impose.

At the same time, the action also focuses on restoring freedom of movement to the waterways that empty into the sea. These waterways, some of which are open streams while others are confined to pipelines, cross the city from the mountains to the sea, sometimes reaching flood proportions and causing damage and endangering life. Thus, along the natural line of their outlets along the coast, the project proposes to erect new "Beach Villas", special, paradigmatic topical sites that can control the built property, protect the environment and provide sustainable public places.

This was the profound sense of the urban work: to use this opportunity of developing new construction to make of it a great project focused on ensuring the safety of the city; not through works of hydraulic engineering – not by constraining and regimenting – but by freeing all this through a redesign of the architecture of the city and of the waterfront itself.

(A) The "Beach Villas" and canal system

(B) Birdseye view toward the port of Messina
(C) Rapid elevated transportation system

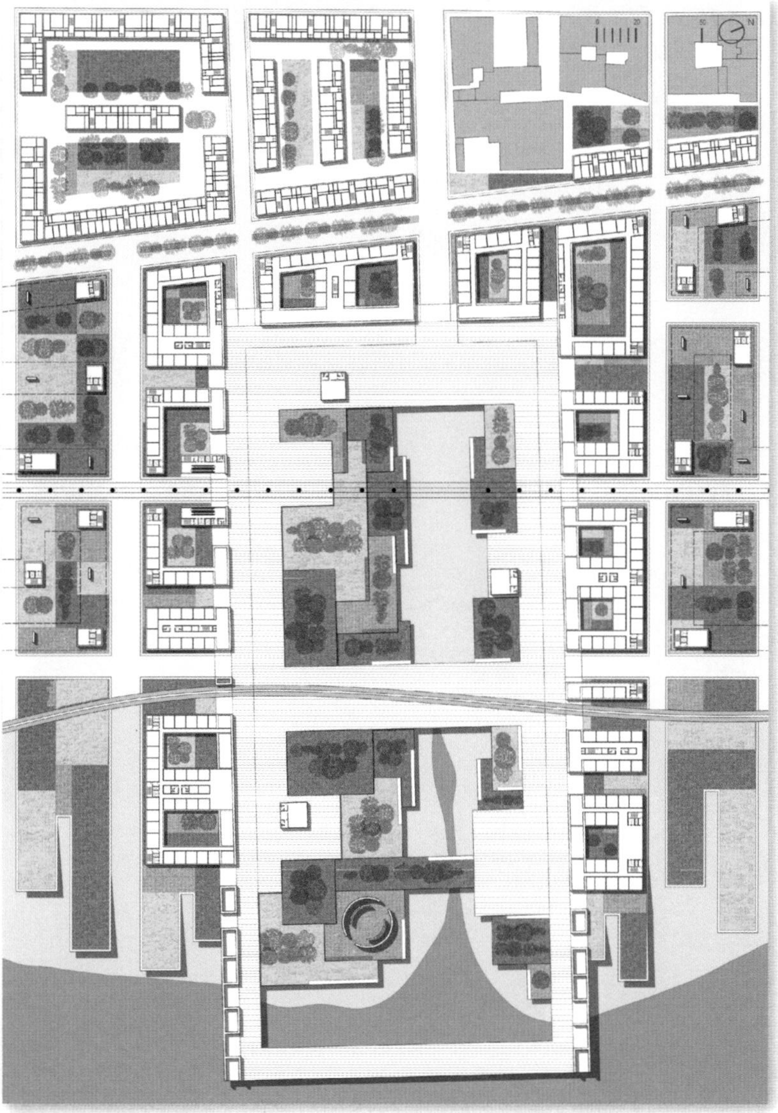

(D) General urban plan and overview of the residential districts
(E) Close-up of floorplan of the Santa Cecilia Beach Villa

(F) General view toward the gardens and a canal

1.2 NORTH-SOUTH, EAST-WEST... BRINGING ORDER TO WHAT WAS BROKEN, DIVIDED, FRAGMENTED

Recovery of the Spreebogen area, Berlin, 1992

We clearly recollect when, against all reasonable argument, we decided to participate in this competition that marked the end of the division of Berlin. A new foundational act, a new heart of the city, a new identity for the return of the capital to Berlin.

The entire project centred around the construction of an Agora, a Capitol capable of creating a new identity and, at the same time, of housing the great public institutions of Germany: the Parliament, the Chancellery, the Lander Parliament.

In the organisation and dialogue between the North-South and the East-West axes, the idea of the central place was grounded. It would be the soul of the new Germany. No longer divided and separated. Whole again, around this great Esplanade, a perfect and perfectly monumental location, capable with its absolute perfection of giving powerful meaning to this new unity.

We cannot believe that the city's sites always have to have a domestic value, as if belonging to a city and calling it home meant we could not accept and be proud of the dimensions and scale of its monuments. All the scales, that of the public, the collective and the private must exist together, but the collective identification is possible if the location of the great democratic government institutions has some memorable characteristics.

(A) View in perspective of the Capitol

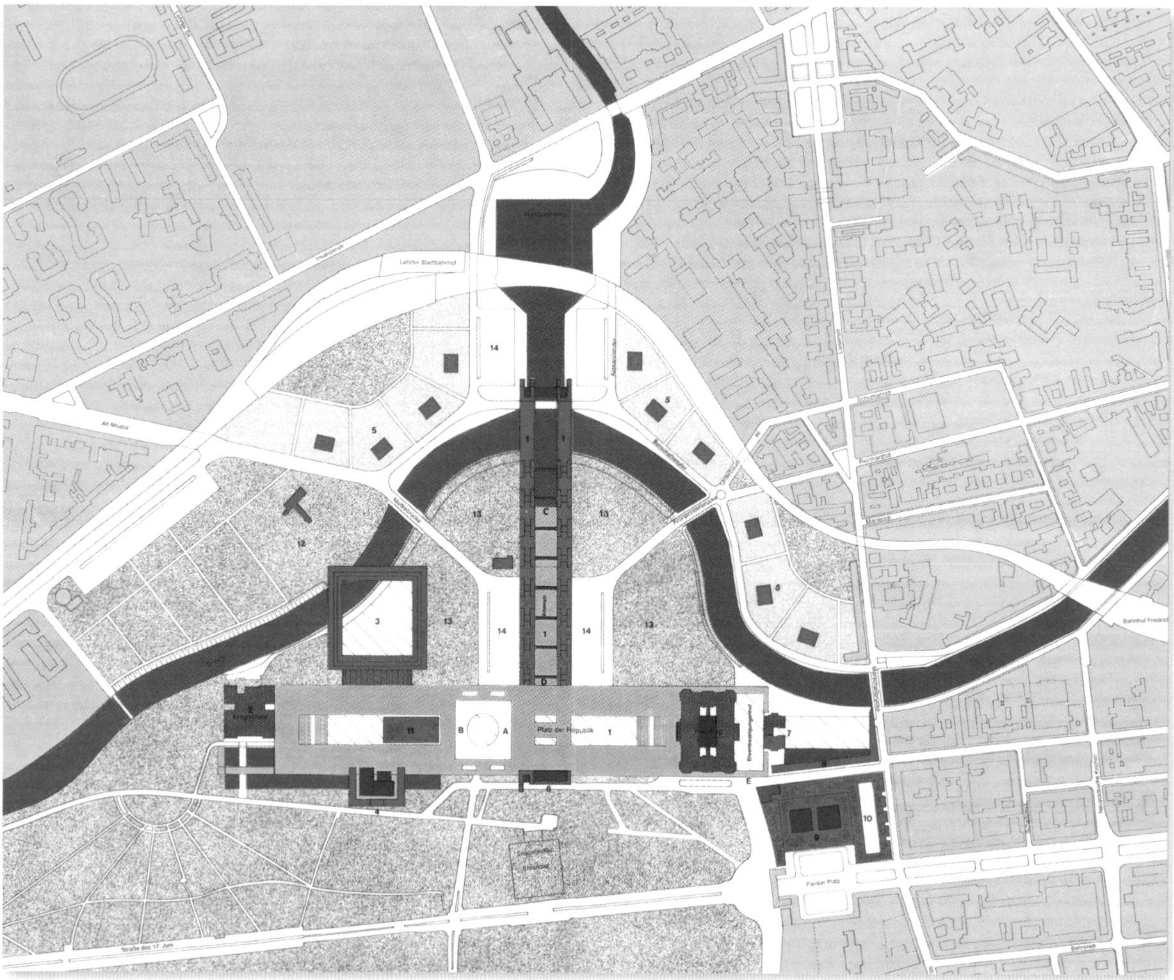

(B) General layout of the project

 (C) Photo of the model entered for the competition

(D) Axonometric overview

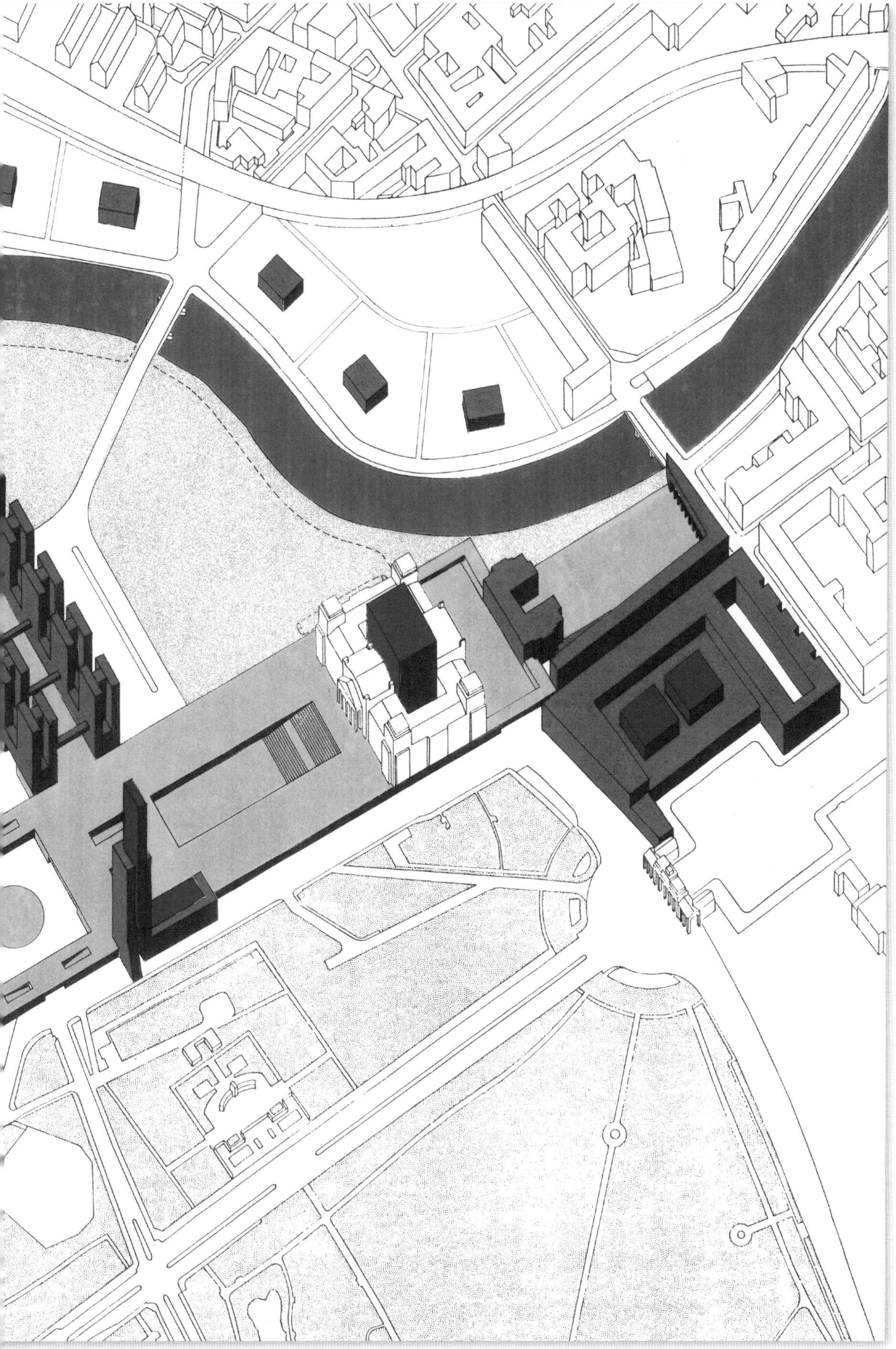

1.3 A NEW DISTRICT, RISING ON NEW GROUND
Residential complex on the site of the former "Tuscan Wolves" barracks, Florence, 2016

Transforming a decommissioned military base, isolated in the countryside and enclosed in itself, into a new satellite district, independent and self-sufficient, interconnected with the rest of the metropolitan city but still tied to the layout of the area, was the project challenge behind the conversion of the former "Tuscan Wolves" barracks.

The project called for demolishing most of the existing buildings and replacing them with a residential complex, a compact project that would, however, leave the memory of the historical background of the military base.

We could define the project "Isolotto 2.0": a green district with low population density, compact, consisting of residential clusters made up of public and private housing, neighbourhood services, office and administrative buildings, shops and artisanal companies as well as businesses of the latest generation, personal and collective services. It was not to be a ghetto!

The backbone of the settlement would consist a system of *people movers* running at a height of 5 meters above ground and connected to Line One of the tram system and the hospital area.

This infrastructure would form the central urban axis for mobility within the district and to and from the metropolitan city, but also as the backbone of the urban services, water, gas, electricity, central sewer system, remote heating: a contemporary Roman aqueduct.

The geometrical design of the system replicates the plan of the Tuscan Wolves barracks: general north/south orientation and east/west alignment. It is the same orientation as Florence had in Roman times, indeed, the *castrum* was no more, originally, than a military encampment which later grew into a city.

Starting from the residential section, a three-dimensional plot, the layout consists of a virtual volume with a built portion and a service portion. In other words, a small house with garden positioned at any height above the urban soil. The juxtaposition of these three-dimensional lots created a construction pattern made of "blocks of villas", a new type of residential construction that was a contemporary reinterpretation of the concept of the "immeubles-villas".

The new raised ground, as well as the low traditional ground, became public spaces but were protected, with sports fields, public parks and urban vegetable gardens, pedestrian paths, bike paths, parking spaces, open areas for cultural events and playgrounds.

(A) View from the public driveway

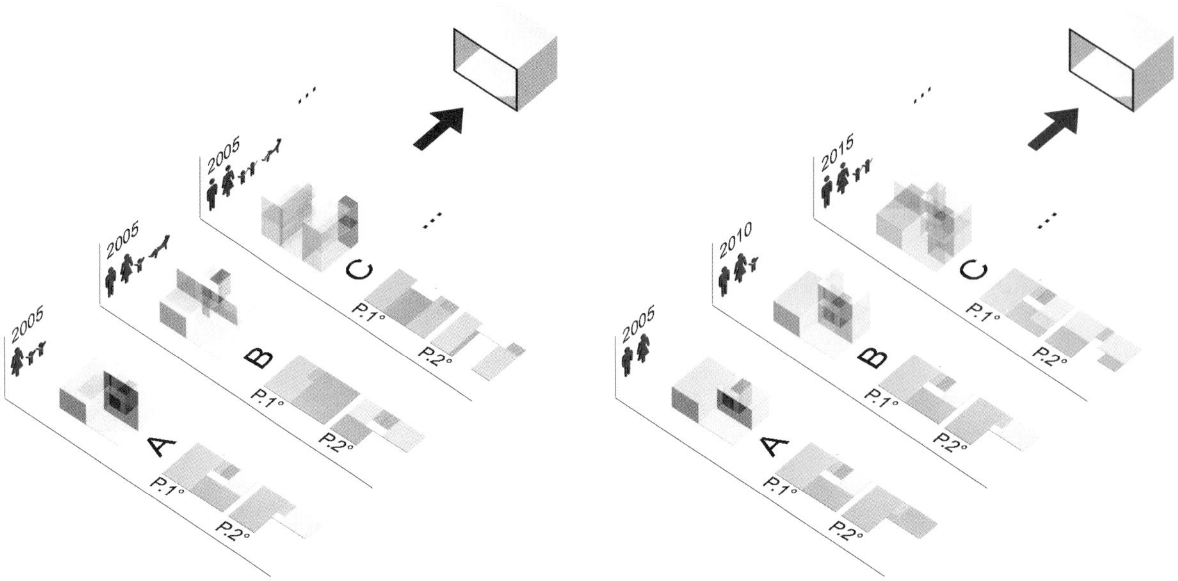

(B) Composite layouts of housing units
(C) Typical cross-section of building blocks

 (D) 3D overview

(E) The new district served by the people mover

1.4 TO EACH HIS OWN HOME, LIKE A CHARM BRACELET
Living at Milano/2, Milan, 2005

There was a powerful determination here to build a housing unit that would encompass all the features that contemporary collective housing should have, where different needs have to share common spaces. Starting from the realization of a courtyard that gives meaning to a collective space separate from the external public space, but not enclosed. A limit, consisting of a built border, but not impassable, rather open and porous. A built border, continuous and uniform that gives the sense of unity but, as soon as it is crossed and passed through, allows people to enter a world that is, on the contrary, fragmented. Here, in the great common courtyard, the porches and balconies of the houses jut out, each separate and different from the ones near it, so as to be identified and recognized. To the point that each resident can say that that one, just that one there, is his.

With a configuration similar to that of a large coral atoll, the buildings are arranged like a "coastal line" around a protected inner space; the portico along the perimeter guarantees freedom of access and passage, and the reciprocal perception both of the inner space and of the surrounding landscape.

At the same time, the sinuous border of the building creates an underground road, a circuit where public and private parking is located. At the top of this built border, similarly, a terrace, a roof garden, provides another circuit, this one a bike path.

The goal is the construction of an interior landscape in which the perception of space is changed with a gradual passage of scale, from the serial and impersonal typical of the large urban outskirts to a more domestic view, identifiable by the variety of buildings and the singularity of places.

(A) View in perspective

(B) Typical layout

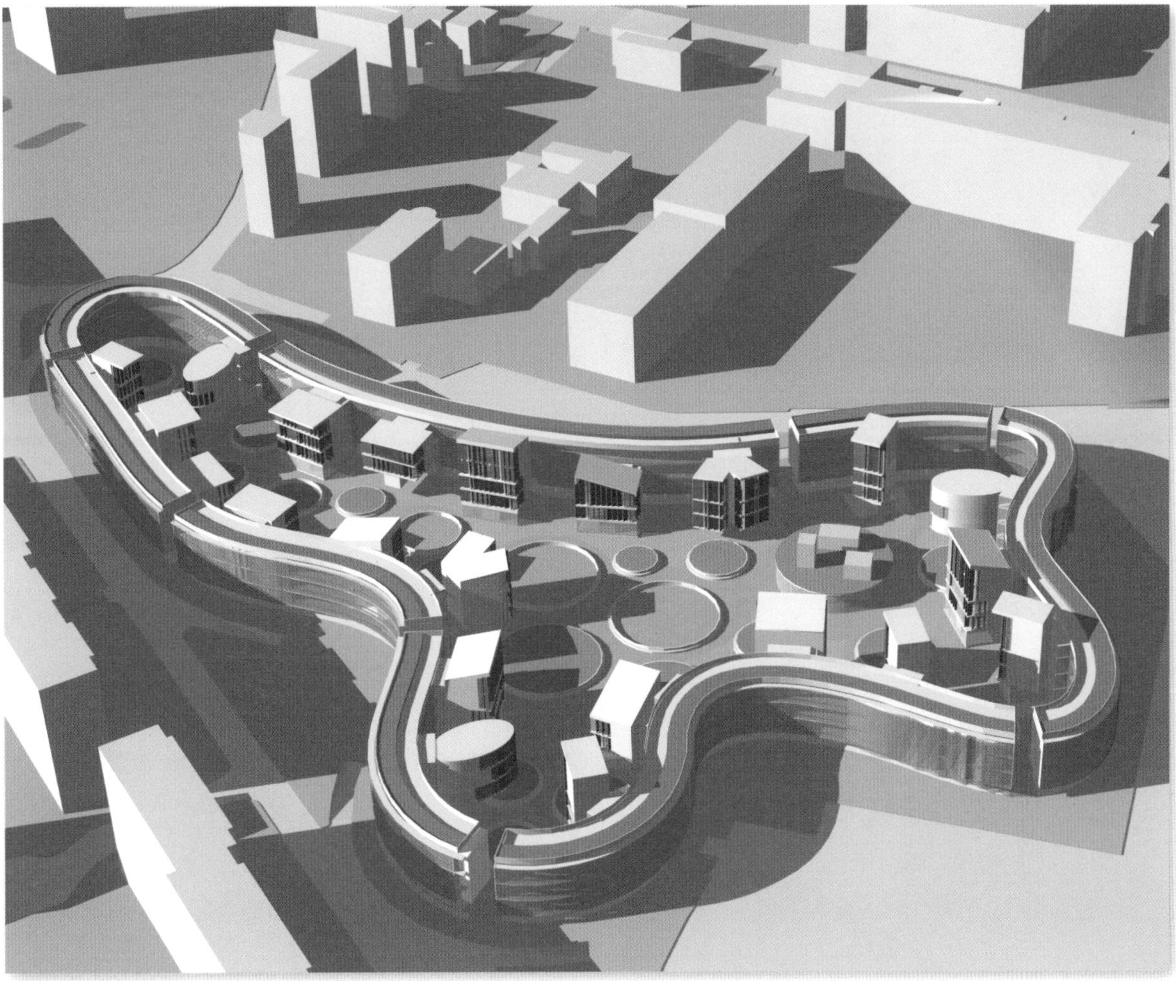

 (C) Overview of the project

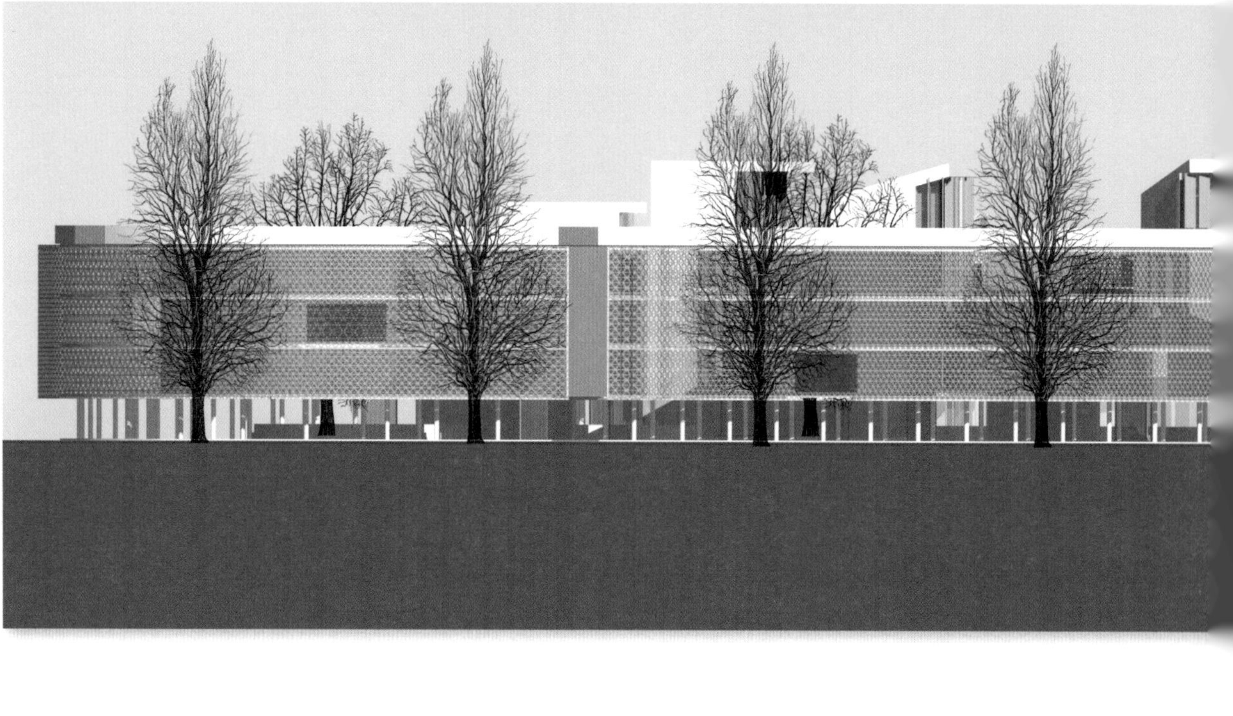

(D) The inner court and the residential units
(E) Elevation

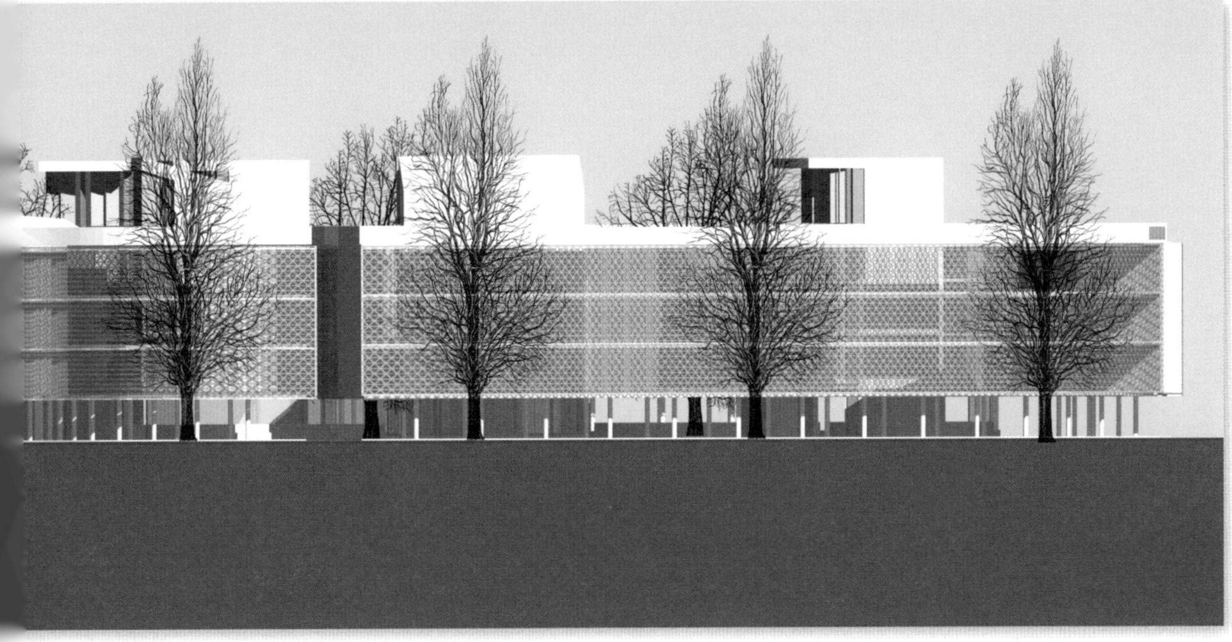

1.5 SMALL TOWERS RISE ABOVE THE GUTTER LINE
Flaminio Project, District of the City of Science, Rome, 2015

Unlike the barracks of the Tuscan Wolves, the principle applied in the case of the Flaminio District was to maintain not only the existing layout but most of the built portion as well, only demolishing parts of it. Its transformation was achieved through integration, starting from the existing structure, to develop an original conversion.

The action consisted of extruding portions of the existing line of buildings, extending them precisely and skilfully and elevating them disproportionately above their gutter line. The result of this action is a forest of towers that stand atop a base of built structures and make this an authentic and original place to live. On the existing structure, as it on an open field, we are building the new identity, a new residential district.

Located, as it is, in sight of the MAXXI, how could we fail to perceive what our role should be? Our choice is to act as the backdrop for an exceptional solution.

The intention of the work is to consider the existing portions of the long, shed structures like a pentagram on which to draw musical notes, with accentuations and pauses.

Producing a residential complex where there is only a group of indistinct but emblematic specialized constructions can be a way to bring them back into the game, relative to the development of the city, thereby responding to those “moralistic” claims – people who support the idea that the less we do, the better – those who view any change to the city as bad.

(A) The existing buildings and the new towers

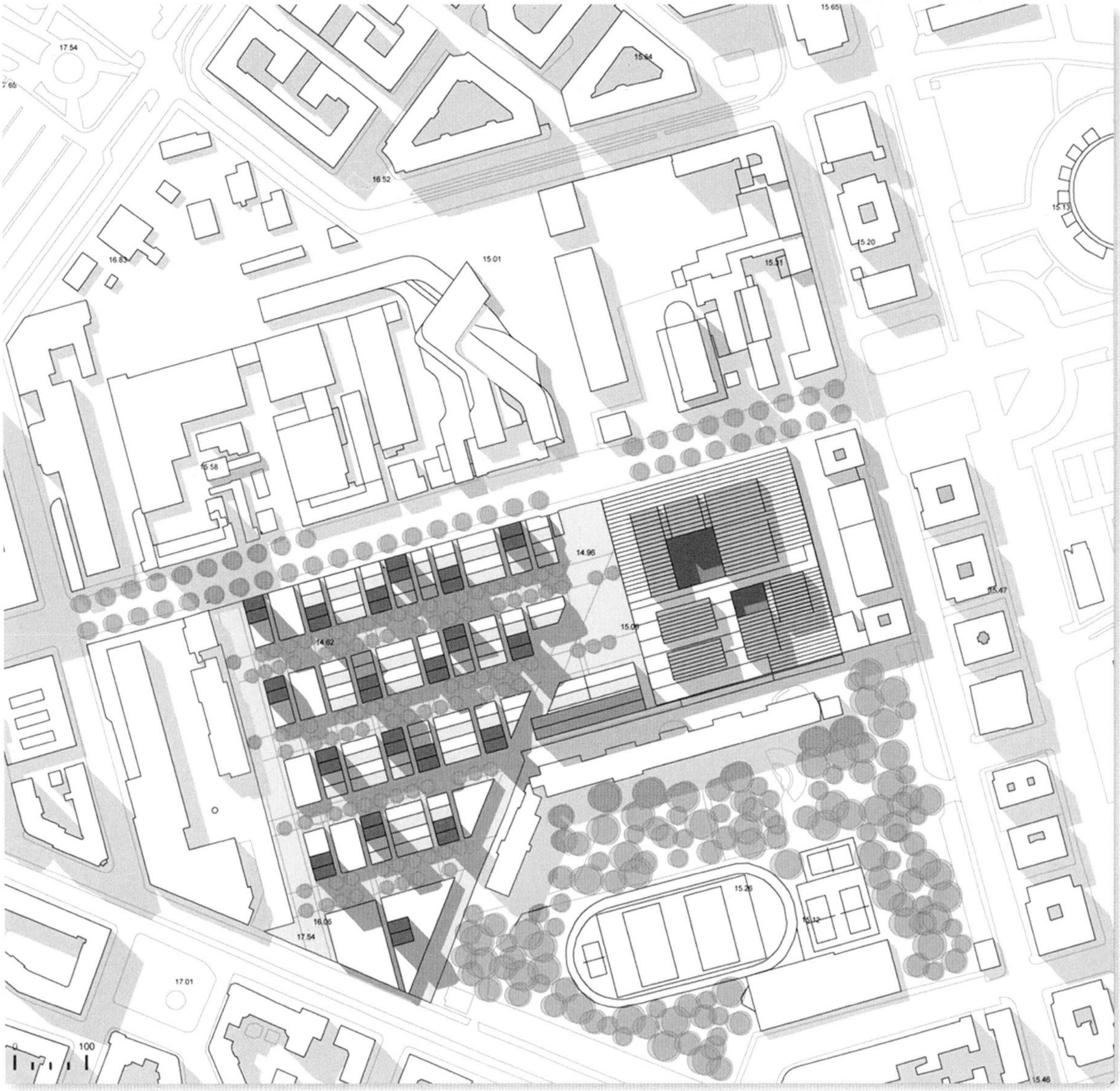

(B) 3D overview

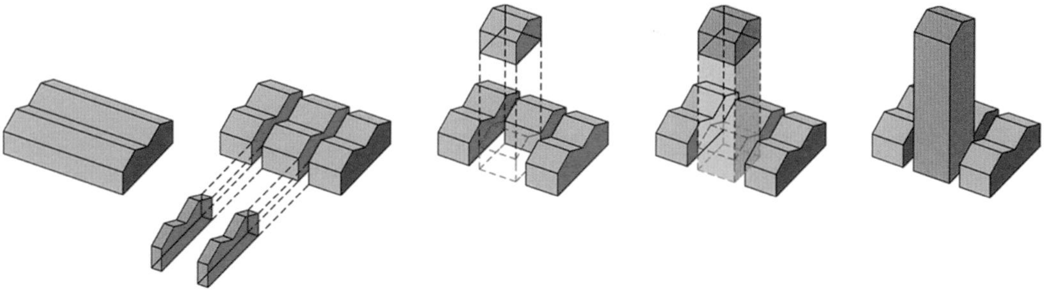

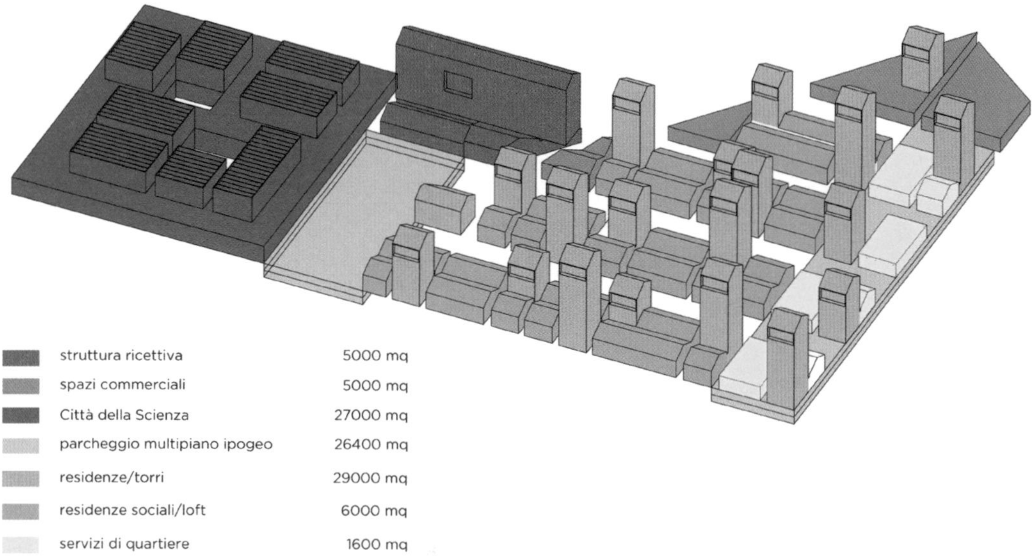
struttura ricettiva 5000 mq
spazi commerciali 5000 mq
Città della Scienza 27000 mq
parcheggio multipiano ipogeo 26400 mq
residenze/torri 29000 mq
residenze sociali/loft 6000 mq
servizi di quartiere 1600 mq

 (D) Overview of the Flaminio District

1.6 EXCAVATING ROOMS IN THE OPEN AIR
Urban park in the former Boschetti area, Padua, 2015

What is the nature of a contemporary park in a solidly historical city like Padua? What is the role that the area in question holds in the urban fabric in which it is located? The proposal is based on a reinterpretation of the matrix of public spaces present in Padua and their symbolic and formal value in a contemporary understanding. At the same time, the configuration proposed for the park responds to the desire to leave space available for daily enjoyment, with a degree of flexibility that will permit a differentiated use, in relation to the diverse and changing needs of a continuously growing city.

The former "Boschetti" site, not currently qualified as a public space but only as a place of linear passage along the bank of the Piovego canal, appears as little more than an unresolved break in the margins of the historical fabric.

The space of the new park is characterized for its topographic variation on two levels, which describe two ways of using it: as a path across on the one hand, and as an activity area on the other. The formal structure that creates a pattern of empty space is assigned to ellipsoid figures such as are found in other parts of the city, representing green islands in a paved area whose geometry is not clearly identifiable. This choice enables us to bypass hierarchies and rules of order which would be hard to establish in such a formless area, generating a field of free relationships, shaped by recognizable spatial patterns.

The green islands are sunken into the soil in depressions 1.8 meters below the surface of the site, creating open-air rooms. At the same time, these sunken rooms maintain their contact with the city above through a tidy division of the sides obtained by corrugating the borders.

The dip thus acquires an architectural characterization given by the topographic variation of the ellipsoid figures that is also a useful expedient for defining the spaces for the activities of the new park, separate from the system of pathways.

(A) The system of pathways between the green islands

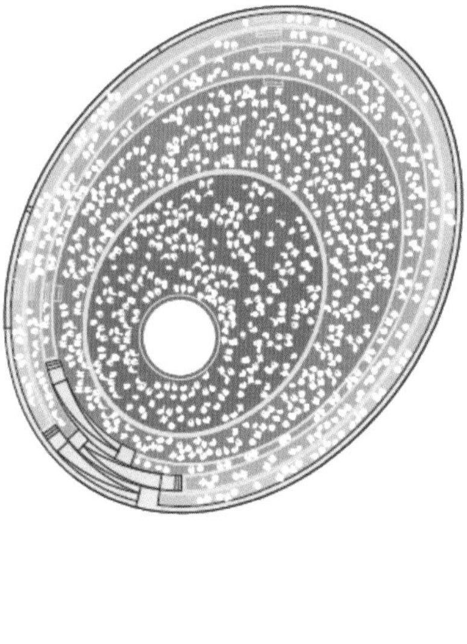

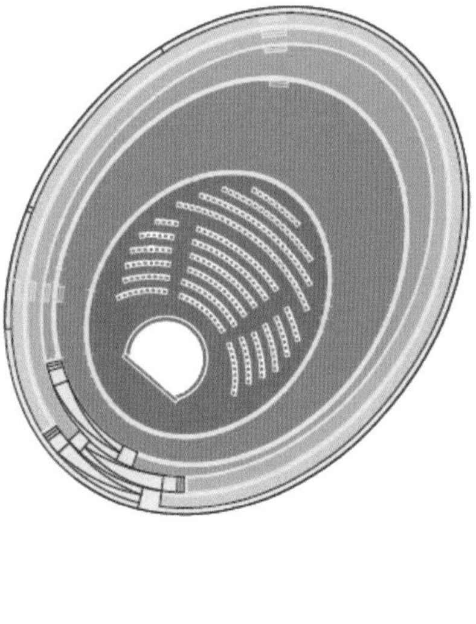

(B) General layout
(C–F) Flexibility of use of the green islands

0 10 20 50 100 200m

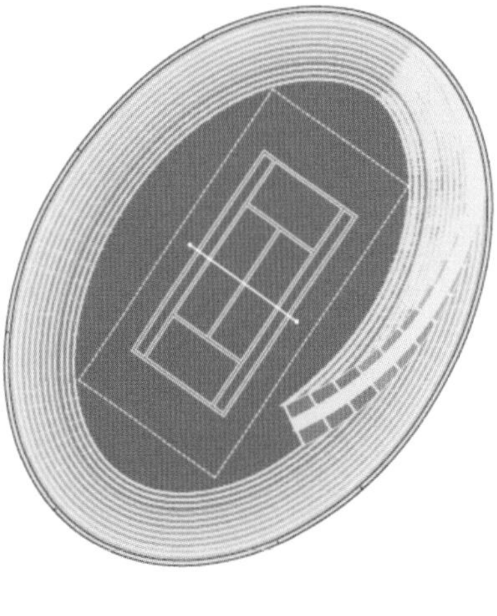

(G) Aerial view of the urban park

2. Freeing the land, rising above it. Trying, desperately, to touch the ground as little as possible. Aiming for elevation so that the earth can flow uninterrupted below.

The idea of disconnecting the building from the ground, so that the green plantings grow all around and under it, is a quality that belongs internally to the history of the modern movement. The way in which this new relationship is developed over time depends on the sensitivity and skill and on the ability to perceive such a solution as feasible.

Many authors come promptly to mind, but above all Le Corbusier. However, the real achievement is not simply the idea of erecting a few pillars, as in the best modern tradition, but the fact of emancipating structures from the surface of the earth. This gesture in some way wants to be a reparation: a sort of healing of the earth after having allowed past construction to take root in the soil. We attempt to occupy as little soil as possible, to become independent of the earth.

This condition appears so novel as to require a new architectural language, which views the detachment from the earth as a singular condition. At the same time, not resting the building on the ground, not raising it out of the soil, creates a new and different way of appreciating the structure. Putting it on stilts, on legs, disconnecting it from the ground creates an idea of movement, as if the building were looking for other places, other shores on which to take root. Actually, this mode of standing on the ground offers the opportunity to create an urban space for collective living, a park, a covered plaza that is not enclosed but rather opens on the city. A space under the building acts as a projection of it, and acquires its own identity as a *place*, and not merely as the result of a subtraction.

Historically, buildings were only raised off the ground for defensive purposes. In ancient times, stilt houses made it possible to live in hostile environments, swamps, ponds, floodlands.

On the contrary, this group of “unborn” projects based on the principle of rising above the earth was not imagined with the specific intent of defending it, but rather as a new, alternative way to enter a building, a complex. Not from its perimeter, not from one side, from a border of the buildings, from the walls, but from the centre, from its heart, and from there move not inward toward the centre but outward, toward the edges. The possibility of entering from below, achieved by raising the building, represents a new way of conceiving the architectural structure of the building.

2.1 ATTEMPTING TO DETACH THE SHADOW FROM THE GROUND! New provincial headquarters, Arezzo, 2005

This project for the new Provincial Headquarters of Arezzo is an introverted project, one that does not reject the goal of identifying and representing the *site of the Institution*, but that shows itself, when necessary and at the same time, as 'open' or 'closed'.

It is a building that attains the ability to reconnect the two roads existing in the area (an older road and the new ring road) in such a way that the new construction does not obstruct the passage through its *public* parts. It is an introverted building in its working parts, which face inward in the *private* sections.

It is an enclosed complex, surrounded by 'walls' that open dramatically to create a passage that, over ramps and stairways, leads to the public portion in the fullest sense of the word, the 'plaza'.

The building is designed as a series of horizontal planes, interacting with the city through the metaphor of the walled and turreted 'citadel', elevated above the ground, that restores the area occupied by the projection of the building to the more urbane use of the green and of the parking areas, linking the two parts of the city. The intent was to avoid any physical or visible blockage to the city's full utilization and permeability.

The Provincial Headquarters develops around the idea of the turreted citadel, appearing from a distance and through the gaps that open as it ascends toward the main 'plaza'.

The towers, which are simply stairwells, elevators and air shafts (wind tunnels with their intake openings), rise above the flat line of the terrace in a sort of reciprocal emulation, between those that stand tall and slender and those that dominate with their mass.

The architectural image is achieved through the use of a single, traditional material. The outer walls are clad in terracotta tiles, solid or open depending on the designs, which form changeable patterns or lacy scrollwork, interrupting the walled curtain and allowing shafts of light to pierce through to the inner corridors. In particular, the openwork design is reminiscent of ventilated walls in terracotta on old Tuscan barns with their triangular tiles arranged in various configurations on the walls, from solid to semisolid, to open, producing a changeable effect from the total opacity of the solid material to the complete transparency of the light element.

(A) Detail of one of the inner courts

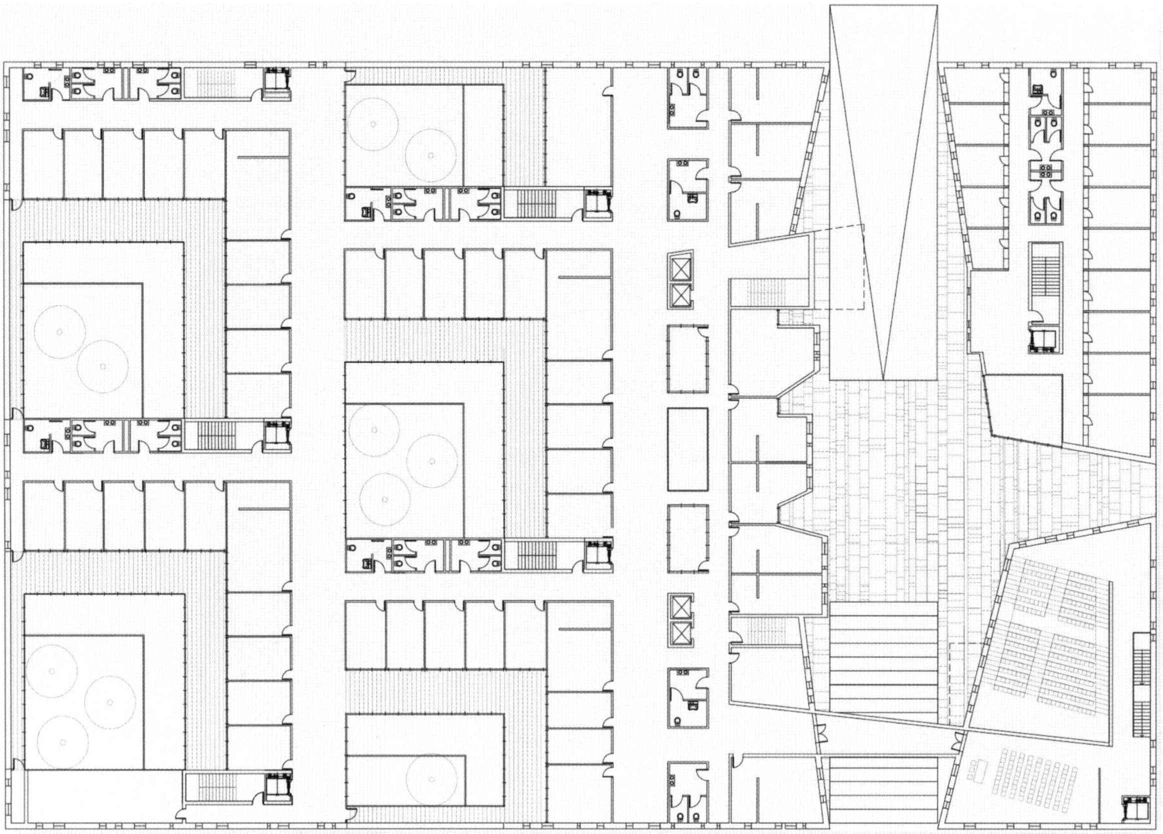

(B) Floorplan of the second floor

(C) Model of the project
(D) View from the front

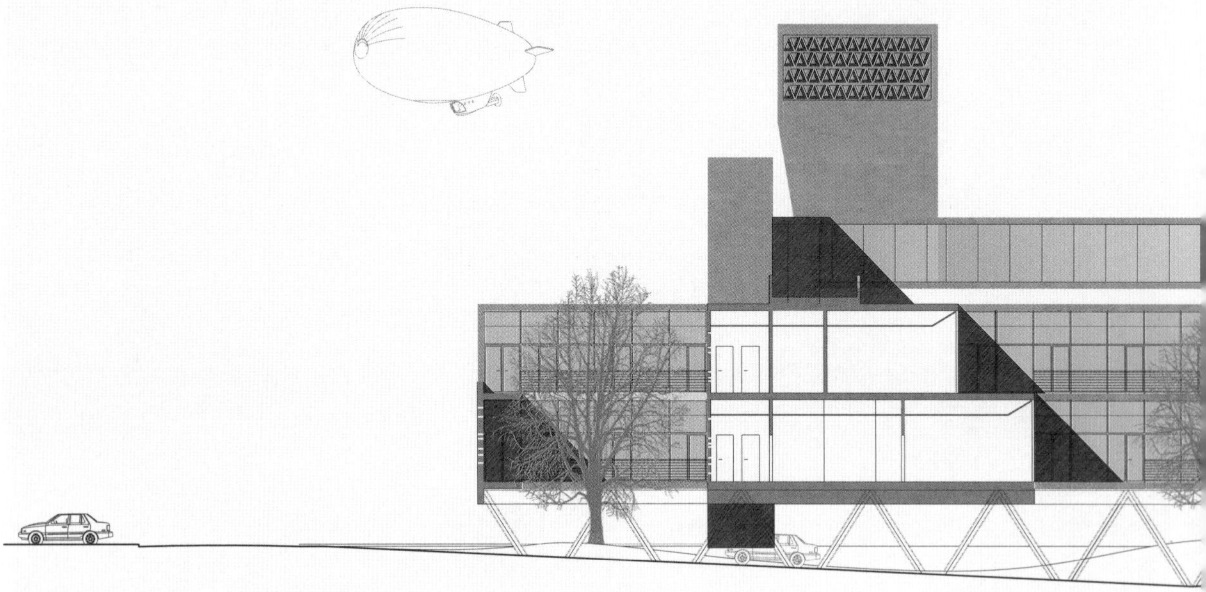

(E) View from the front with the main entrance ramp
(F) Elevation in cross-section view

0 2 4
1 3 5 10 m

2.2 FLOATING ABOVE A PARK
"La Romanina" school complex, Rome, 2004

A single building, ensuring the total usability of the site and at the same time protecting, almost isolating the community of children and their teachers a world of their own. This idea led us to think of the school as a sort of ark that shelters, protecting them from the imponderability of the contemporary world. If the metaphor of the ark represents the need to preserve, first, and then to restore, the act of lifting any object off the ground and using the space underneath it means, in terms of urban architecture, creating at the same time different but interconnected conditions. A single low structure lies suspended over the land, barely visible to the eyes of observers from a distance, and transparent to the people who pass through it.

The school is as if spread over a large plate, as wide as the school and long enough to allow for the rational organization of spaces in respect of the residential principle: the idea of an "urban system" that has determined the elevation of the building to enable the school and the city to live together spatially.

The building, constructed on two levels, develops in a strongly sectional concept with an extruded profile that emphasises and defines its structure. The open space underneath provides a park for the enjoyment of the neighbourhood.

(A) Open and sheltered space connecting the classrooms

(B–C) Views of the north and south ends

(D) View from below at the public park level
(E) View of a patio adjacent to the classrooms

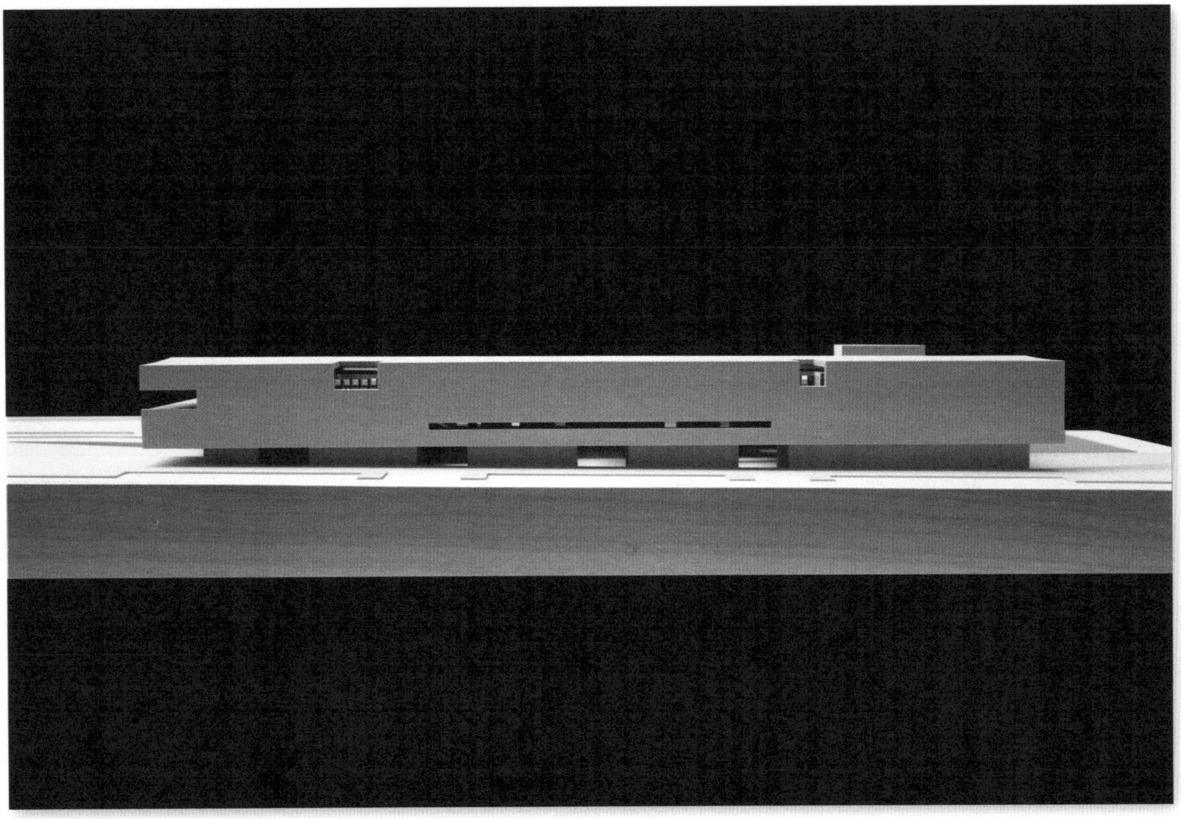

(F) View of the model from the west

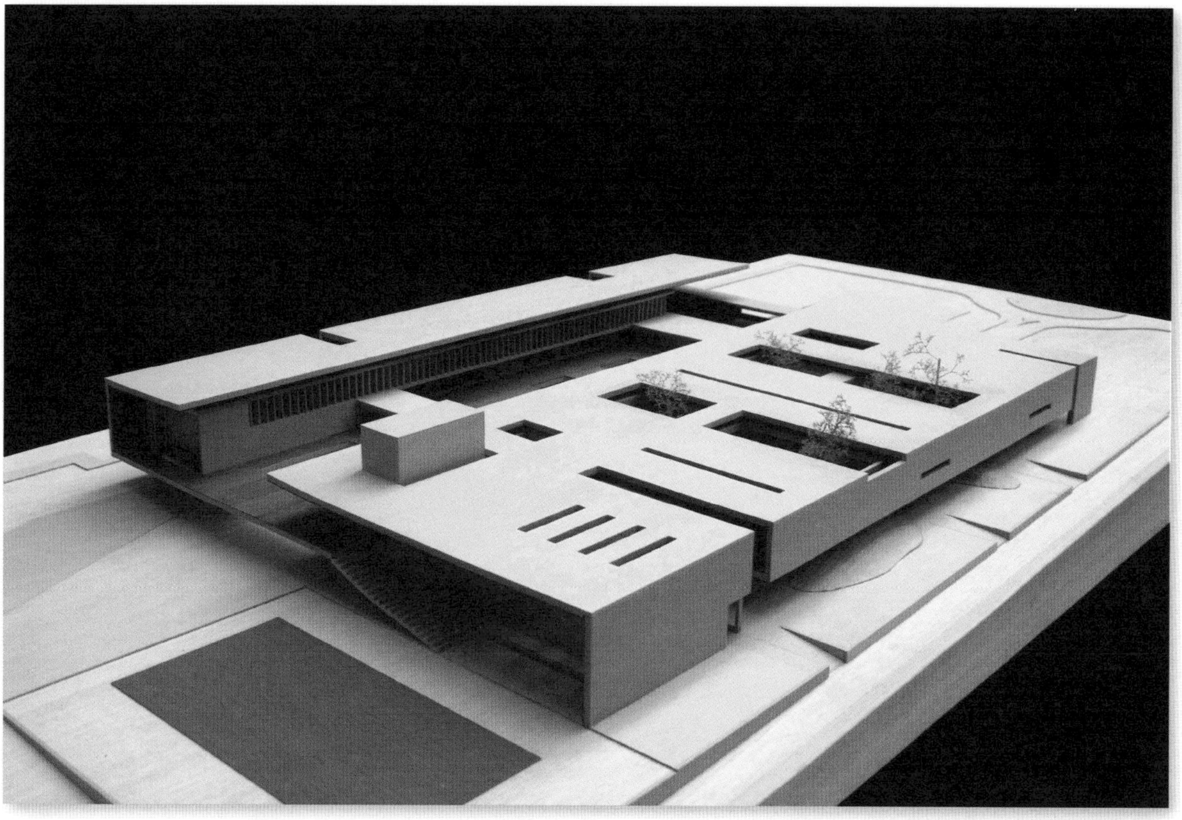

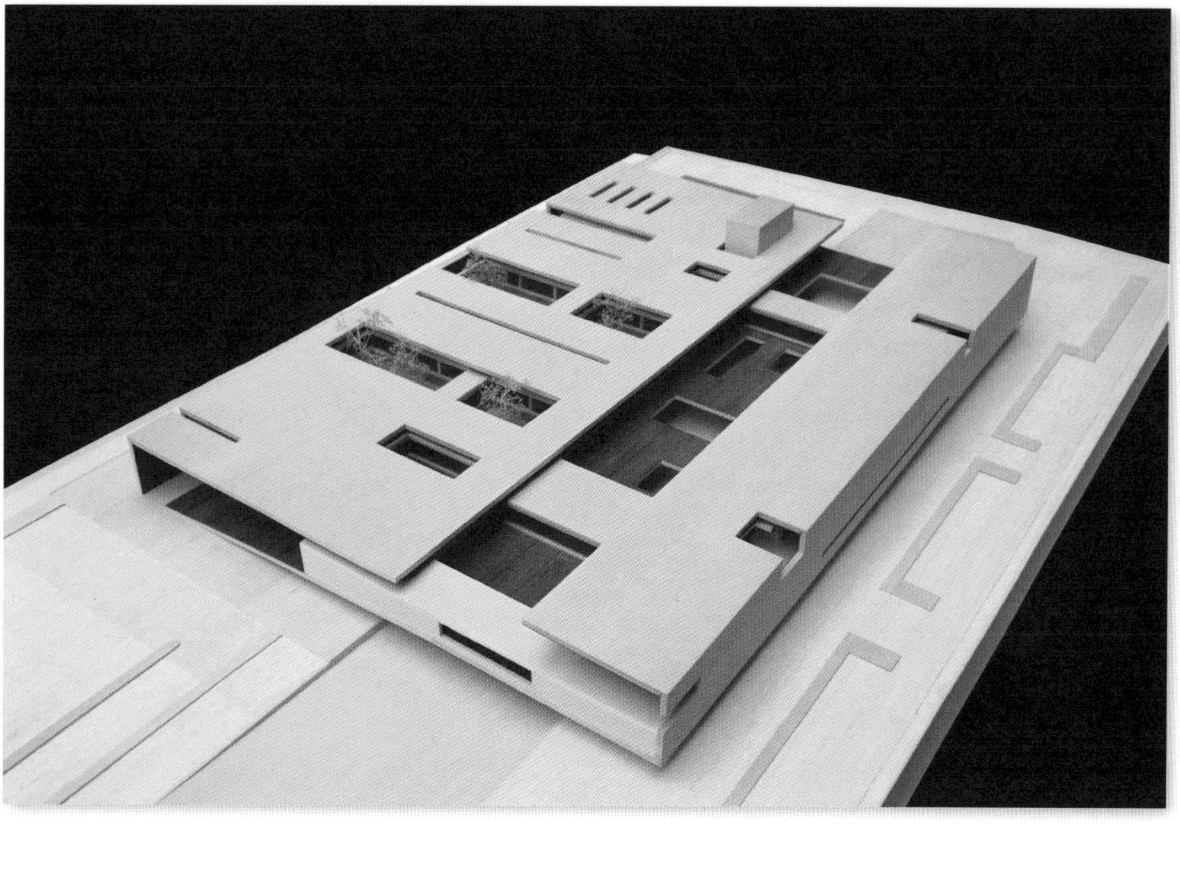

(G–H) Views of the model from southeast and northwest

2.3 IN PLACE OF THE WALLS AROUND THE ROOMS, OPEN SPACE
Daegu Gosan Public Library, Daegu, South Korea, 2012

The province of Suseong-gu decided to build a new library for the municipality of Daegu in order to create a structure capable of meeting the growing need for the transmission and accessibility of information, going beyond the idea of a mere container of knowledge, indifferent to the changes occurring in the world outside.

Simplicity and recognizability were the guidelines of the project. The former viewed as a principle of reality, capable of ensuring the legibility of the layout and the precise division of space. The latter, instead, interpreted as a feature able to foster the integration of the new building in the dense urban fabric and as make it a real attraction for the users of the future library.

Starting from the compact volume, we developed a separation into different functional areas: *open user space*, *culture and lifelong study space*, *office/maintenance space* and *common space*. Then, we made a further subdivision which gave us distinct spatial units, actual "*rooms*".

An assembly of *rooms* suggests and illustrates an idea of "urban fabric". The room, as an elementary unit, is configured as an intimate, domestic place, where a person can study, develop ideas and at the same time exchange and share them. What could seem a chaotic collection of rooms is really an organized set of spaces systematically arranged.

Every element is part of a route or, better, a circuit, that connects functionally uniform rooms; in turn, this circuit is connected with other sets of rooms, where the different functions of the library have their place.

One of the characterizing elements of the project consists of conserving almost entirely the space allocated to a garden, located at the level of the city, through the elevation of the volumes that house the library. The rooms are raised on concrete slabs, thereby freeing the ground of their mass.

The action of elevation creates almost total permeability and use of the park by every inhabitant in the district throughout the 24-hour period.

Suspended boxes and green space, linked by close relationship, influence one another reciprocally: the library's rooms open to views of the sky filled with light and the garden offers visitors and students at the library ideal places to rest and stunning outlooks.

(A) View from the park of the elevated volumes

 (B) Overview of the library

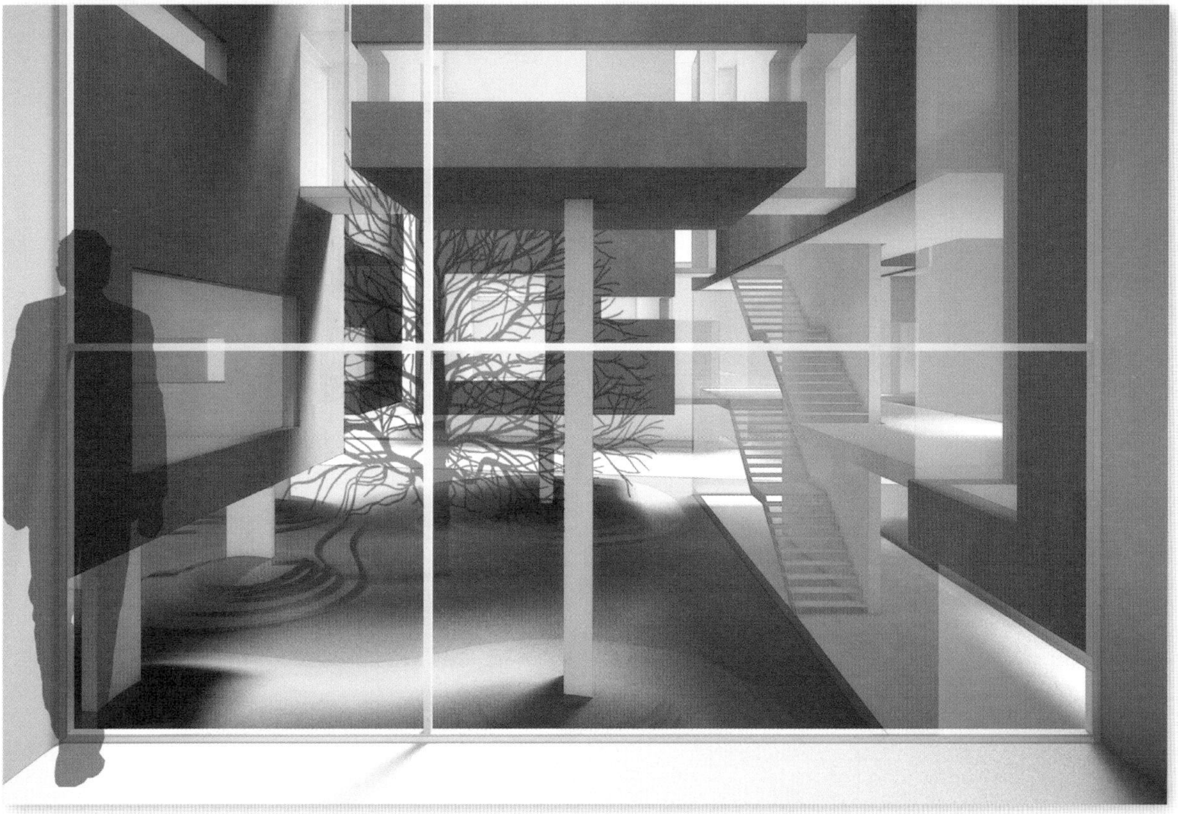

(C) The interior consultation and reading rooms
(D) View of the “rooms” that make up the library

(E) Main front view of the entrance

2.4 A CASTLE APPEARS, SUDDENLY, AMIDST THE MULTITUDE OF HOUSES
Region of Sicily Office Building, Palermo, 2020

Intended as a clear and notable element with respect to the surrounding landscape, an "outsized" work of architecture, the new complex is built around an immense suspended base, with high towers accentuating and dominating the view. It is a peremptory sign of the new city skyline that should find in this work an element of extraordinary recognisability.

The structure of the building is configured as a quadrangular base element that develops on seven level; above it rises a system of four towers of varying heights (from a minimum of 13 storeys to a maximum of 29).

The entire structure appears suspended over the land so as to ensure ample permeability of the entire planted area below that is offered to the city as a garden – named after *Luigi Pirandello* –, which underlies or encircles the building and is characterised by a particular design of the vegetation.

The building is meant to appear as a peremptory figure with respect to the skyline of the urban landscape; even more, it should represent a significant visible landmark along the line of Viale Regione Siciliana. The architecture features stereometric choices that act as guides and suggest subsequent options with respect to the figurative character of the entire structure: a compact front view externally, marked by a sequence of circular openings that echo the design of a "mashrabiyya" – and, on the other hand, a highly transparent, entirely glassed-in aspect from the other side, overlooking the belvedere plaza named for *Giovanni Verga.*

Centrally, with respect to the base element, and on the imprint of the volume of the auditorium, a circular pedestrian ramp connects the building with the subway station and with the terminal of the bus lines, flanked by the line of shuttle buses. The ramp distributes all the levels from the garden to the lobby. On the roof, a belvedere plaza offers views in various directions of the surrounding landscape. At the centre is an orangerie, which outlines the central part and encloses a small cafeteria pavilion, while the four towers are the "points" of a sort of crown, an image that we can take as a figurative metaphor of the new complex.

(A) View from Luigi Pirandello Park

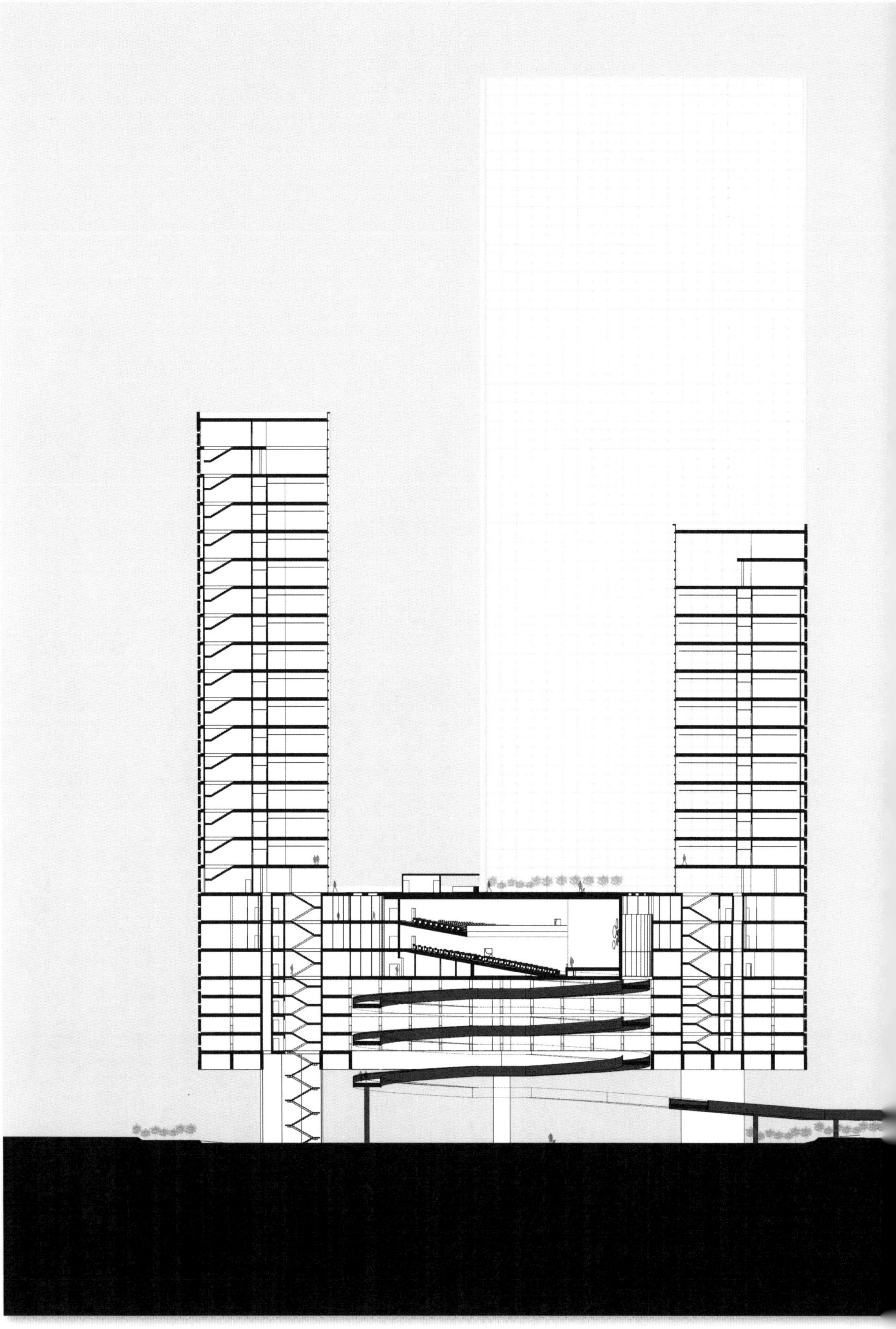

(B) Longitudinal section on the auditorium
(C) Southeast elevation

(D) Aerial view

(E) View from east toward the coast

2.5 SKATING AMONGST THE ICICLES ABOVE GROUND LEVEL
National Museum at Vestbanen, Oslo, 2009

The idea of the museum is to create an iconic, highly characterised location, the opposite of neutral wherever possible; it wants to be a museum in which the rooms can valorise the work of art to the point of exalting the visitor's perception of it.

The museum is intended here as a public but also a personal place, with which to establish an intimate relationship with the work of art or a part of the building. It wants to stimulate the visitor, also by offering alternate spatial structures, some in scale (human) and some outsized, turning the visit to the museum into what is effectively a sensorial experience.

The image of the crystal, of the iceberg and the forest, the desire to probe the intimate relationship between land and the water that is intrinsic to Norwegian culture: these were the impressions that inspired the project.

On the basis of these images, at the compositive level, the museum acquires an iconic, recognisable character, defining a new urban skyline and generating a new centrality, a reference that is not merely cultural but also figurative for Oslo. The structure acts as a sort of lantern, which continues to reveal itself as a civil and cultural institution even at night, its high towers illuminated and rapidly becoming part of the collective image of Oslo.

The floors above and below the great roof should become public spaces, freely usable not only by visitors to the museum but by the populace in general.

From the ground floor, passing through a forest of columns, it is possible to walk freely up a circular ramp to the roof, which becomes a panoramic terrace overlooking the fjord and the city, but also the skating rink, at the centre of which stand great monoliths of ice and crystal.

The *Main Station*, as the ancient access gate to the city, is also involved, becoming the new entrance to the museum complex. The heart of the building remains the museum, however, which comes to life inside the hollow portion of the monoliths, creating an immersive voyage in an extraordinary, enchanted landscape, as only Norwegian landscapes can be.

(A) View of the towers from the rooftop skating rink

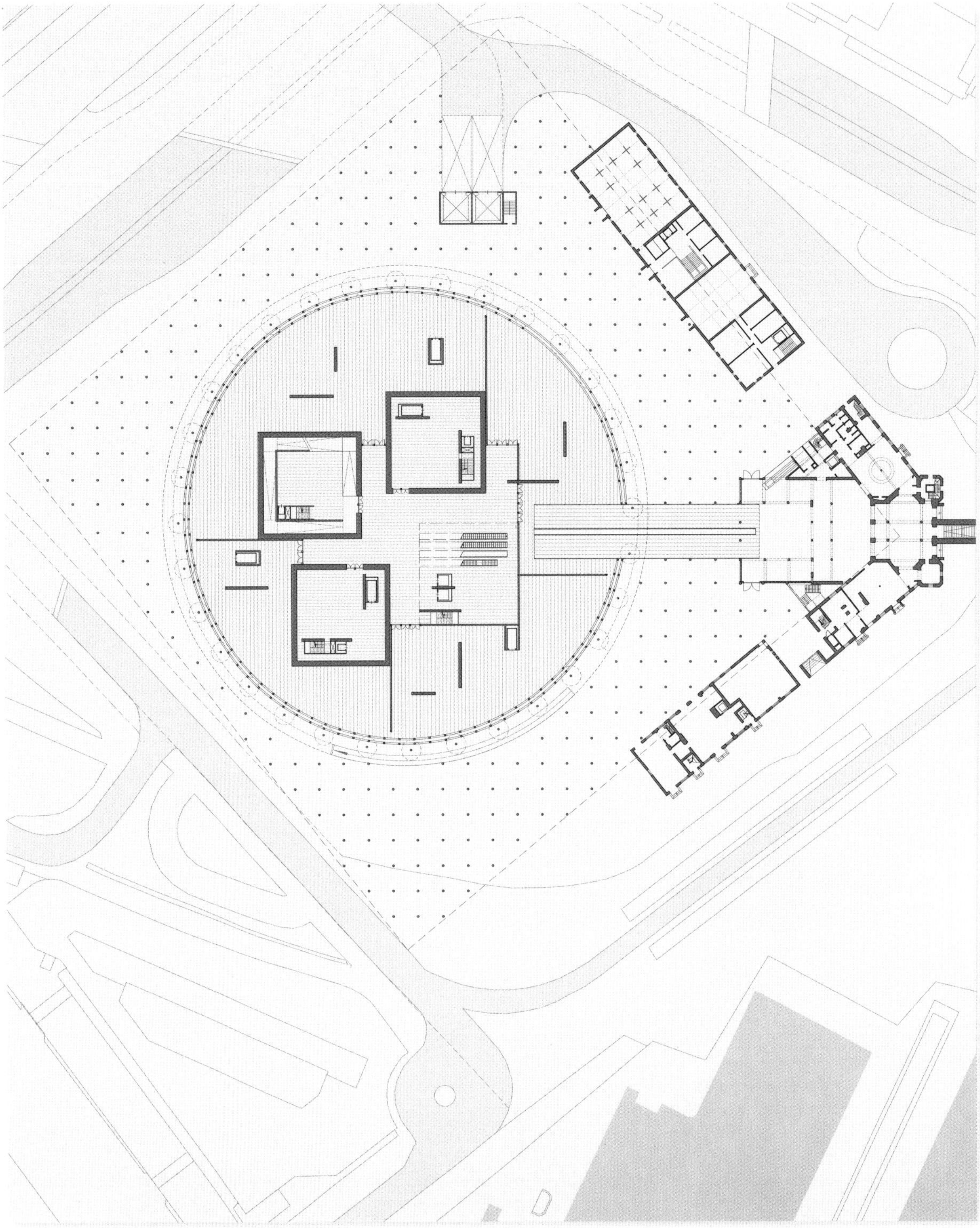

(B) Layout of the ground floor

 (C) Overview from west

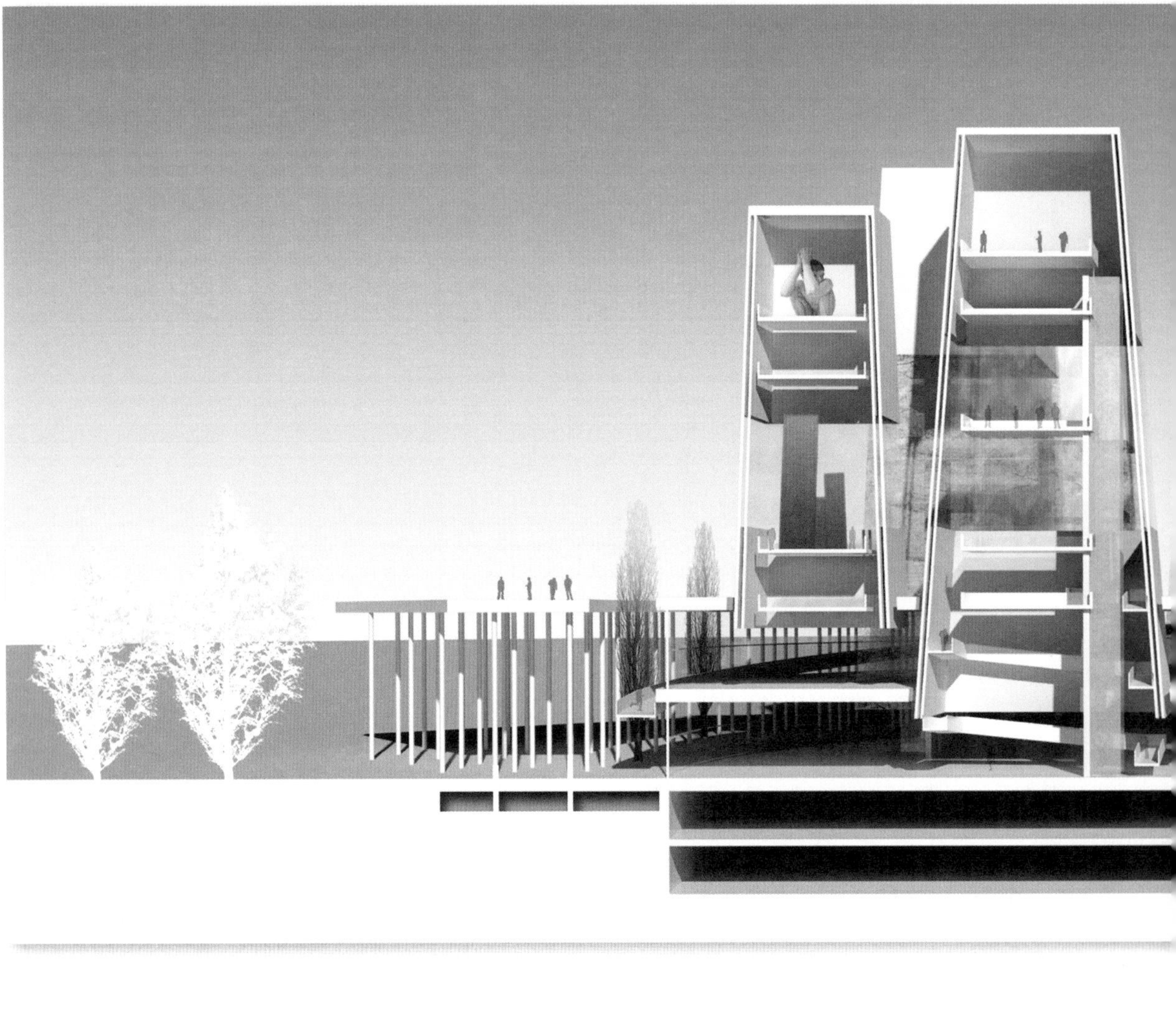

(D) Front view from oceanfront road
(E) Cross section elevation

2.6 SHELTER AND PROTECTION FOR BOOKS, TREES, PEOPLE
BEIC European Library of Information and Culture, Milan, 2022

The construction of the European Library in Milan has a long, complicated story. When the first competition was announced in 2001 – later assigned to Bolles-Wilson – we participated with an interesting idea, a great container that absorbed part of the park into its structure.

When the competition was announced again in 2022, it seemed natural to us to participate again, perhaps with the idea that we might have deserved some sort of reparation: of course, that's not the way it went.

Stubbornly, we imagined that our original idea, placing the relationship between the library and the park at the centre of the project, or rather making the library the backdrop and stage of the park, was the right one; that letting the park enter below the building without integrating it completely was the way to achieve it.

The new BEIC is based on the interpretation and emphasis of the connective and infrastructural value of the park, allowing it to flow without interruption along the route already drawn for it by the open space. The project is shaped like a loggia, seeking a dialogue with the scale of the setting, settling itself on the border opposite the rail line and opening on the park to define a space of hybridization between the city and the landscape.

The border along via Monte Ortigara is occupied by a wall of residential buildings that curves to become a block weighing on the land, the projection of which provides the space for the development of the building and interaction with the context The loggia offers its outlines as the result of a meeting of two archetypal urban models: the gallery and the plaza. On the one hand, the plantings link the structure to the park to the east, and extend westward; on the other, the projection of the roof line creates an evocative picture of the spatial quality of the great 19th century interiors.

The building is formed by the extrusion of one section outward so that it looks like an upside-down letter "L", but it is actually a "C", considering the underground portion that anchors it to the soil. The development lies entirely on the surfaces and is defined according to two registers: one focused on the more external surfaces facing toward the city; the other, in glassy material, which faces on the park and the belly of the loggia.

(A) View from the vast urban loggia

(B) The main front entrance

 (C) The interior spaces for consultation and reading

(D) The vast urban loggia that faces onto the park

3. Being part of the perpetual motion that is the city's growth. Replacement, expansion, addition, ways and shapes whereby the new becomes part of the existent elements.

Architecture always acts within something: a landscape, a city or a building, and needs to define its borders each time, to determine its position in the context. Architecture is never built in the abstract.

Buildings are the result of external conditions, as well as the product their internal organization. The conditions, constraints and requisites of the environment do not refer only to physical characteristics – dimensions and geomorphology – but also to cultural and historical, anthropological and socioeconomic factors. All these elements can contribute, to different degrees and in a range of conditions, to determine their design.

In order to build a within the landscape of the city and its buildings, we have to be informed, aware and responsible. The "context", as reference, premise, condition a priori, is not enough to determine the nature and characteristics of the architectural project. Designing within requires a certain ability to interpret, to listen and to establish a feeling with what we have before us, so that we can develop, through the project, not only the permanent features but also, and above all, the potential for expression of a beauty that opposes the simplification of parameters; this is achieved through immersion and interpretation. Addition-expansion, restructuring, crowding, then tearing down and rebuilding appears to be the only way we can build within the city. In a constant exchange between new and existing structures, between what wants to emerge as new and what has already emerged and is the state in which the lives of all of us exist and intersect.

The meaning of the expression "being part of the perpetual motion that is the city's growth" is to say that the growth and development of a city is not the deterministic result of actions that occur in a constant, linear and gradual flow leading, inevitably, toward a perfect balance, but recognizing that the nature of all things, and thus even of cities, is changeable.

We have to acknowledge that there is no set method for dealing with change, only an attitude, a way of dealing with reality, some ethical guidelines that, depending on the circumstances of the case, will define the nature of the work, the conflict that is generated between the respect we have for what was there and our desire to change it.

The built work alone can tell us whether the conflict we created has resolved itself and peace has been restored. With regard to our unborn work, we have to think that it might have been a positive opportunity... but we can't swear to it!

3.1 INSIDE THE MURATE... BOOKS INSTEAD OF FELONS
New Library of Architecture, Florence, 2006

The location of the Library of the University's Department of Architecture inside an extension of the protected complex that was the former men's Murate prison, raises a fundamental question: how can something new arise without raising the issue of the state of things? Not an easy question!

The answer focuses on exalting, through a clear, if muted, figurative design, the nature of the spaces in which the library will be housed. Figuratively, the only new elements appear to be the great circular tanks visible over the crenelated crest of the walls. But it is in the experience of passing through those wall that the architecture is revealed, and it is precisely in the fact of entering the structure that the novelty appears in all its power. A dead structure comes back to life, a closed, inaccessible place – whether a prison or a convent – opens to the city.

The new Library of Architecture, housed in the complex of the Murate prison, borders on the complex of Saints Verdiana and Teresa, a former convent and now the home of the University of Florence's Architecture Department.

Literally, the project is housed inside the structure of the Murate prison and is characterised by its respect for the particularity of the place, attempting a sort of independence and a reciprocal recognition between what is new and what came before, to the point that the former remains alongside the latter, still legible. The open space of the structure, its courtyard surrounded by the high walls of the prison, which used to serve as the outdoor area where the prisoners were allowed an hour of fresh air, becomes the central nucleus of the place, a study hall, the reading room.

The two wings of the "panopticon" designed by the 19th century prison are reused on the upper floors as "cells" with open shelving for the consultation and deposit of books; on the ground floor for such public functions as the bookshop and librarian offices, on a sort of urban gallery or passage that leaves the building completely open to the community.

The surrounding walls, whose conservation has been decreed by the Historical Heritage Supervisory, have been embellished with a sort of bow-window overlooking the city, leaving the façade independent, in glass and metal, of the new building and ensuring that the "new" and the "old" are clearly discernible. The peremptory image of the walls is thus maintained intact, but its perception is altered, making the walls more of a noise-abatement barrier, a screen for introspection and a diaphragm for the light, benefiting the people as much as the books. The roof of the new building is designed as a hanging garden of stone.

(A) Entrance to the library from piazza della Madonna della Neve

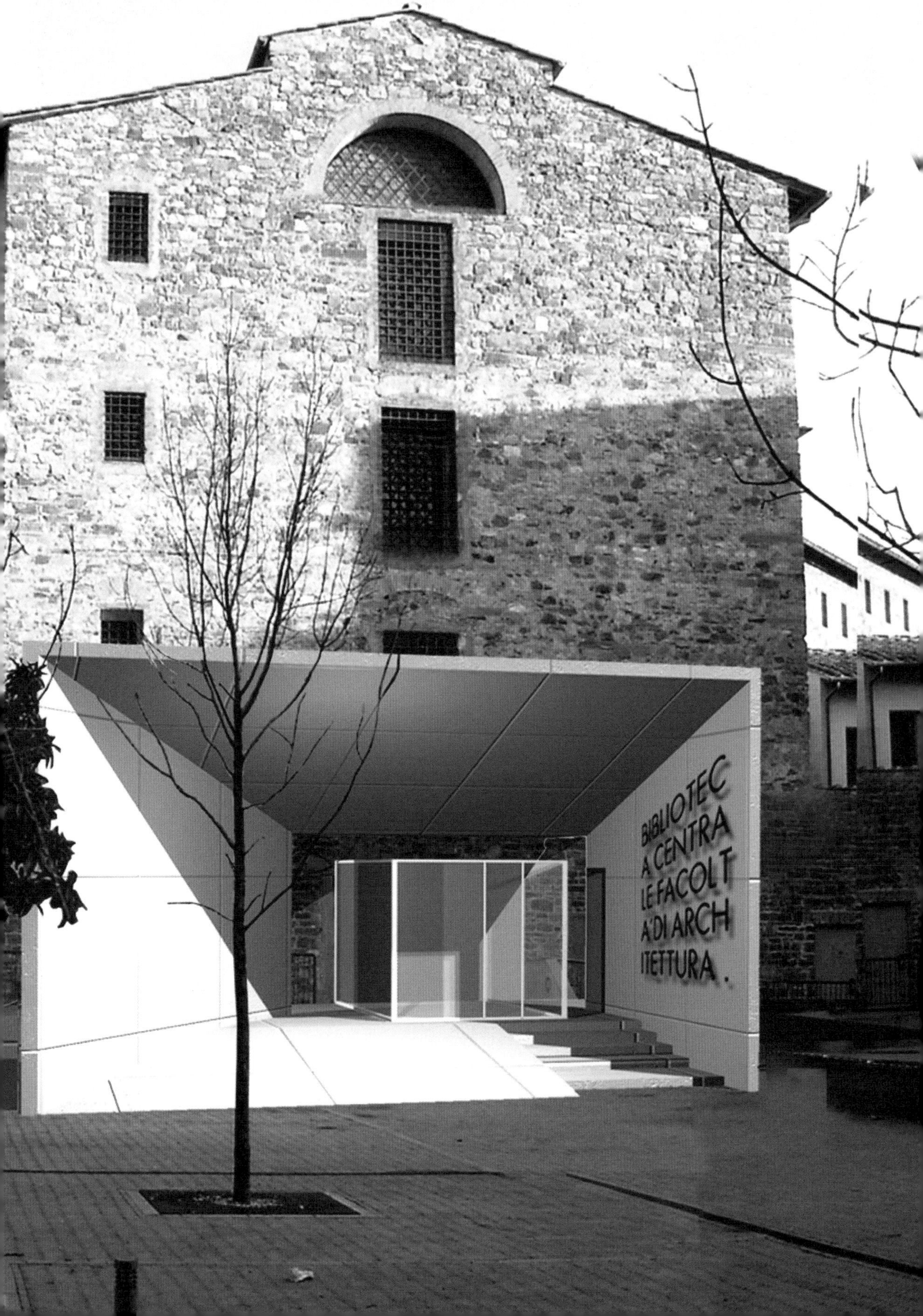
BIBLIOTEC
A CENTRA
LE FACOLT
A' DI ARCH
ITETTURA .

(B–C) View of the model from outside and from inside the Murate complex

 (D) Detail of the ramp to the newspaper and periodical library

(E) Entrance to the library from viale della Giovine Italia

 (F) Bow-window overlooking the city from the external surrounding wall

3.2 THE DESIRE TO LEAVE EVERYTHING AS IT IS AND THE DESIRE TO CHANGE

Citadel of assisted living, Riva del Garda, 2010

Following careful study of the existing structure and its characteristics, and a thorough inspection of the urban setting and the types and features of the architecture, everything possible was done to save the original structure rather than demolish it.

The project proposed focuses on the conservation of the existing buildings their structural layout, the glassed connections and green areas.

The choice to recover and restore to a more modern aspect an existing complex derives, beyond the cultural reasons, from ideas linked to memory and tradition, also expressed by a principle of construction.

Not to demolish the current structures offers the additional advantage of not having to set up a complex, invasive construction site that could hardly be reconciled with the simultaneous need to continue with activities of care and assistance. We would be able to have a compact, clean worksite. In other words, we would carry out a sort of "dry" assembly of the additions and new structures.

The increased volume of space necessary to respond fully to the functional, dimensional and technological demands of the competition are achieved with the creating an additional floor below the existing space under the roofs, through a reinterpretation of the roofing elements. The operation is viewed as the transfer of a "light" element (the roof) which, with a simple formal remodelling, will serve to frame and at the same time modernize the project in question.

The inclusion of four small volumes in the existing courtyard area between the pavilions serves to complete the new organization both from a functional standpoint (new meeting places between the different zones) as well as from that of the overall composition.

(A) Interior view of a collective space

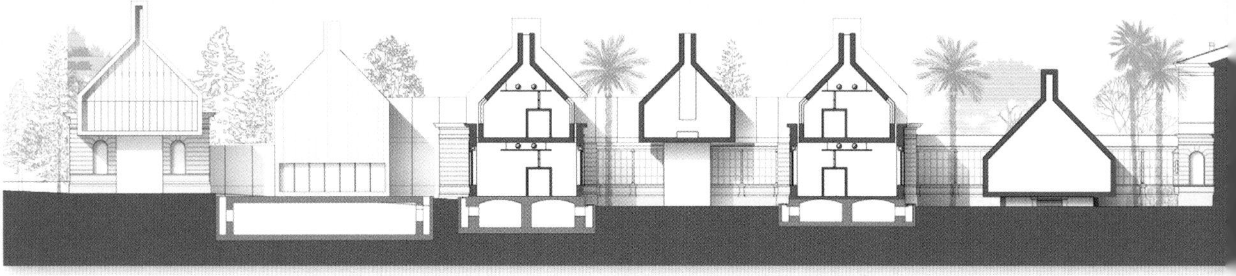

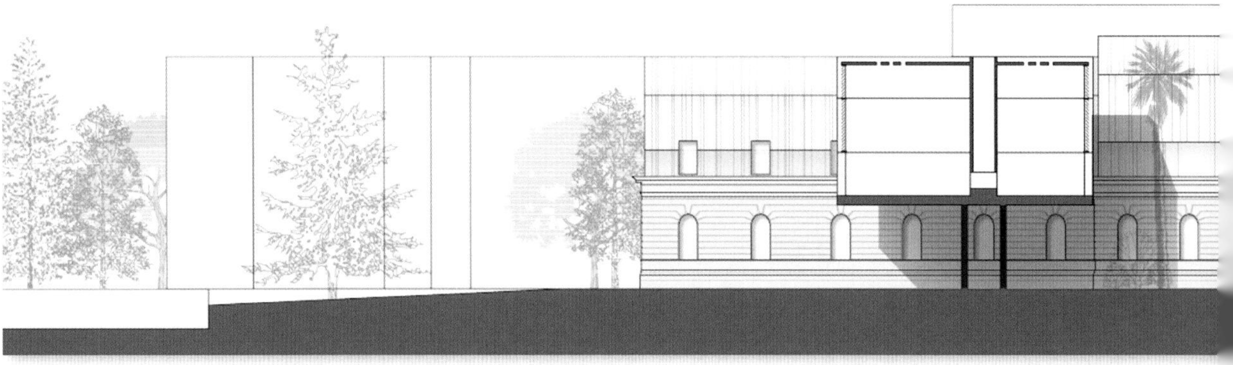

(B) Cross section
(C) Longitudinal section

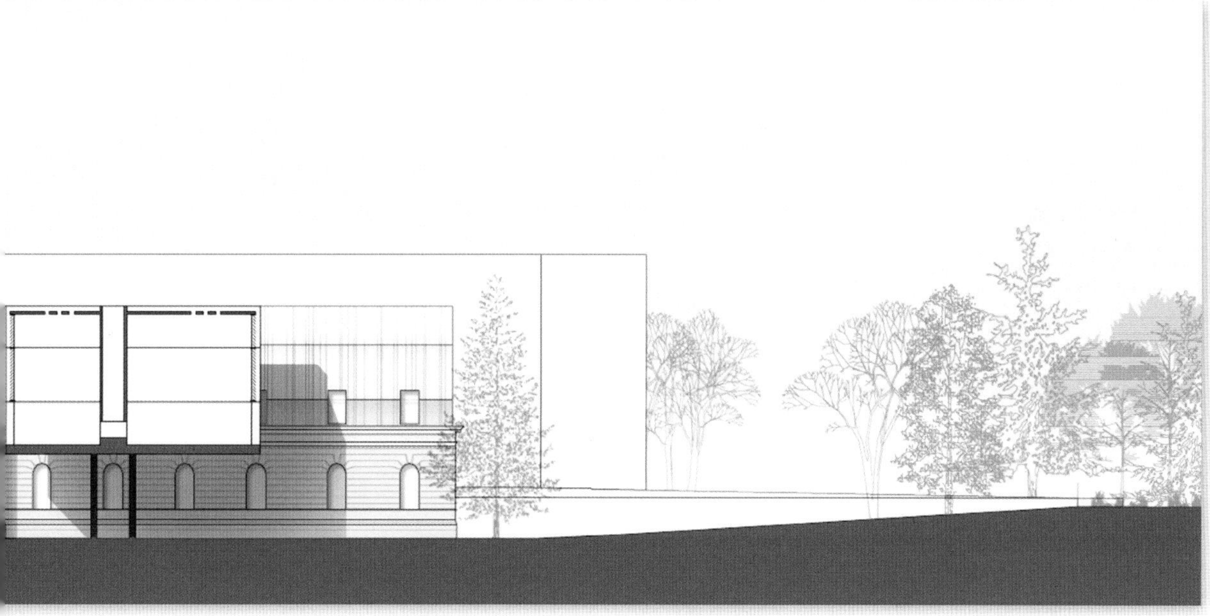

 (D) Overview of completed facility

3.3 NEVER TO BE FORGOTTEN
MEIS, National Jewish and Shoah Museum, Ferrara, 2010

A museum that wants to honour the history of the Jewish people in general, and the Italian Jews in particular will have to draw its inspiration, also architecturally, from the dynamic conception of what it means to be Jewish. The building, located between the city and the dock, is itself a mediator between the anthropic space (static) and the river (dynamic), just as the Jewish people live in themselves the complex and often problematic condition of exclusion/inclusion and have been, and still are, an element of mediation between different cultures. It is a dynamic meeting place of artistic, cinematographic and theatrical experimentation, combining past, present and future.

Transforming a prison, a place of suffering and exclusion – that closely echoes the entire cultural and historic existence of the Jewish people – into a place of life and culture, converting it into a completely different condition, induces us to apply two fundamental principles:

→ obliteration of the prison through a definite action that "cuts" one building and "spreads" its volume over the courtyard and open space remaining to be restored;

→ transforming the restored portion of the former prison into the "inner sanctum" of the museum, turning it into the heart and memory of a culture and a community.

The project attempts to respect the general imprint of the prison building and at the same time exalt and overcome the structural elements remaining after the demolitions.

In a random manner, at the level of the layout and floor plan, the prison layout – a structure enclosed in a fence – offers us a possibility of conversion that takes us, metaphorically, to the theme of the holy place of tradition, the concept of the temple within a sacred enclosure. The removal leaves the masonry visible and, above floor level, we have a "podium" that becomes the base for the museum structure.

From the open space of the courtyard, two new towers rise from the "podium". They are diaphanous towers, translucent, in constant communication with the city, a clear sign and manifesto of the new museum. On the highest part of the towers, images will be projected suggestive of the museum's dynamism and, at night, they will indicate its presence as large luminous bodies.

(A) Inside the summit of the towers

(B) View of the main entrance
(C) View of the moat and podium-garden

(D) View of the towers in cross section elevation
(E) Entrance hall and permanent exhibition

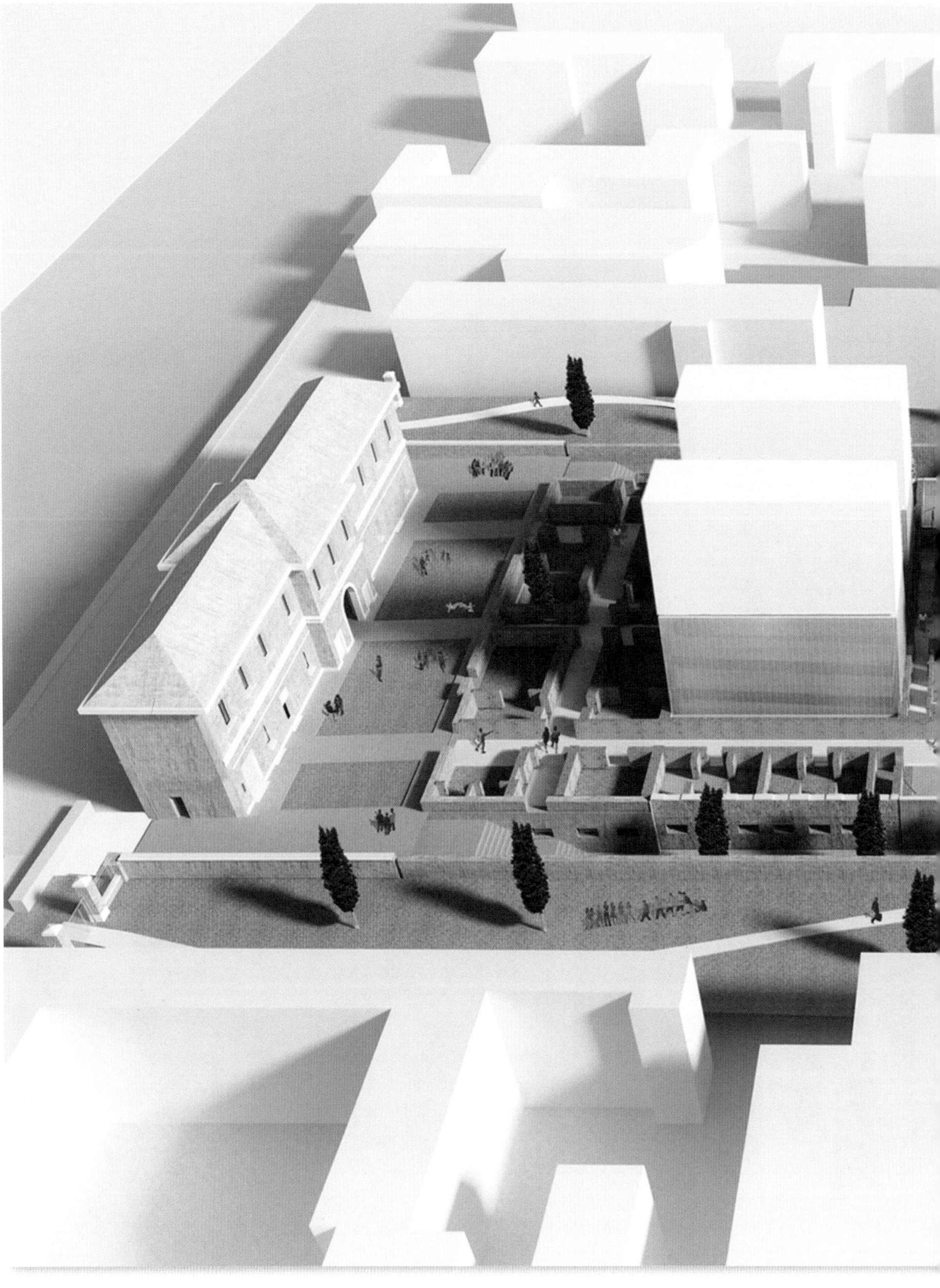

 (F) Aerial view of project

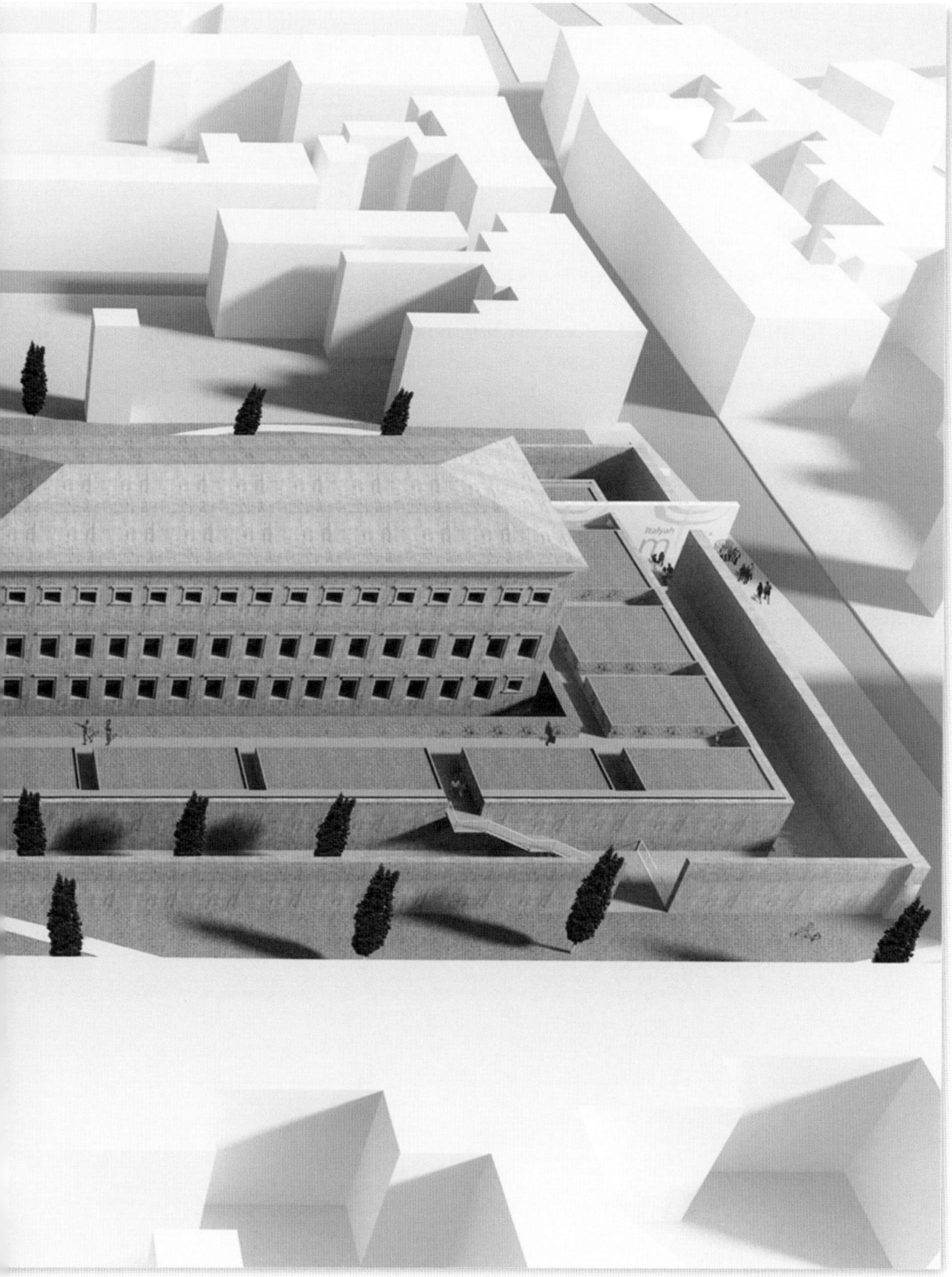

3.4 LIKE A MATRYOSHKA
P.L. Nervi Stadium and Campo di Marte, Florence, 2022

Seeing Nervi place a skeleton of concrete in a structure
is a magnificent lecture.
Don't ever put anything vulgar. Only elegance! He doesn't
call himself an architect but he is better than most of us.
(Le Corbusier)

The entire project grows out of an approach of extreme respect for the work of Pier Luigi Nervi as a true "modern monument" that must be restored to the city. Respect for history led us to conceive of a new stadium as a dual system, remembering Brunelleschi, between a historic treasure chest and an innovative, new, technological marvel shaped like a bronze leaf.

The original design of the stadium, once all the accretions have been removed and its historic structure restored through meticulous study, becomes the absolute focus of the entire project, while containing inside it the "new bronze leaf" that accepts the role of bit player alongside the pre-existent monument.

The project for the new Franchi Stadium can be summarized semantically as: "a stadium within a stadium". The architectural idea took shape, however, as a coordinated response to a set of inputs and analyses of a different kind. Among all, the desire to respect the testimonial value of the work of Pier Luigi Nervi, restoring it to its original integrity and making it perennially visible from the outside. But there was also the need to exalt the experience of the fans, bringing the seating as close as possible to the playing field.

The 40,000 seats envisaged by the project are arranged in five sectors, all covered. The covering, except for the existing portion, is equipped on the terminal section with special shades to optimise visibility. Indeed, the entire "stadium-in-stadium" approach, with the seats near the playing field, is functional to the focus on visibility and maximum enhancement of the spectators' enjoyment.

(A) Birdseye view of the stadium and the Campo di Marte district

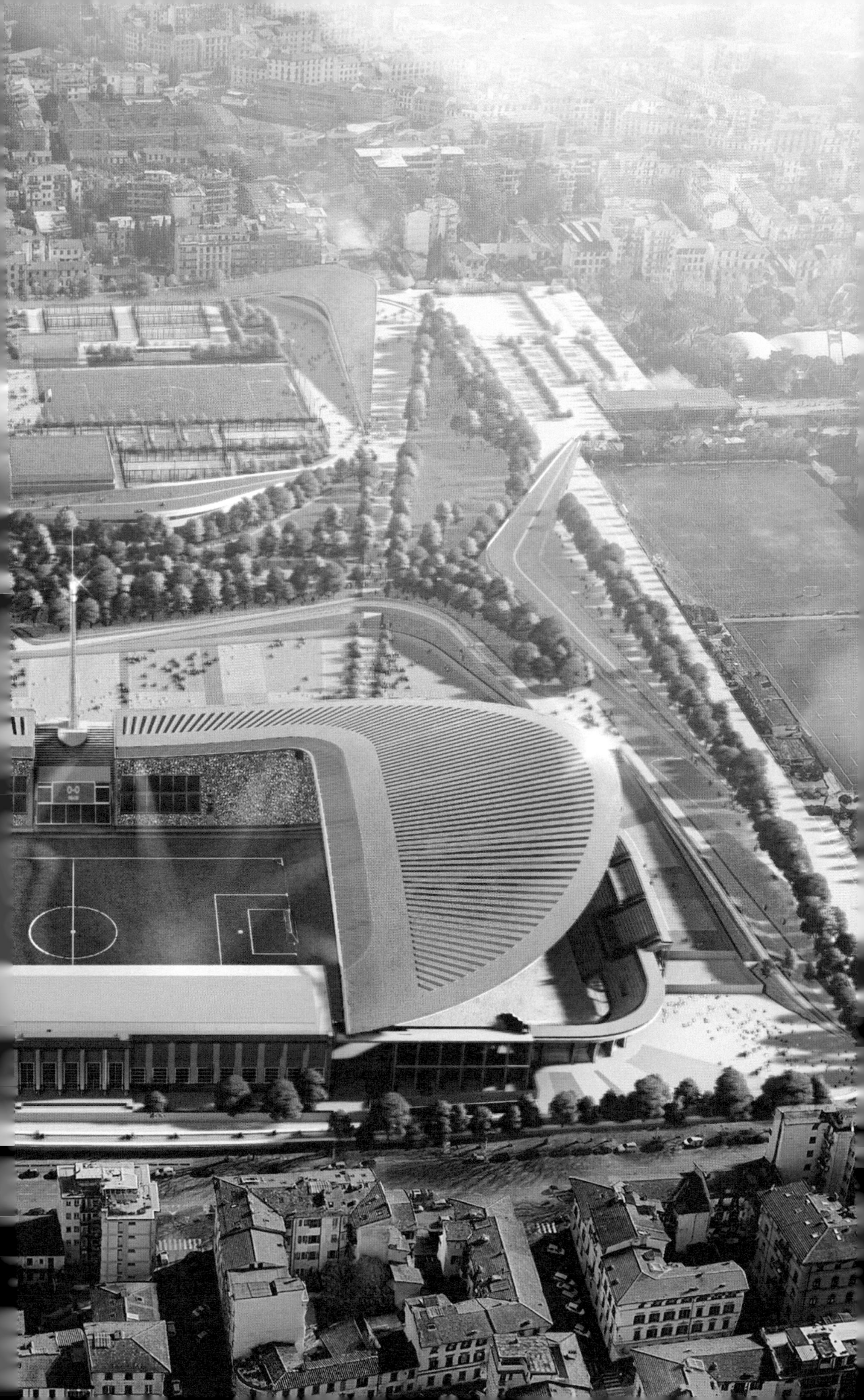

(B) View of the new stadium from the railway side toward the hills of Fiesole

(C) Restoration of the Nervi gallery, the daily market

(D) Existing bleachers that become space for sports events, exhibitions, recreation
(E) Relationship between pre-existing monumental work and new structure

(F) The new Fiesole bleachers
(G) Interior guest facilities and access to the Fiesole bleachers

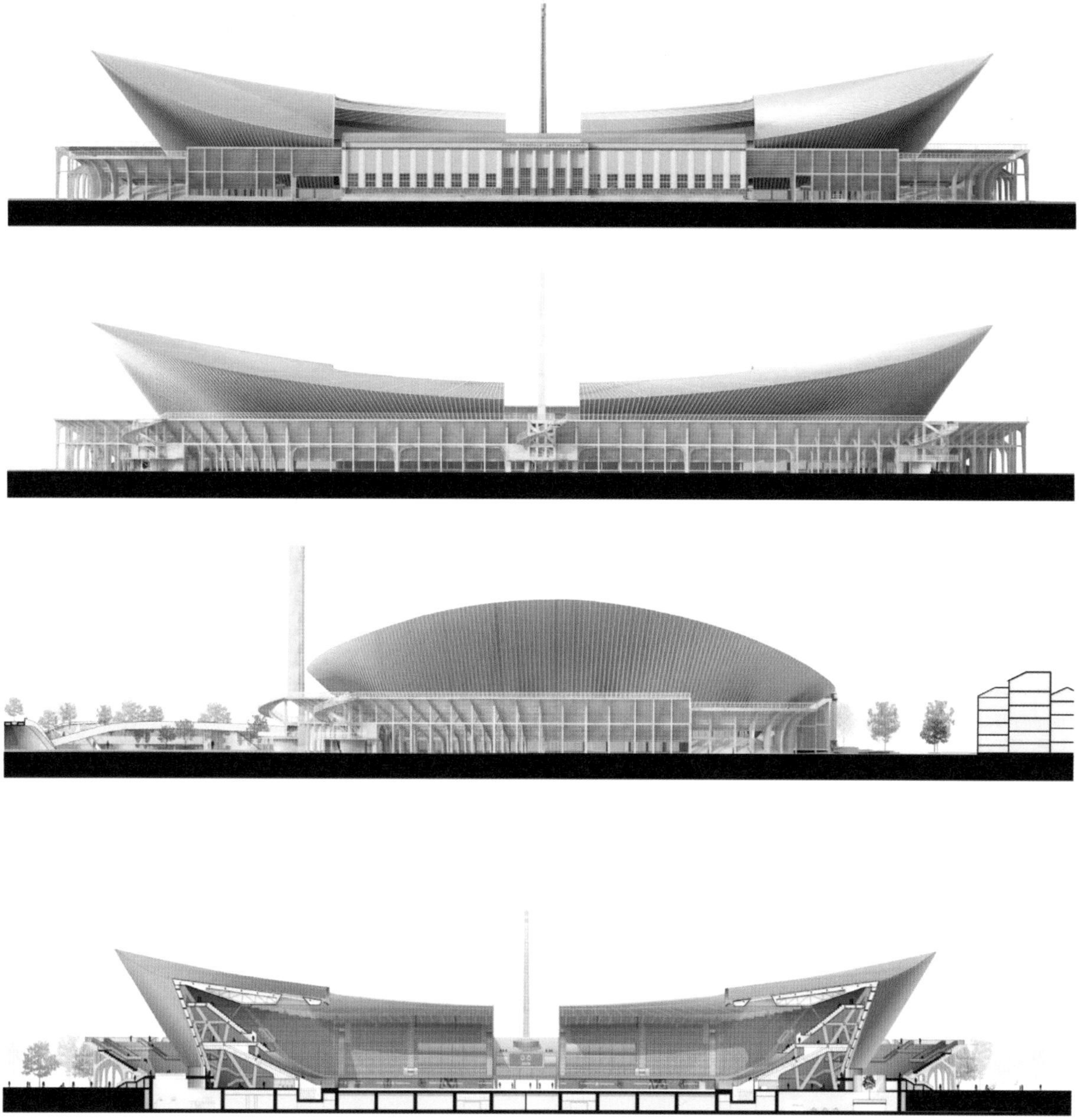

(H) Elevations and longitudinal section

3.5 NOTHING BUT A DIAPHRAGM SEPARATES US
Aluartforum, Zagreb, 2014

The project for the Aluartforum is part of the pre-existing structure, establishing relations of a volumetric and architectural character with the surrounding buildings and the project as a whole. It was meant to establish a strong continuity with the existing structural fabric, acting as an element of completion of the street view in which it would be inserted.

While the intention of this project proposal is, on the one hand, to connect the façades, establishing a visual continuity of the urban fabric, on the other, however, it was also important to emphasise the break with the past from the architectural and stylistic standpoint.

The museum appears to the eye of the visitor as a vertical sequence of suspended spaces, featuring a monumental stairway that alternates in a fluid, airy back and forth that is immediately comprehensible in its entirety. The stairway is characterised by its monumentality, generating an exhibition *promenade* and acquiring the role of exhibition space itself. This creates the need to enclose and contain the sequence of staggered floors through an element of cladding.

This cladding resembles a bellows and is characterised by a vertical structure that generates a dialectic relationship between the museum and the city according to a constant rhythm of apertures and closures, lights and shadows. It creates the impression of a rather insubstantial element of connection and union, serving to close the block but ready to open wide at the visitor's touch and reveal the art it contains.

(A) Detail of the vertical structure of the façade

 (B–C) View of the two exterior fronts

 (D) Perspective section

 (E) Interior exhibition space and monumental staircase

3.6 HOPING, WAITING FOR THE SOLUTION, AND MEANWHILE THIS PLACE RECEIVES ME

Expansion of S.M.A. Hospital, Bagno a Ripoli, 2012

The main generator of the New Admissions Building at the Santa Maria Annunziata Hospital was the need to make the facility more efficient and also more welcoming. This latter issue was resolved by proposing access to the hospital through a single large lobby, the very definition of a public space, that could attempt, at the same time, to be domestic.

The many limitations enforced on the area – the construction limit, in response to the problems of noise pollution deriving from the vicinity of the motorway and the need to provide an opening toward Florence and toward the Chianti district – restricted the architectural possibilities, but in this case offered an opportunity to develop technological responses through the project.

The type of structure reflects the Tuscan experience of the loggia-gallery concept launched by Giovanni Michelucci, and represented in particular by his project for the Santa Maria Novella Station, where the ample open loggia, entirely covered, provided a public connecting point between the parts of the city but was, at the same time, an open, welcoming place. The gallery becomes a huge container that can house all the function of incoming, organized in an independent way and characterised by a high degree of flexibility.

The new admissions building provides a connecting point between the needs of the city and those of the healthcare structure; it is a place of transition for the public with regard to the details of admission, information and communication, as opposed to the very private needs of treatment and assistance. What is new with respect to the current admissions building is obvious: it replaces the simple access to the hospital with a specific public place, a link between the outside world and the inside of the hospital structure.

(A) View of the interior of the hospital entrance lobby

 (B) Connection of the entrance structure with the existing hospital

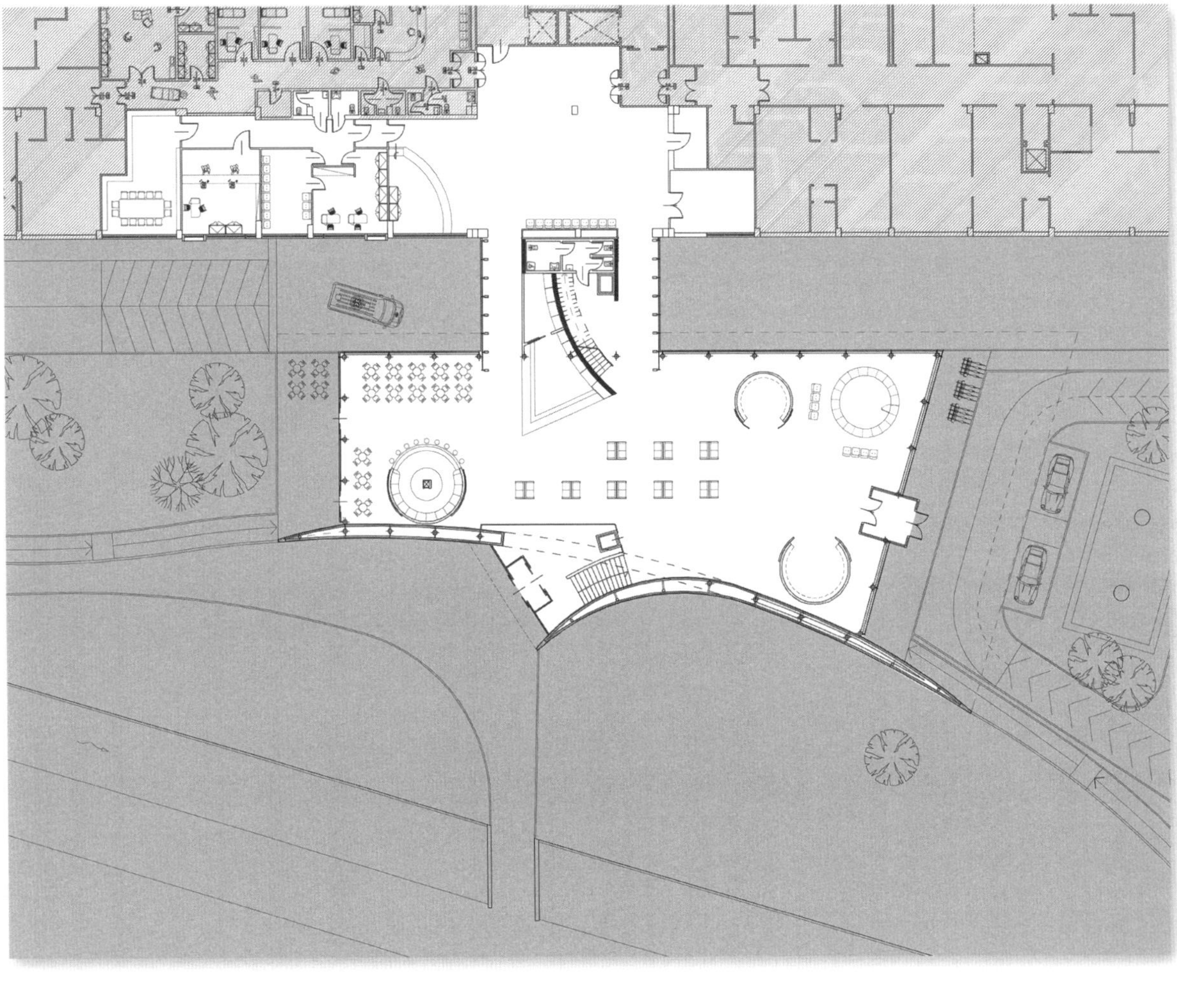

(C) View of the entrance from east
(D) Floorplan of the ground floor

 (E–F) Interior views of the gallery-loggia

3.7 TRYING TO MEASURE UP
Pedestrian bridge over the Valley of the Temples, Agrigento, 2013

A bridge. A path.

If it is not an arc, not a rope, it is simply a plank.
A trilithon. Two posts and a lintel. A minimum, essential, tectonic gesture, as the temples are tectonic, with their columns and entablatures. This bridge aspires to be a fragment of a discourse made of many fragments, scattered over the landscape, between nature and artifice, of the Valley of the Temples. A fragment, a monolithic block, a product of the technology of our time, yet able to communicate with that of the past. An open-profile, U-shaped beam in precompressed, reinforced concrete, produced in the finest tradition of Italian construction.

The project for the design of a walkway connecting the two areas of the Hill of the Temples is defined as the completion of an existing path in the southwestern sector. The basic desire expressed by the client was to rebuild the original connection between the east and west sectors of the hill, to give the visitor a unified topographic perception of the ancient "holy road" of the sector involved.

The idea behind the project was to rebuild the passage between the two sectors of the park through a type of link belonging, in the logic if not in the form and aspect, to the architectural and building culture underlying the archaeological zone itself.

The walkway presented offers the solution to two issues: one *in itself*, and that is, in the nature and form that the bridge has to have in order to perform its role as a crossing; the other, *beyond itself*, which refers to the way in which it is situated in the landscape, and how it establishes its role as an *anti-mimetic fragment*.

The *beam*, the architecture of the beam, its shape, in our project, is not simply a structural element on which to apply a pavement and create a path, but rather an organic structure that, by its nature and shape performs, on its own, the function of walkway and railing all in one. In that way it conveys and protects the people who walk across it.

The project of the bridge expresses its role as a *fragment*, that is, as a part, a significant but silent element of the composition of ruins and remains of the archaeological park; as such, it indicates an anti-organic approach with the context, avoiding any mimetic pretension.

(A) Perspective section of the pedestrian bridge

 (B) View towards the Hill of the Temples

(C–D) Sketches of the project

(E) Elevation
(F) View from the road

3.8 OVER A BRIDGE
Expansion of the OBV Hospital, Mendrisio, Switzerland, 2015

The project fills the urban void existing between the current structure of the hospital and via Turconi, in the attempt to create a public space linking it to the city. The addition to the hospital marks the edge of the public space created by the project for the plaza.

The project is configured as a linear structure connected at right angles to the main façade of the hospital, while minimizing the overlap between the two. Its function as a distributive block and the morphological breakdown into banks makes the volumes appear to advance and withdraw, a physical and functional connection that finds its tangential point in a blind area on the southwestern front of the current hospital. The organization, with its strongly specialised format offers multiple distributive possibilities within each floor, with a high degree of flexibility.

The parking and storage areas, as well as the technological control rooms are located underground and there is a public space on the ground floor, including a cafeteria and shops; the office block is located on the first floor and the examination rooms are on the second. The Dialysis and Nephrology sections are on the third level and the Post-acute treatment area is on the top floor.

Flexibility is the guiding principle of the entire expansion project. The sequential aspect of the project is stressed and highlighted both in the structural principle and exterior design of the façades.

The extroflexion of the structural elements allows for great freedom of the layout, where the positioning of the internal partitions can be adapted to the greater or lesser needs of space of the individual functions. All this is possible thanks to a clear static outline that is simple and rational, consisting of a construction system of just two elements: the bridging beam in reinforced concrete and the three-dimensional framing in steel, which is serial and flexible to respond to the specific functional and physical context.

The plastic/masonry and elastic/wood combination that characterises the style is the theme that guided the development of the project solutions for expansion of the Beata Vergine Hospital.

(A) Connection between the existing hospital and the expansion

(B) View of the linear structure from via Turconi

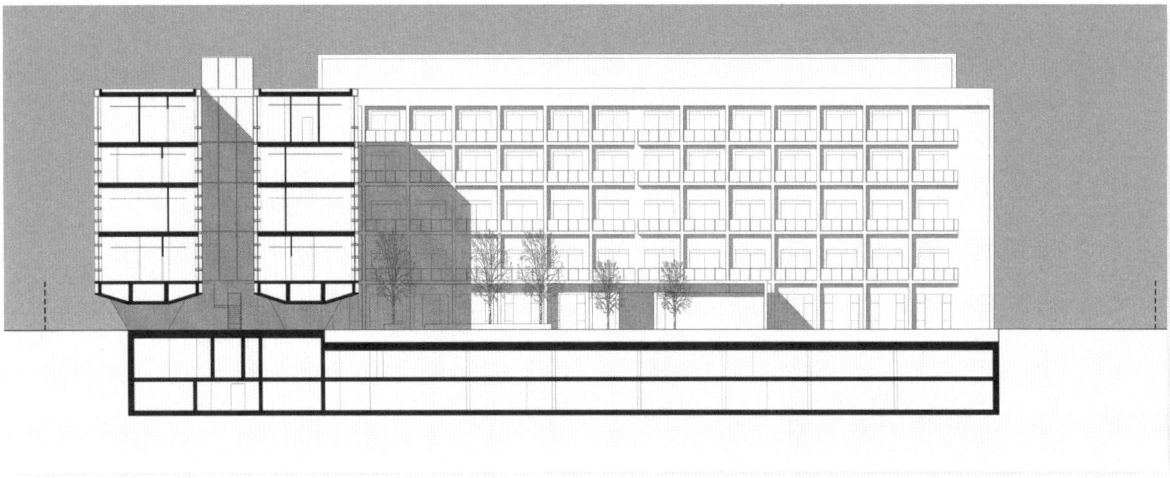

(C) View from the plaza
(D) Cross section

(E) Spaces of internal distribution and detail of the façade
(F) Public space on the ground floor with cafeteria and relaxation area

3.9 AN EXHIBITION SPACE IN THE SQUARE
Library and municipal services, Brescia, 2009

After identifying the specificities of the project, the proposed goal was to valorise the entire area, interacting with the existing structures and at the same time making it an attractive and iconic location in the central district of the city.

With this project, we wanted to bring new life to a part of the city that has great significance for its strategic location with respect to the university campus and other main plazas of the downtown.

It aims to become a point of attraction and fulcrum of activity, with a strong feature of identification thanks to the functions it provides for the many users: from the university students who can access its reading room, study rooms and lobby; to the tourists and citizens who can make use of the infopoint and Urban and Business District offices. Moreover, the exhibition space with its large wall-screen facing on piazza Rovetta becomes a reference for all the citizens.

The potential offered by this building is its ability to interact with the external environment, attracting the population at different times of day: in the morning, it is available to students and in the evening the interior spaces as well as the giant screen can be used for video projections.

(A) View from via S. Faustino towards Palazzo della Loggia

(B) General view from the plaza

IL FORNAIO

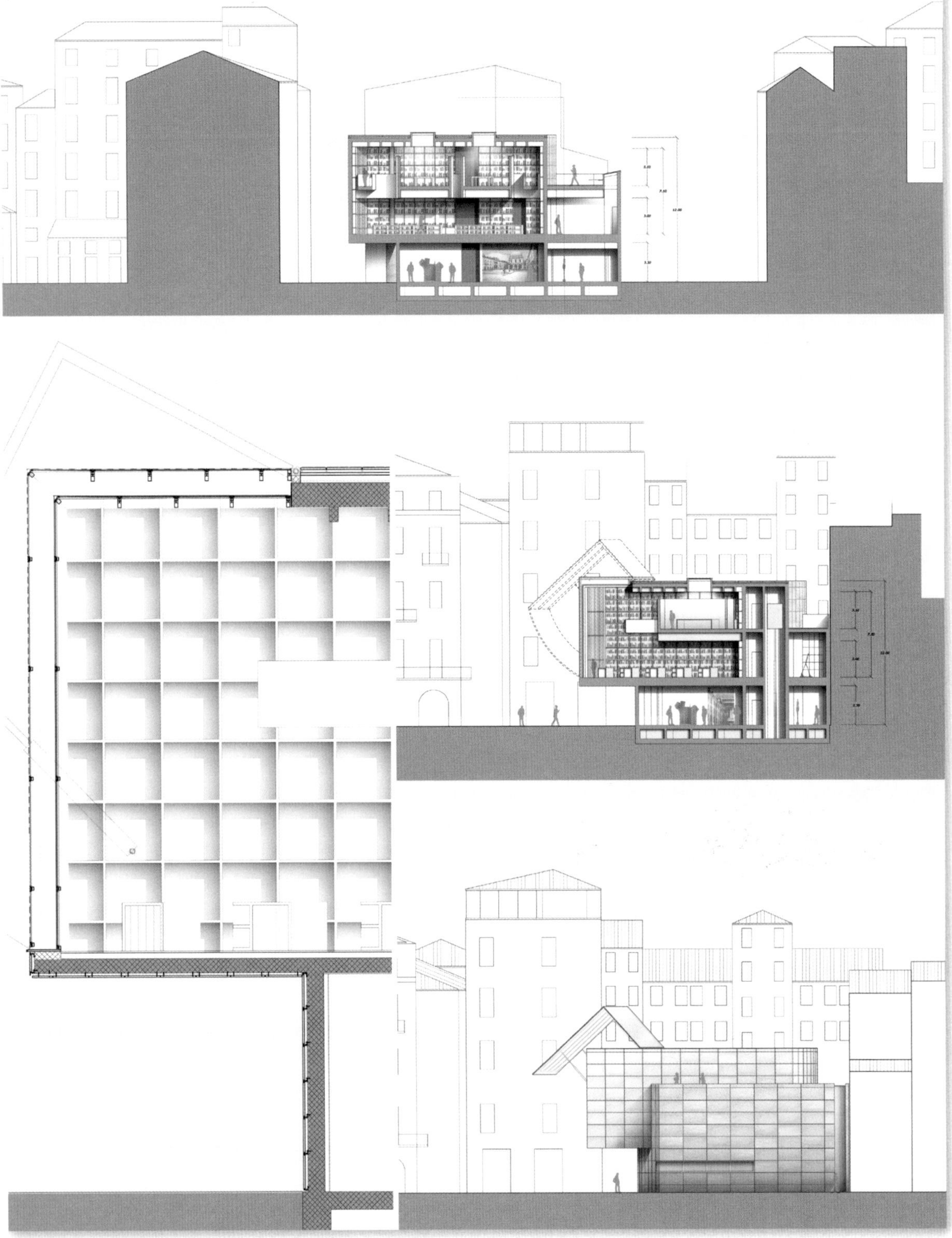

(C) Cross section, detail of section and eastern elevation

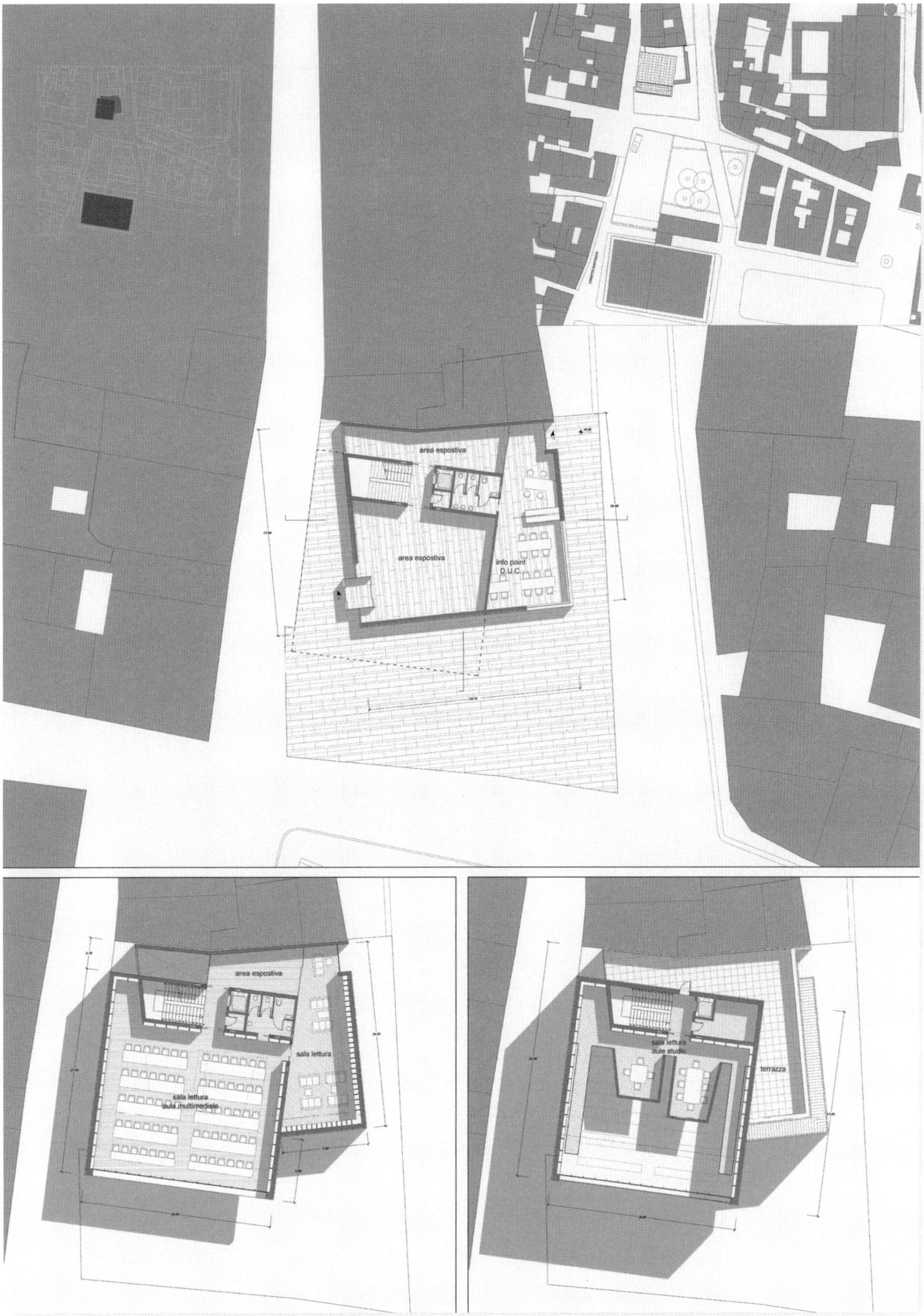

(D) Floor plan of the ground level
(E) Floor plan of the first level
(F) Floor plan of the second level

4. Architecture that reflects in the water.
   Many live near it, on it, around it.

There is a theme that links many of our projects; if we think of the work in Copenhagen and, years later, of that in Venice and, even later, the project for Helsinki, what links them is the fact of being on or near water.

This detail indicates a particular condition that is a fundamental part of architecture: its narcissistic dimension. A condition that underlies the project of architecture, beyond the need to pursue its substantial character, is that of appearing, of showing itself.

What better opportunity could there be if not that of being on the water, near the water, of having the possibility to look at oneself, to enjoy the effect of reflecting and mirroring one's image?

We have to say that this fascination with duality that grows within us certainly serves to highlight the very nature of a building's structure. Water, however, is not really a mirror, it is changeable; its ability to reflect is conditioned by many factors: the light, the height of the ripples, etc. In addition, the other phenomenon to take into consideration is refraction, that condition that splinters an image. However, aside from the aspects related to physics, reflection and refraction, architecture on the water, or even in the water, offers extraordinary impressions and sensations that can influence the very genesis of the design process.

The myth of Narcissus, however, warns us of the risk we run when we try to reflect ourselves in the water: that of missing the measure. Being near the water, for a building, means testing the dimensions of that limit. A changing limit, because it belongs to the contrary dimension, between solid and liquid, between land and water, it is a constitutionally unstable relationship. However, there are works of architecture that rise from the water, that merge with it, as in Venice, where water is its "foundation": Venice was born from the water, like Venus.

Other structures barely touch it, some even cross it without getting wet: bridges reach beyond its borders and connect the shores. But other buildings are there, waiting for the tide. They look as if they could be carried away by the sea, like a piece of the coast that becomes an island; other structures appear like floating cities, like the great transatlantic vessels that artists found so fascinating in the 20th century.

4.1 REFLECTING IN THE LAGOON
Ca' Venier dei Leoni, Venice,1985

Cà Venier dei Leoni was chosen by Aldo Rossi as a work to be studied and interpreted, as part of the 3rd Venice Biennale of Architecture. A building never born, but only suggested. Only the base portion of it exists and still today is the headquarters of the Guggenheim Museum.

To those who participated in the Biennale that year –1985 – this was the query proposed: imagine the complete building starting from what remains of it.

The idea was to imagine a conclusion that would either be a continuity or a contrast. We chose the former, a continuity that set itself the problem of how to develop the project as outlined: a specialised serial building arising from the general aspect of the urban structures along the Grand Canal, but also from the nature of the built portion remaining.

Cà Venier dei Leoni appeared, and appears, to be formed, in addition to its base portion, by the walled garden at the back, a classical secret Venetian garden. The heart of the system is the missing "Palace", consisting of three units, one of which organises the others symmetrically and acquires the value of compositive and spatial centre. In the project of redesign we imagined, where the classic Venetian hallway should have been, this first unit contained the invention of a space within the space, like a treasure chest, one literally opening into the other. The other two units, offered another variation on the Venetian palace, from a distributive standpoint as well as dimensionally.

The other parts we imagined for the complex were: the Galleria and the Scola.

The gallery occupies two levels and makes use of the existing wall. The "school", in the Venetian usage, disposes of its own space and expresses by its presence the asymmetric dissonance of the entrance.

This latter confirms the independence of the parts and marks the presence of the building on the mainland side with the small "Byzantine" dome, which accentuates its spatial quality.

(A) Detail of cross section

 (B) Main elevation

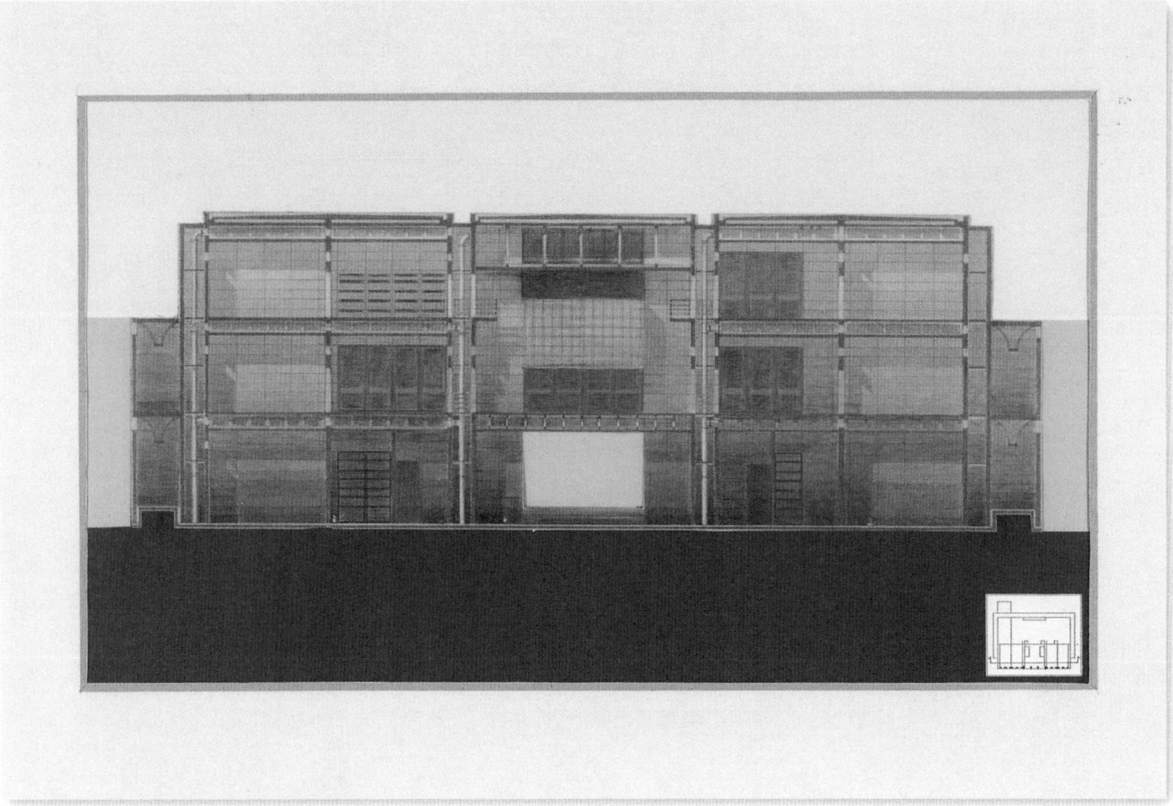

 (C) Longitudinal section

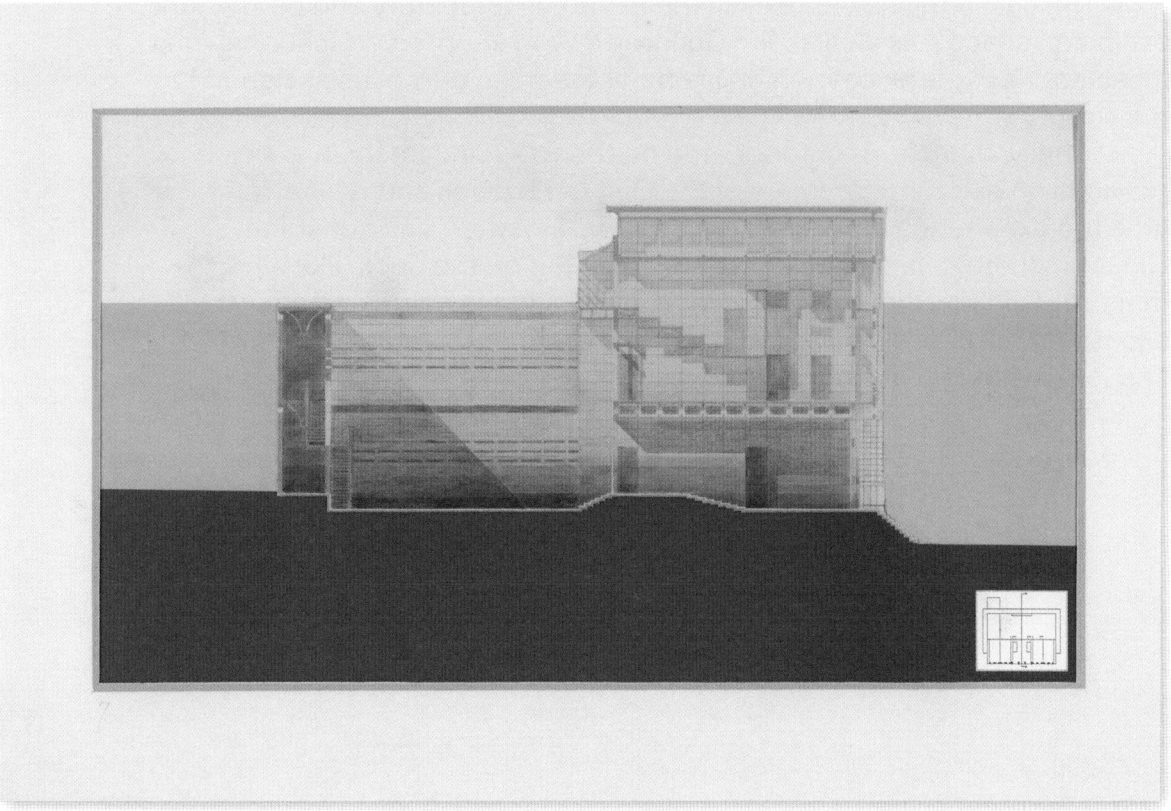

(D) Longitudinal section
(E) Cross section

4.2 UNDER FULL SAIL IN SEARCH OF THE SUN RATHER THAN THE WIND
Science Centre, Naples, 2015

What was left after the fire of March 4, 2013 that destroyed part of the main building of the Science Centre is a place without origin, an orphan of a building.

There were two possible choices: to rebuild exactly as and where it was, or to build something new and meaningful in its own right.

Our choice was to design a building that could interact with itself, built atop the area of the pre-existing building but leaving the remaining portion, which would acquire the role of a ruin.

It is a structure, a non-building, that calls to mind the memory of the former one. An ark that does not float, but is under construction, awaiting a flood that is to come. A new reality that does not forget what came before.

Moreover, by placing the building at a height of 3 meters above the ground, we are able to ensure a visual continuity and use toward the sea, so as to allow the visitor the opportunity to achieve a direct relationship with the coast and the gulf.

As such, this ark has a belly, a hold, capable of containing the Science Centre, with access through the only two elements located at ground level: the former contains the entrance, box office and information desk, and one of the two snack bars, the latter contains the lifts.

The space that is the belly of the ark holds temporary and permanent exhibition spaces, as well as the Children's Workshop, an educational area for scientific experiences, which is one of the main purposes assigned to the structure.

Finally, there is an outdoor area on the roof/deck of the ark which provides an extraordinary view of the Gulf of Pozzuoli and, at the same time the experience of natural phenomena: air, water and sunshine. Gigantic photovoltaic panels are also installed on the deck, like sails, that turn to follow the sun. They stand alongside the agora and stairways accessing the different levels and, in case of excessive wind, can turn and fold to prevent the sail effect.

(A) Access to the Science Centre and relationship with the existing building

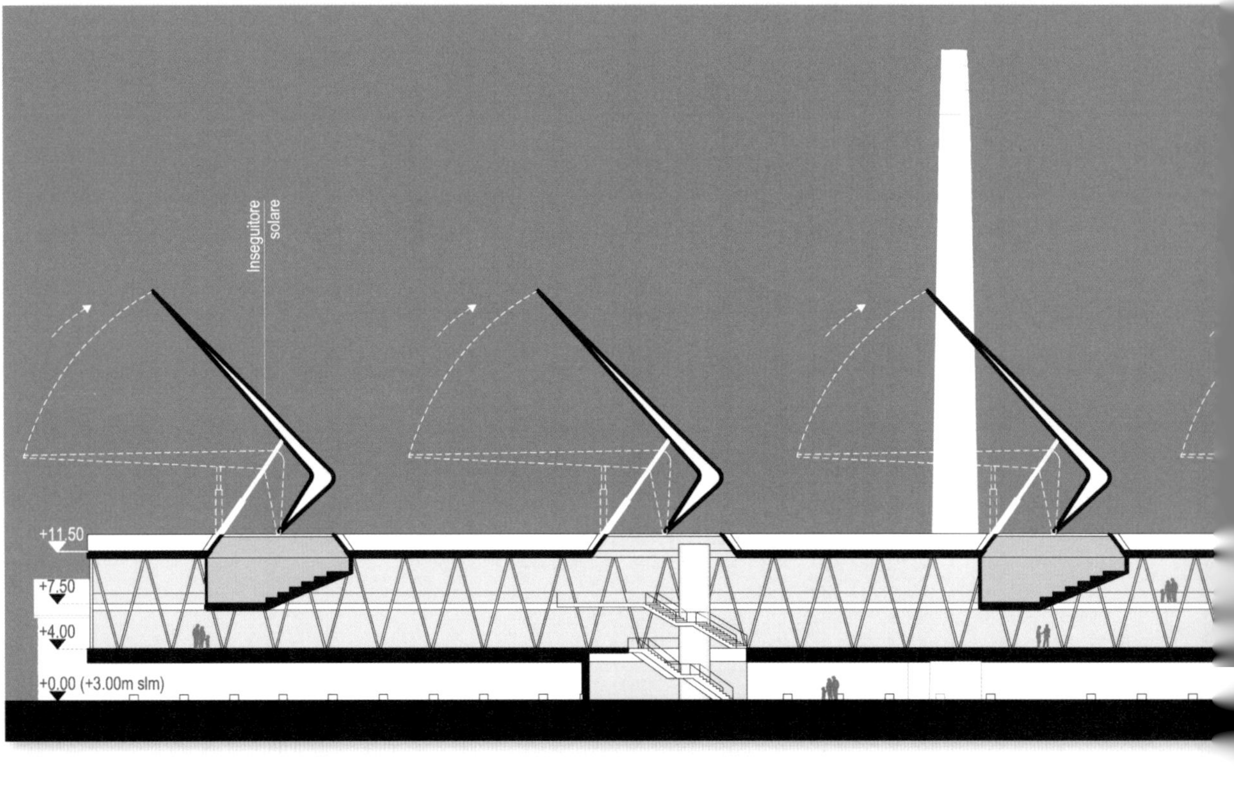

(B) View of the new construction from the sea
(C) Longitudinal section

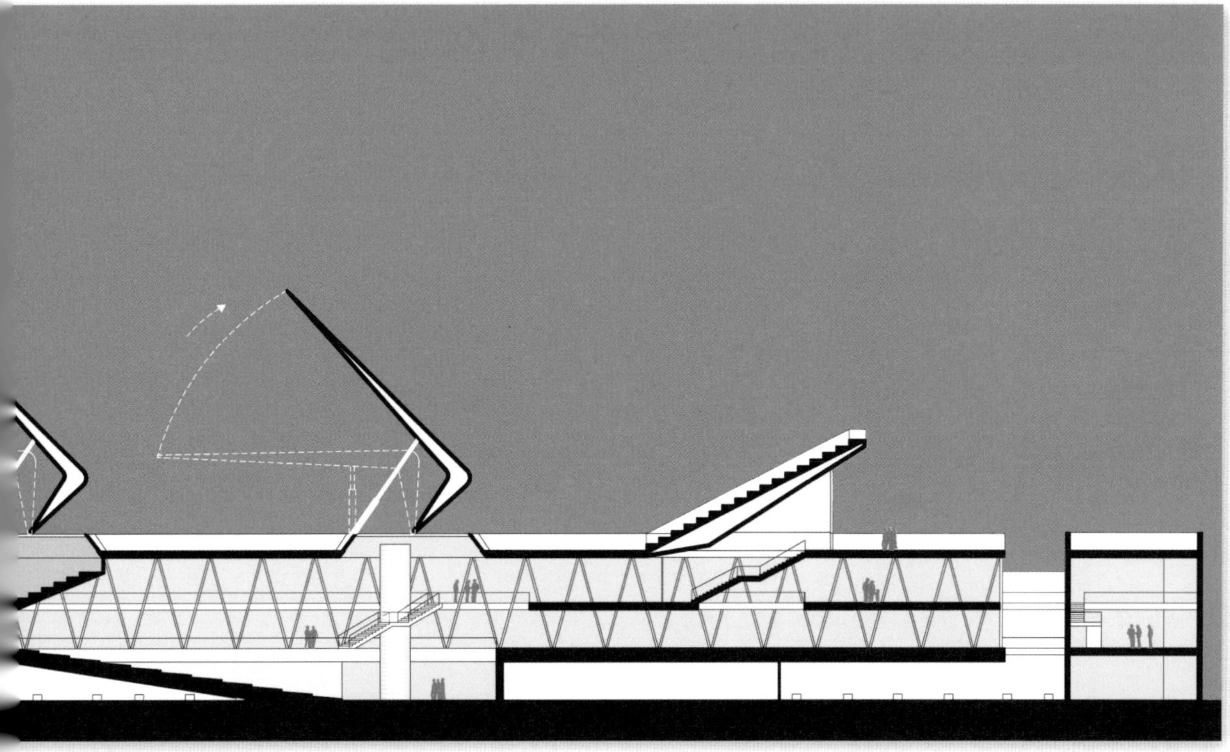

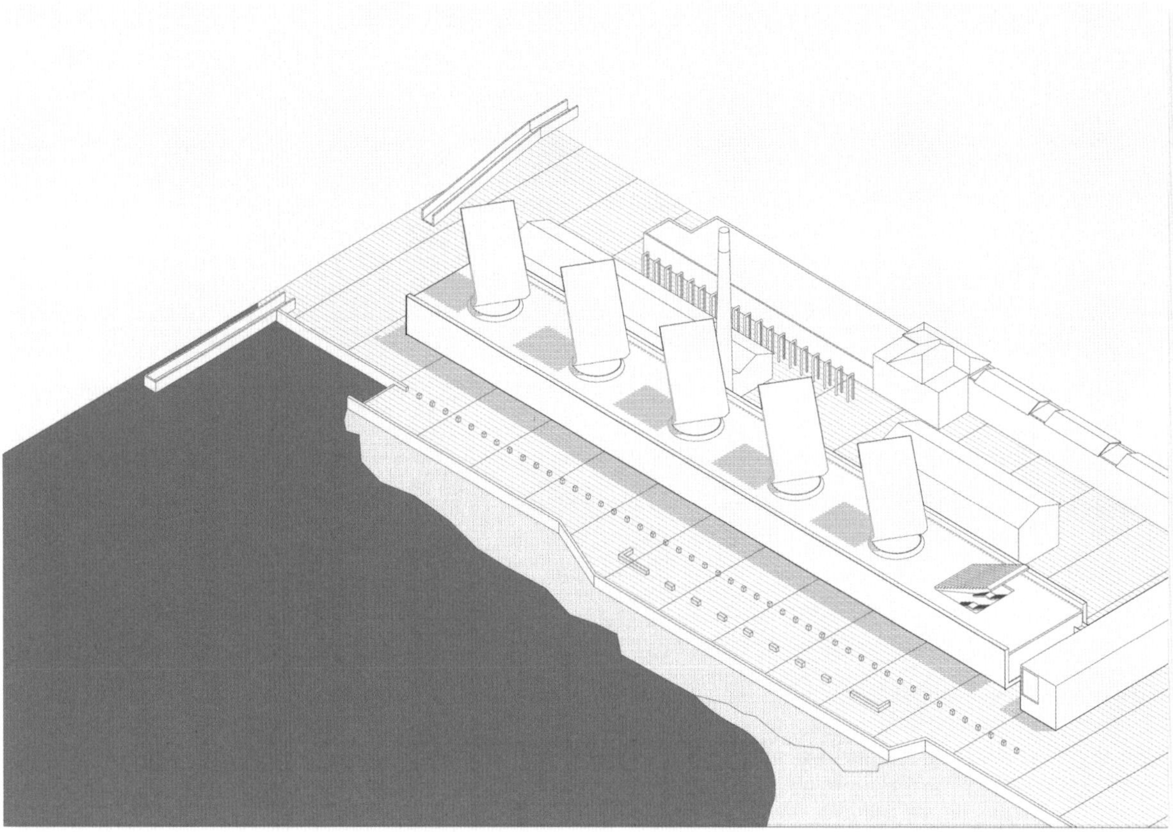

(D) General axonometry

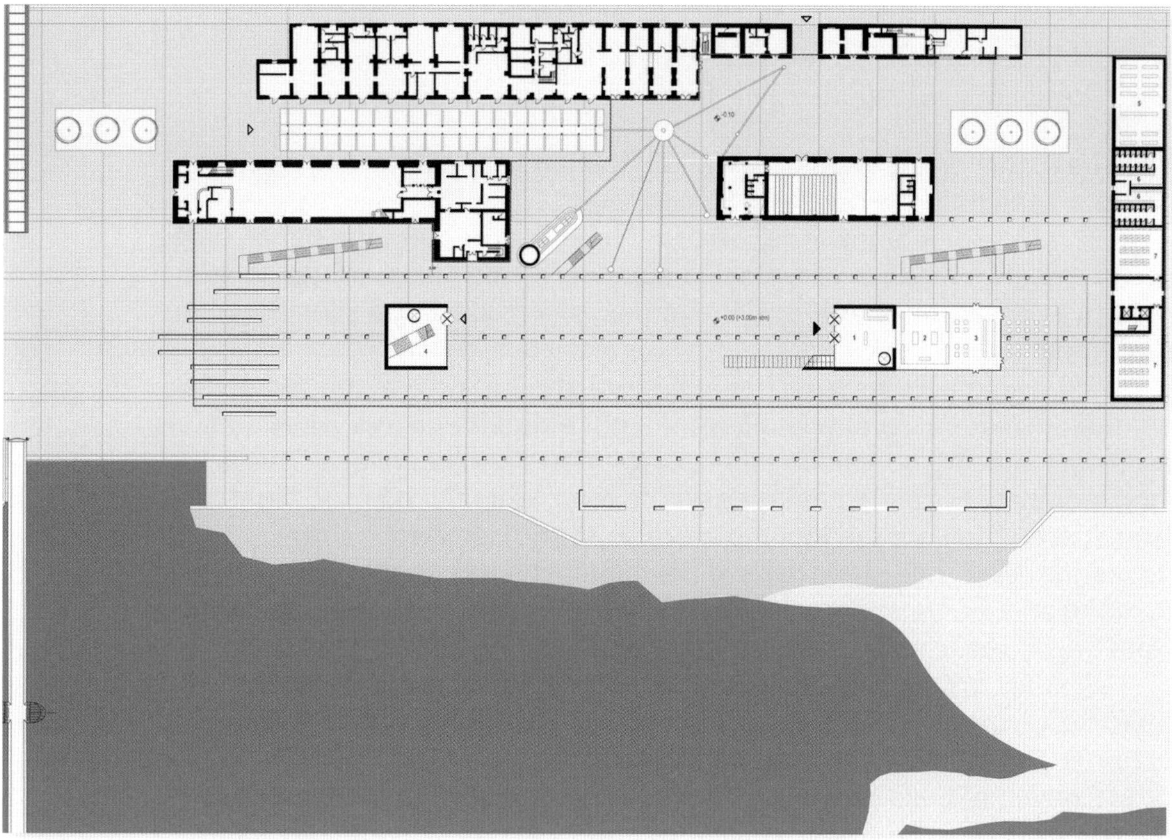

 (E) Floor plan of the ground level

4.3 WHEN THE SHIPS REMAINED AT ANCHOR IN THE HARBOUR, AWAITING THE TIDE
Royal Library, Copenhagen, 1993

The site of this project was on the Slotsholmen, in the decommissioned harbour zone near the centre of Copenhagen.

The project intends to reconstruct a unified front on the canal, using two elements evocative of typical images of the old harbour: the dock, to form a continuous base, and the jetties which, like huge silos, sink into the water.

The two main elements of the system, the "quay" and the "wharves", are then designed using two different architectural registers. The "quay" is actually a building containing some of the new library services. This is a long, compact building that faces on the road, with a tilted roof, "light" and "transparent" toward the top and more solid and compact below, descending in broad steps toward the canal. The reduced height of this building and the geometry of its roof leave glimpses, from the canal and from the opposite side, of the monumental buildings of Slotsholmen.

On the contrary, the "wharves" contain the final portion of the building, connected to the Royal Library and, cutting across the "quay", maintain the rotation with respect to the canal.

The entire building consists of three central portions that cross the Christians Brygge on a bridge-like structure. From the central block the building is divided into five branches, three of which protrude, just like pilings, from the water of the canal.

The jetties, characterized by the lightness and transparency of the cladding in wood and glass, are fitted with adjustable shutters to admit more or less light and enclose the reading room in a single large volume; from the inside, through the closely knit wooden structure visible, the perception of the external environment is enveloping, to create in the visitor the sensation of being in an open space, suspended between the sea and the sky.

(A) View of the model, one of the bridges that extend over the canal

(B) View of the model, detail of one of the reading rooms

 (C) View of the model, detail of one of the reading rooms

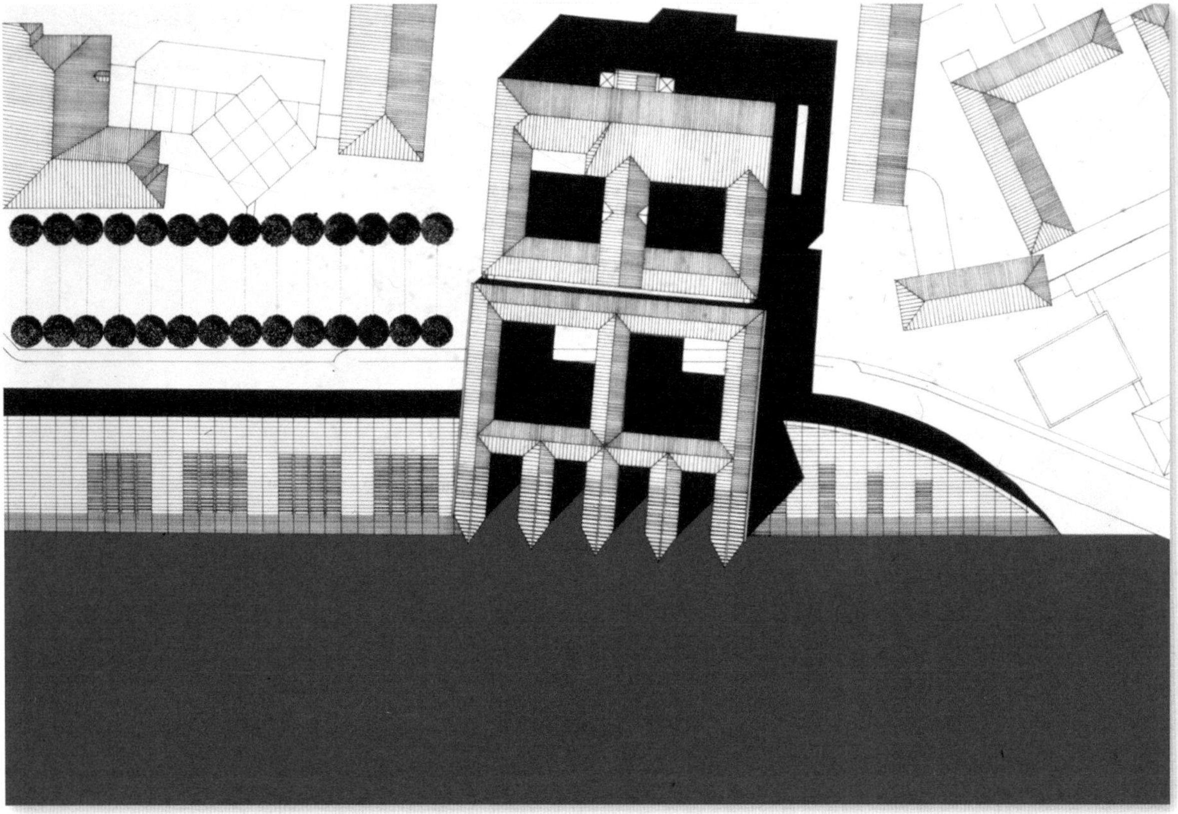

(D) 3D overview

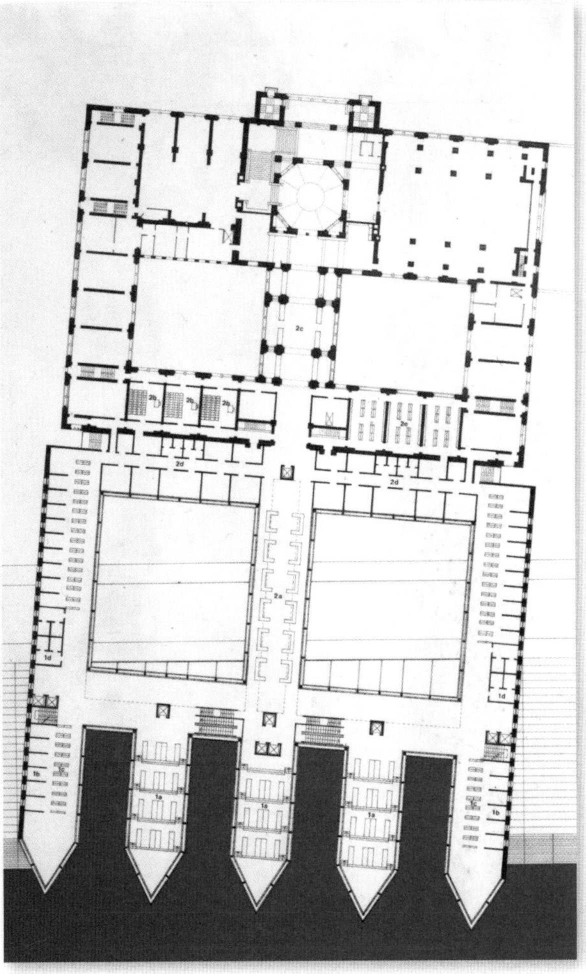

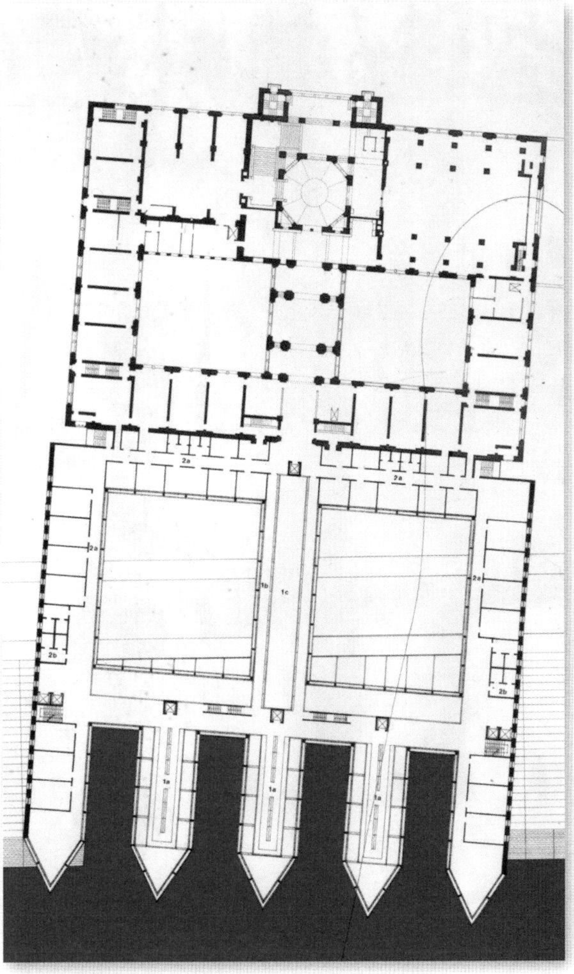

(E) Floor plan of the second level
(F) Floor plan of the third level

(G) View in perspective of the reading rooms on the canal

4.4 MEASURING OURSELVES AGAINST THE VAST HORIZONS OF VENETIAN TERRITORY
Office Complex, Porto Marghera, 2003

This project came out of the desire to comply in every respect with the Plan of Recovery, which was intended as part of a process of redevelopment already in progress in the mainland city, more than to refer to an improbable dream of a "new Venice". An ongoing process of reconversion to new functions, involving broad swaths of Porto Marghera, without losing sight of the significant productive focus that has always distinguished it, but confirming its value through an essential environmental restoration.

The distinctive characteristics of the place made it a sort of metropolitan alter ego of Venice, and any solution imagined for it had to take account of this condition in order to grasp its virtuous contradictions.

The project theme arises from our impression of the site: a place closely tied to the shipping and industrial landscape, connection between an area undergoing a process of rapid transformation and the mainland city; a place subject to a special condition of significant visibility and accessibility, as the motorway to Venice passes right by it. It is a place suspended between a forward-looking contemporary world and the memory of the 20th century.

The main impression that influenced the whole project was the way in which the building complex stood in relation to the harbour canal and is its terminus.

The location of the group of public spaces at +4.00 meters above sea level leaves room on the ground to establish a privileged relationship between the pedestrian area and the water. A series of furnished terraces can be seen, in the guise of docking points, from the tilted ramp that reaches the second level of the business zone, the base of which is similar to the deck of a ship with two bridges: permeable and passable with railings and tunnels, and integrated with the arcaded system that overhangs the portions open to the public.

The office centre, however, is located in the two elevated buildings that extend toward the water. The look of the entire complex is dominated by its imposing structure: a sort of "worksite" that evokes vague memories of industrial activity and, more specifically, of the shipping port business of the place, interpreting and transferring to the project materials that might as well have gone into shipbuilding activities.

(A) View of the interior of one of the suspended volumes

(B) View of the new office centre from the canal

(C) Area of access to parking lot

(D–E) View of the pool in the open and closed configuration

4.5 RISING FROM THE SEA, SHE TURNED TO STONE
New IUAV campus headquarters, Venice, 1998

> The chain of marble cliffs.
> (Marcel Proust)

Venice is, beyond all the dreamy imagery, the civilisation of construction. Designing architecture for Venice is a problem of civilisation: a project for a material and intellectual culture that in absence and in need has found the architectural materials and stylistic inventions that allowed it to be built. The area of San Basilio is detached from the city and in order to make it a part of Venice it is essential to make it like all the rest.

The first act was to redesign the harbour and urban areas. Of the port, the language of the quay remains, connected with the city through the water and a slender jut of land (narrow, a mere strip). The second was the demolition of the Naval Station with its immense size acting as a barrier to relations between the city and the sea. Finally, the pedestrian pathways had to find their way back to the lagoon.

The city extends over the entire area of San Basilio, as if to take back the lagoon for its own. The garden islands line the route of the Zattere. Islands that conceal and protect lovely gardens, like little shards of land floating on the lagoon and recreate with their nearness to the quay and the old port, the memory of those peripheral lots, with their weed-infested borders, that surrounded the city and defined its relationship with the water. After the long harbour building on the quay was demolished, pilings were left in place of the former Ligabue warehouses and became new elements of contact between the sea and the land, extending over the canal like the hangars of an airport.

The new IUAV headquarters are the product of overlapping traces. The structural metaphor of the building starts from the floor plan of the demolished block. The traces remain, with the columns that emerge from the water, changing into something that no longer remembers those old cold storage warehouses. The project becomes a metaphor of the destiny of Venice and this part of the city. From an industrial site to a place of cultural production. The façade on the canal returns to the theme of projects for buildings in Venice: the legibility of the interior structures, both spatial and constructive, the transparency of its parts combined with a fascination for wood borrowed from a mason's experience. Three levels of spaces: public, community, private, each corresponding to a different level of the building. On the Giudecca side, the classrooms, open toward the lagoon, and are transformed into a sort of balcony suspended between the sky and the water. Here, in spaces created in continuity with the classrooms, are sections devoted to seminars, small meeting rooms. The auditorium, under particular conditions, opens toward the little Oratorio square, which becomes the stage. Every classroom, within its physical limits, is not made to border on another space except through the mediation of the light. The sensation, at all times, is of a perception of light, sky and sea.

> The present resurrects the past making
> a continuous metamorphosis of it.
> (André Malraux)

(A) View from inside the jetty toward the lagoon

 (B–C) Views from the canal

 (D) Inside the classroom facing the Giudecca

 (E) Main façade seen from the canal

4.6 A FOREST OF MASTS AND RIGGINGS
Tourist port, Piombino, 2011

The project, located in the area of Poggio Batteria, provides for creation of a Tourist Port with areas for the upkeep and storage of boats and an integrated service complex, with a view to the creation of a direct relationship between the new port and the city of Piombino.

The building that, with its immense "doorway", marks the junction point between the "internal" infrastructure of the marina and those integrated with the docking area has the task of indicating the entrance to the passenger and tourist point, representing a sort of "Gateway to the Sea".

The type and intended use of the works on land – in particular those included in the roster of services that are integrated with the infrastructures of the tourist port as well as with a series of functions available to the public – make the project interesting not only for the creation of a new and important holiday structure but also as a significant work of redevelopment and modernization of the urban context.

The project of the works on the sea developed after a careful analysis of the natural conditions of this portion of the coast. In the marina zone, the jetties lie at right angles to the quay adjacent to the embarkation plazas and the under-watershed zone, with optimum spacing for manoeuvring of the different boats docked there.

The services along the wharf are distributed with very low density and without ever exceeding two floors above ground.

The structures intended for on storage and the boatyard were built near the large plaza at Punta Semaforo, almost entirely occupied by a tent system with which four large hangars are being readied to winter boats of various sizes on land. Air generators and a mini-windfarm will be installed on the pylons of these tent structures.

Along the north-eastern side, the last segment of suspended roofing to the riggings of the tent structure holds the shops and services devoted to the quay for docking the larger yachts.

(A) Gateway to the sea

 (B) Structures devoted to on-land boat storage

(C–D) Aerial views

(E) Quay for docking large yachts

(F) Quay with shops and service structures
(G) View of the sea before entering the tourist port

4.7 TOUCHING THE SKY WITH MUSIC IN OUR EARS
Landmark Tower/U2 Studio, Dublin, 2003

A singular, extraordinary opportunity: Ireland, Dublin and the U2. One of the most prestigious bands on the musical scene in the last decade was associated with the construction of a tower which would have to house their recording studio. Conceived and planned at the point where the two canals of the port of Dublin converge.

The idea of working with such an iconic theme: a tower and a band, messengers of the new Ireland, appeared highly stimulating. To measure ourselves with a place where water plays an absolute role, but also with the mists they create, attracted us greatly, even having no other references beyond that of the towers scattered through the Irish countryside. In fact, this was one of those projects located in place we have never visited or known, except in literature and in our own imagination.

Would it be impossible to design a project without our physical knowledge and presence? We don't know, but we have often felt that the distance and the imagination can facilitate the vision of extraordinary things that, vice versa, excessive knowledge of a place might prevent us from perceiving or suspecting.

The elements of this configuration are a horizontal structure and a vertical one. They interact and define an absolute image, a monolithic block in concrete that dissolves in the mist at the top, on its summit, with a series of crests on which stands the cube, partially in glass, of the recording studio, with its amazing, inspiring view.

(A) View of the tower from one of the canals in the port of Dublin

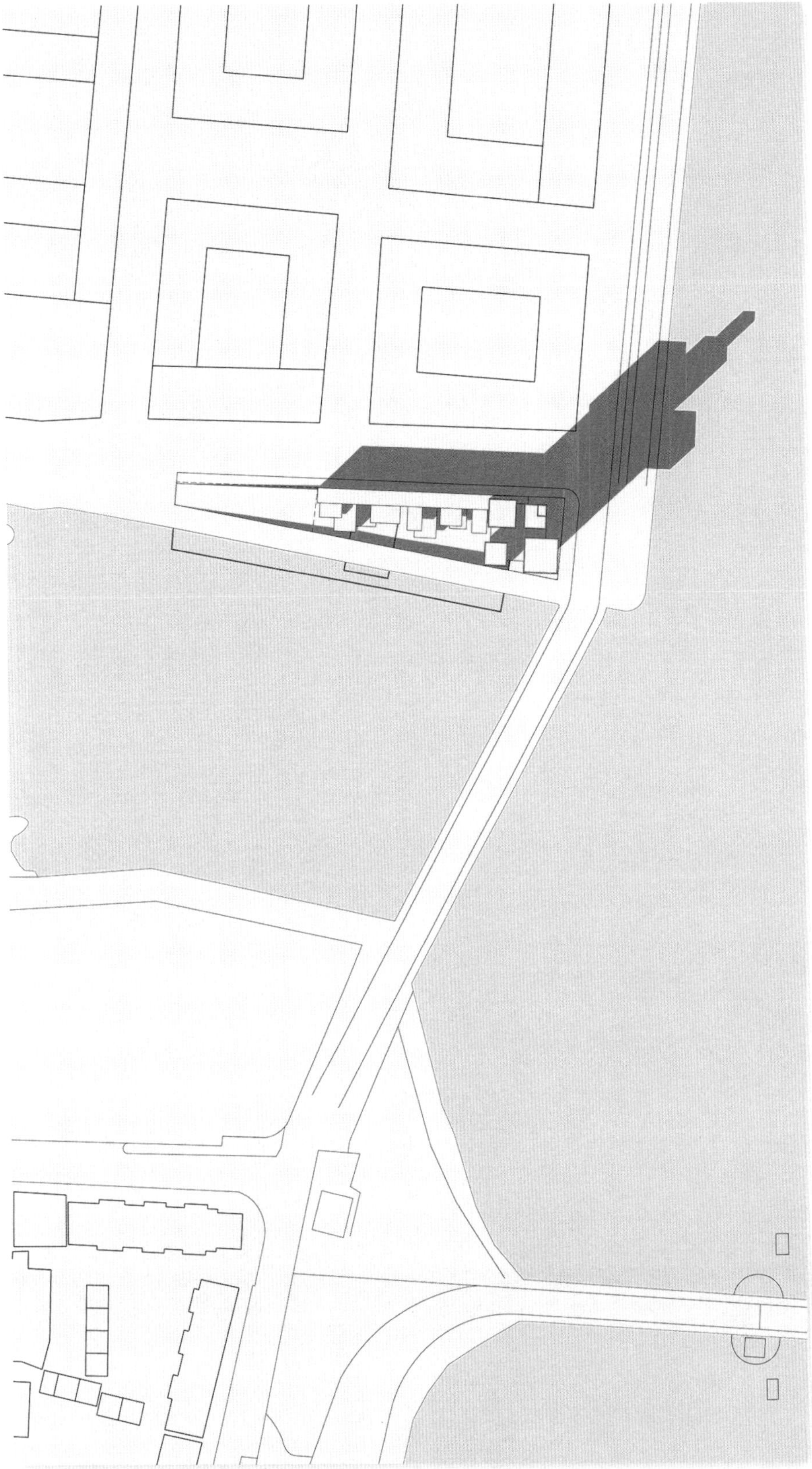

 (C) 3D overview

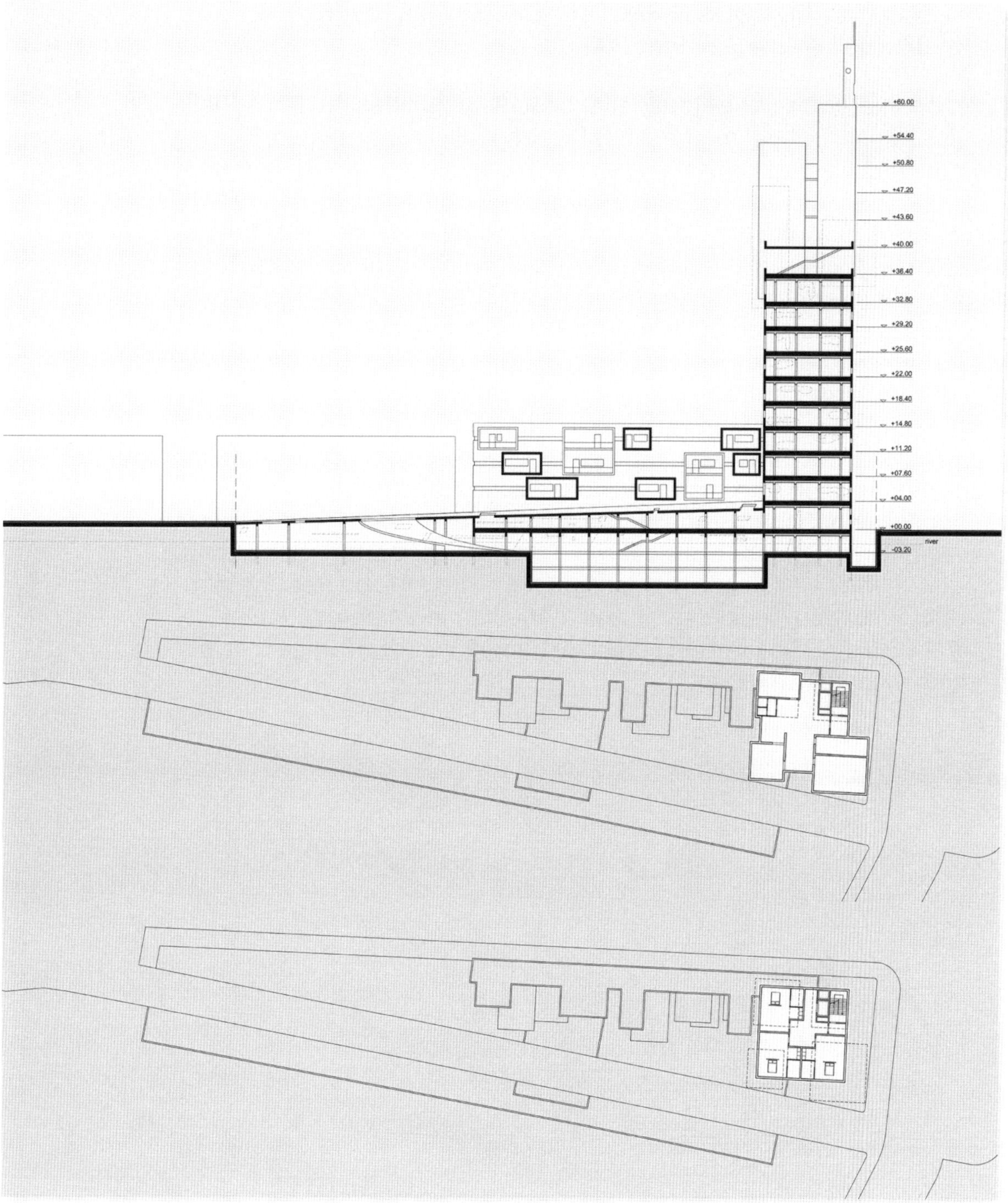

(D) Longitudinal cross section, floor plan of recording studios, floor plan of residential and office floors

4.8 UNEXPECTED COUNTERPOINT ACROSS THE RIVER
Ponte della Musica, Rome, 2000

Point-counterpoint is the slogan that best distinguishes the Ponte della Musica [Music Bridge] on the Tiber River but, like every slogan, it came after the fact.

The profound reasons for the project are rooted in the desire to create an inviting, not hostile, pedestrian bridge, one that treats the users to fascinating views of the other side of the river and, at the same time, shelters them – rather than exposing them. The idea of this pedestrian bridge is to emulate the Old Bridge in Florence or the Rialto Bridge in Venice, where the water, in its entirety, comes into view suddenly, when one arrives at the centre.

A pedestrian bridge as the ideal continuation of the riverside road.

An *inhabited bridge*, that grows out of the desire to pay tribute more to the stonemason's art than to a more elastic wooden tradition; its references generally classical and Mediterranean. It is not antithetical to the expressive richness of so-called lighter structures, but is an attempt to achieve the same impression of lightness through apparent weight.

A monolithic block contrasts with the dominant perception of lightness as a necessary and sufficient condition; it is a bridge that is nothing more than a beam.

(A) View of bridge intrados

(B–C) View from above and general view of model

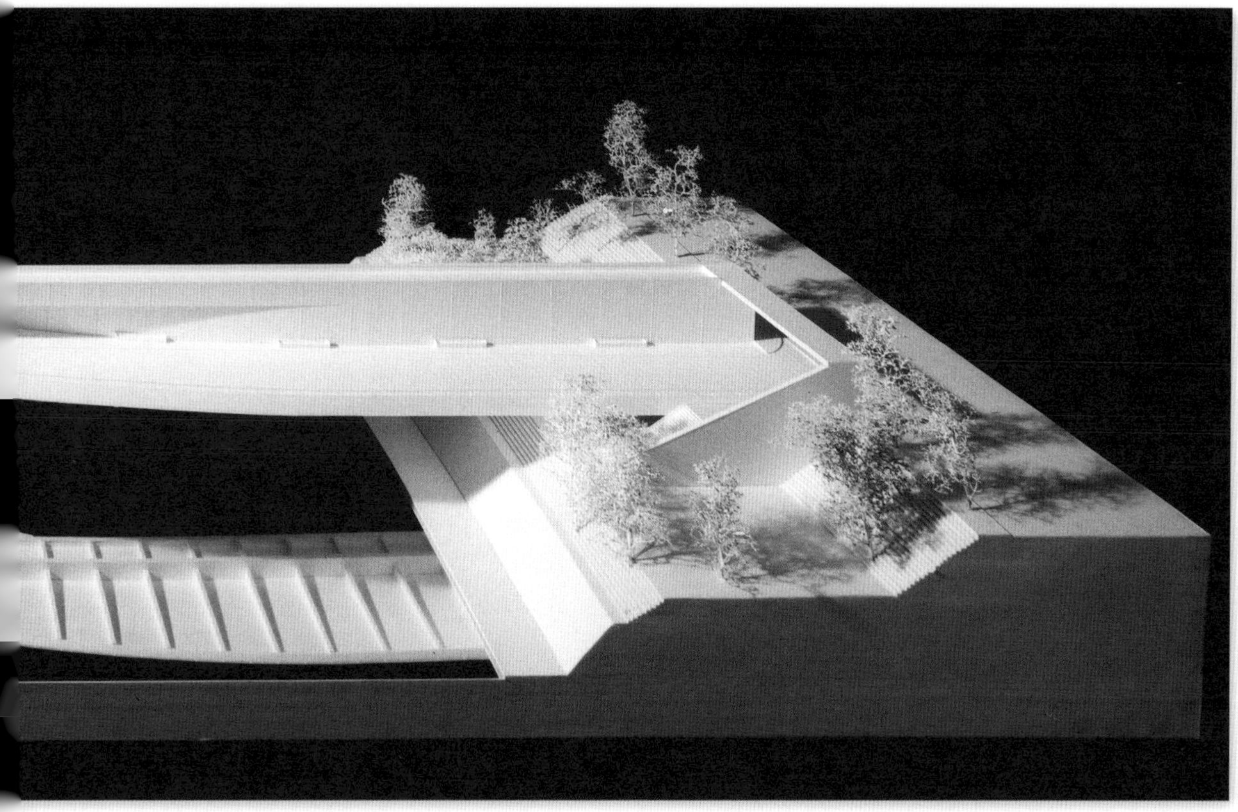

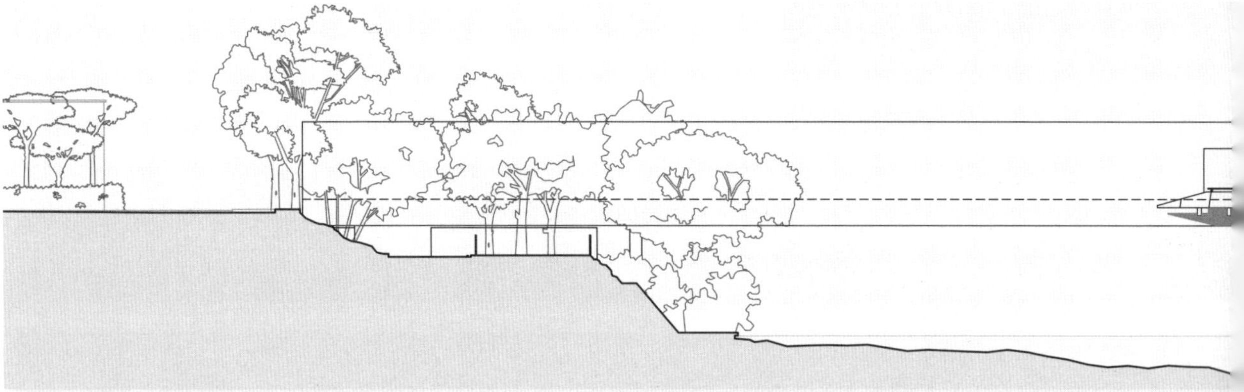

(D) Photomontage inclusion of the bridge in the landscape
(E) Elevation

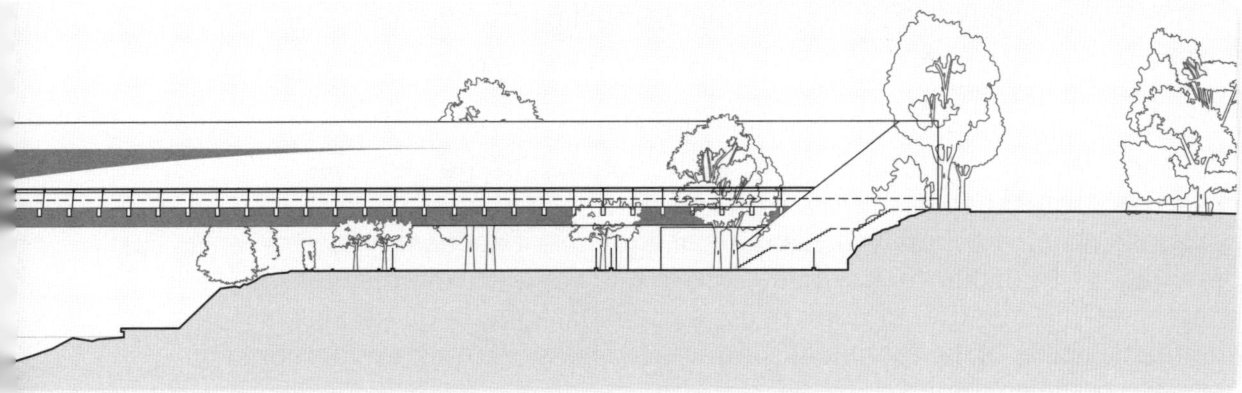

4.9 TURNING POETRY INTO BARCODE
Guggenheim Museum, Helsinki, 2014

The project concept behind the Guggenheim in Helsinki is to design it like a "theatrical machine" where artists can experiment with the various forms of contemporary art.

The idea arises directly from the impression of the site, a place firmly anchored to the dockyards and industrial landscape. The building is located in an urban setting, according to a parallel matrix, with east-west axes, perpendicular to the edge of the quay, a barcode that controls the spaces and functions entrusted to it.

The eleven volumes, like ships docked in port, rise parallel to one another as if placed on a long crosswise structure elevated above the surface of the quay.

The museum is laid out on two levels: the ground floor, at quay level, contains the storage spaces and areas devoted to maintenance, loading and unloading of the works, the lifts and all the compartments and cabinets necessary for the technical systems.

This lightweight base is transparent, almost permeable and passable, integrated with the system of walkways, and in some ways could be said to represent the deck of a ship, its "topside".

The visitors enter on the first floor, which has spaces for events, workshops and an auditorium. Seven of the volumes of the first level house exhibition spaces, flexible environments consisting of a technical section in which machinery and technical equipment necessary for the preparation of exhibitions is housed. The inner rooms are simple neutral containers in which the variation of the systems of light modulation, and the flexibility of the technical solutions facilitate the full development of the dramatic action.

The character of set machines is also assigned to the mobile openings on the fronts of the buildings, which permit the variability of the inside/outside space ratio.

One of the distinctive features of the project consists of its almost complete preservation of the space assigned to the plaza, at the quay level, through the elevation of the volumes that house the museum, permitting the holding of outdoor exhibitions, performance and events during the summer in open/enclosed spaces.

(A) Detail of the model

 (B) Aerial view of project

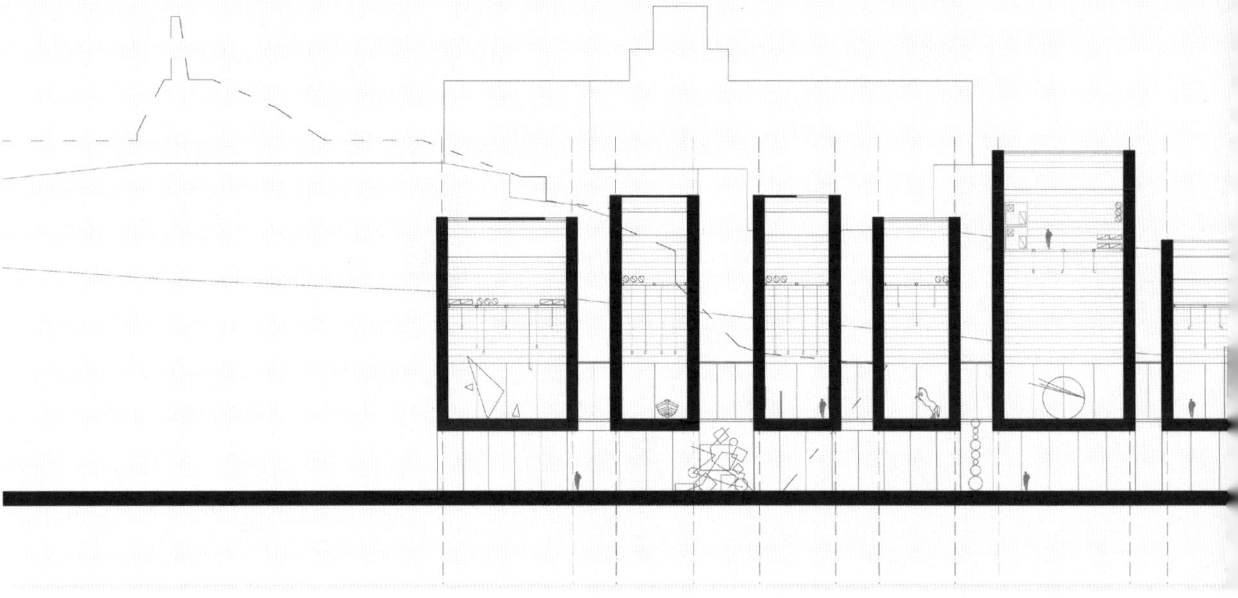

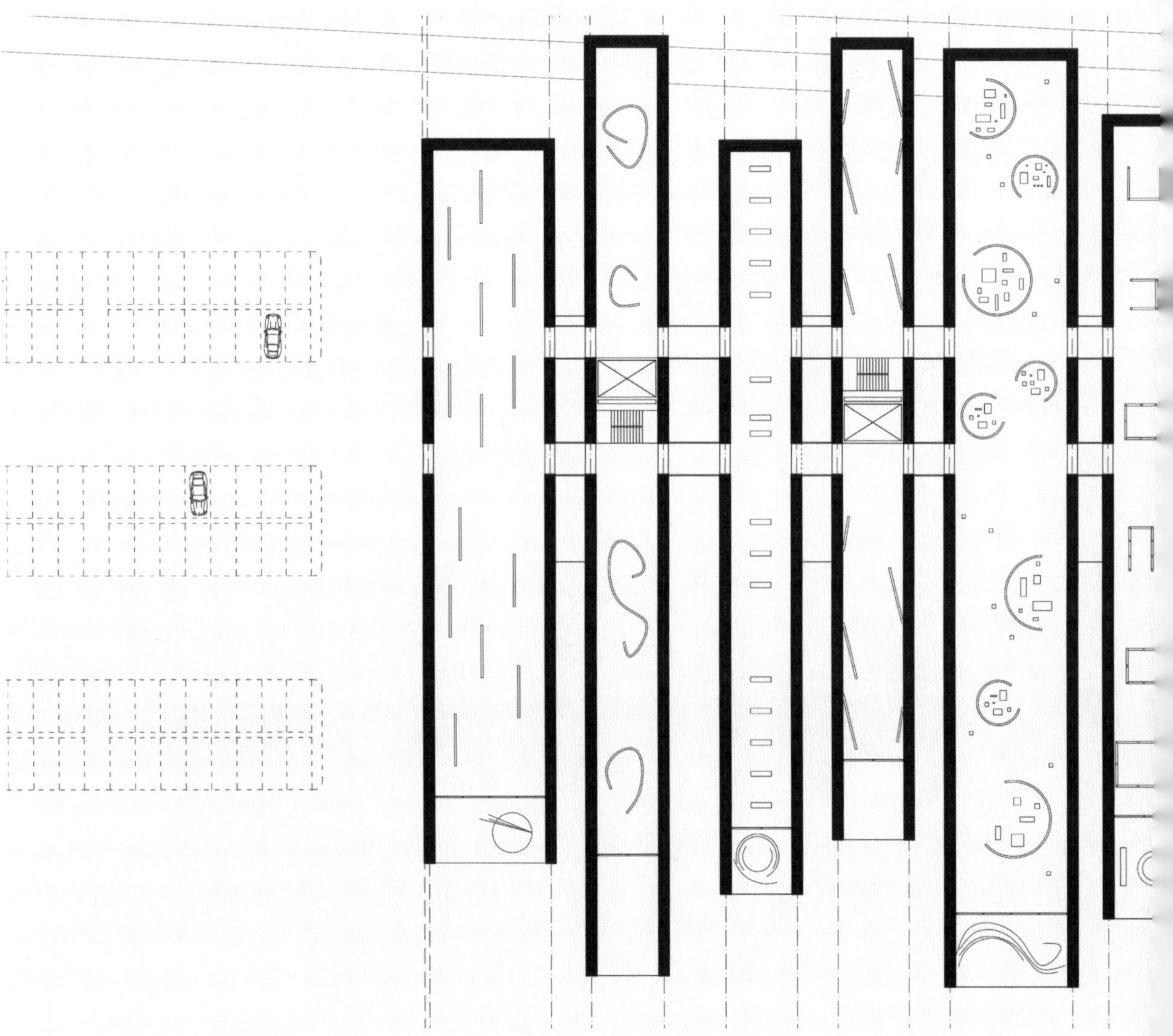

(C) Cross section
(D) Floor plan of the first level

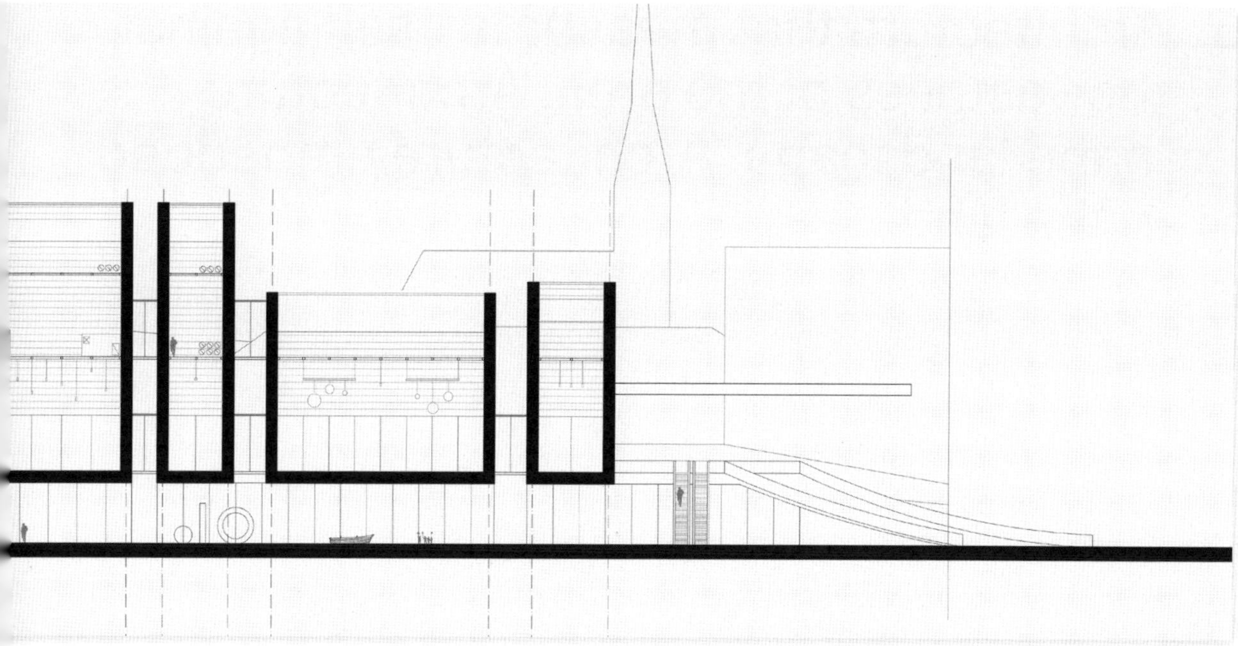

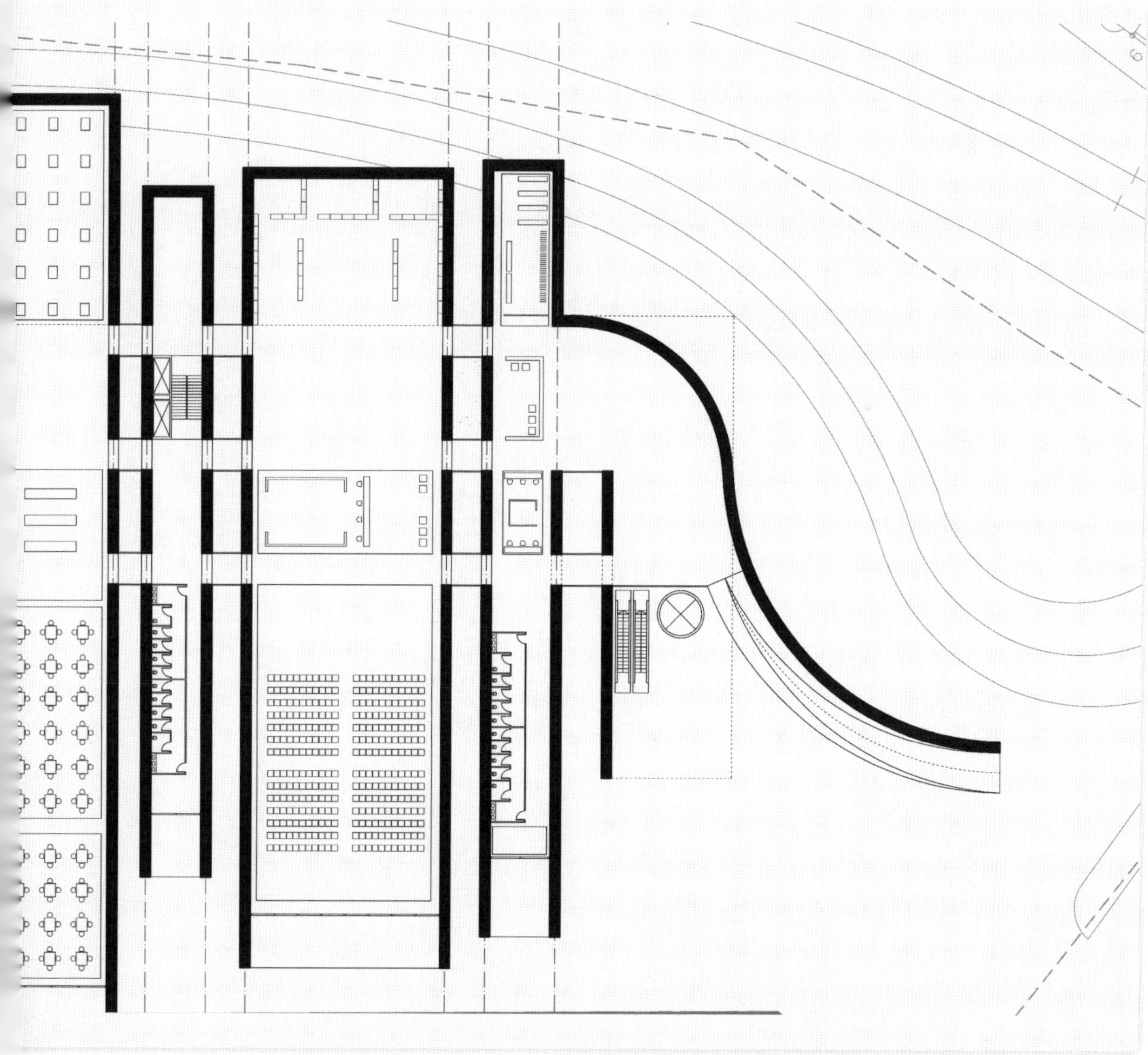

5. Architecture that measures itself against the vastness of the area. Architecture in the landscape. Architecture embedded in the land.

Measuring the physical structure of an architectural project is necessary, above all, to determine the conditions of the forces that act on it internally; measuring how the spaces fit together, how the project fits into the site, and finally, how it relates to its surroundings.

When a building is located in the city, at its heart or on the fringes, this is, obviously, quite different from existing outside the city, with all the many and varied contemporary implications that may have.

The countryside, as opposed to the city, was once marked by very formal clarity, by a sharp separation: where the city ends, there the countryside begins, and vice versa; the city walls stood on the border between these worlds. This is no longer true, and has not been true for a long time. The sprawling city, the extended city, with the outlying infrastructures that connect the entire area now define these places.

At this point, therefore, architectural projects must necessarily measure themselves with this dimension and recreate that lost urban connotation, imagining a measure for themselves which has the capacity to become a place. That is, the architecture has to condense and contain within itself those interior qualities that will effectively establish its identity, so that it is not just landscape architecture which fits into its surroundings so well that it blends with them, becoming part of the landscape, but that draws onto itself the qualities of the site to the extent of making itself a reference point: a work in a setting, not part of a setting.

The architectural project poses new problems when the works are not isolated but included in an infrastructure linked to local mobility – like the railway station or the airport – or when it is no longer desirable to have them in the heart of the city, like a hospital or a market. The design of these structures poses problems of definition by type, because their dimensions and functions are so vast as to elude any possible interpretation.

For this reason, whether we are talking about hospitals, hypermarkets or monofunctional building complexes of any other kind that is strongly identifiable and characterized, they set off an immediate conflict for whoever is called upon to design them. It is a conflict between the desire to integrate and signify the work in the landscape, and the functional reality that is imposed. All this results in a battle, which it is not always possible to win.

5.1 PAUSING TO STROLL AMONG THE RUINS...
Prenestina Zone on the A1 Milan/Naples motorway, Rome, 1988

Travelling a long stretch of motorway alters our perception of the landscape, allowing no more than a large-scale overview of places and horizons.

Within this linear function, ideally linked to the continuity of the route, the rest stop stands out as a singular event and abruptly alters the balance of perception in the scales on which we view the scenery in the motorway-landscape relationship. This intentional perceptive turbulence provided the basis for creating the introverted product of a rest stop designed like a small town, taking the focus off the usual "motorway show" for once.

With a project revolving prevalently around excavations and infills, the site encloses on its premises an internal landscape with an architecture that is expressed with the force of its own layout rather than with the addition of volumes.

Indeed, the evenness with the surface along the top of the infills creates an effect of inclusion in the landscape; the structures turn their back on the flow of vehicles and proclaim the presence of a warp in the linear development of the route merely with the gradual "uplifting" of the embankments, softened by the texture of their grassy covering.

Two symmetrical, tilted clearings, unify the general plan of the two areas, destined for differentiated functions.

We cannot hide that the main source of inspiration for this project was the vicinity of the archaeological complex of Hadrian's Villa. There, the volumetric subdivisions are appreciable in the architectural structures, though ruined, and unclear. Scrubby bushes and stunted trees mingle in a picturesque interplay with the rubble to create a romantic scene that is an essential part of our idea of an archaeological park.

 (A) 3D overview

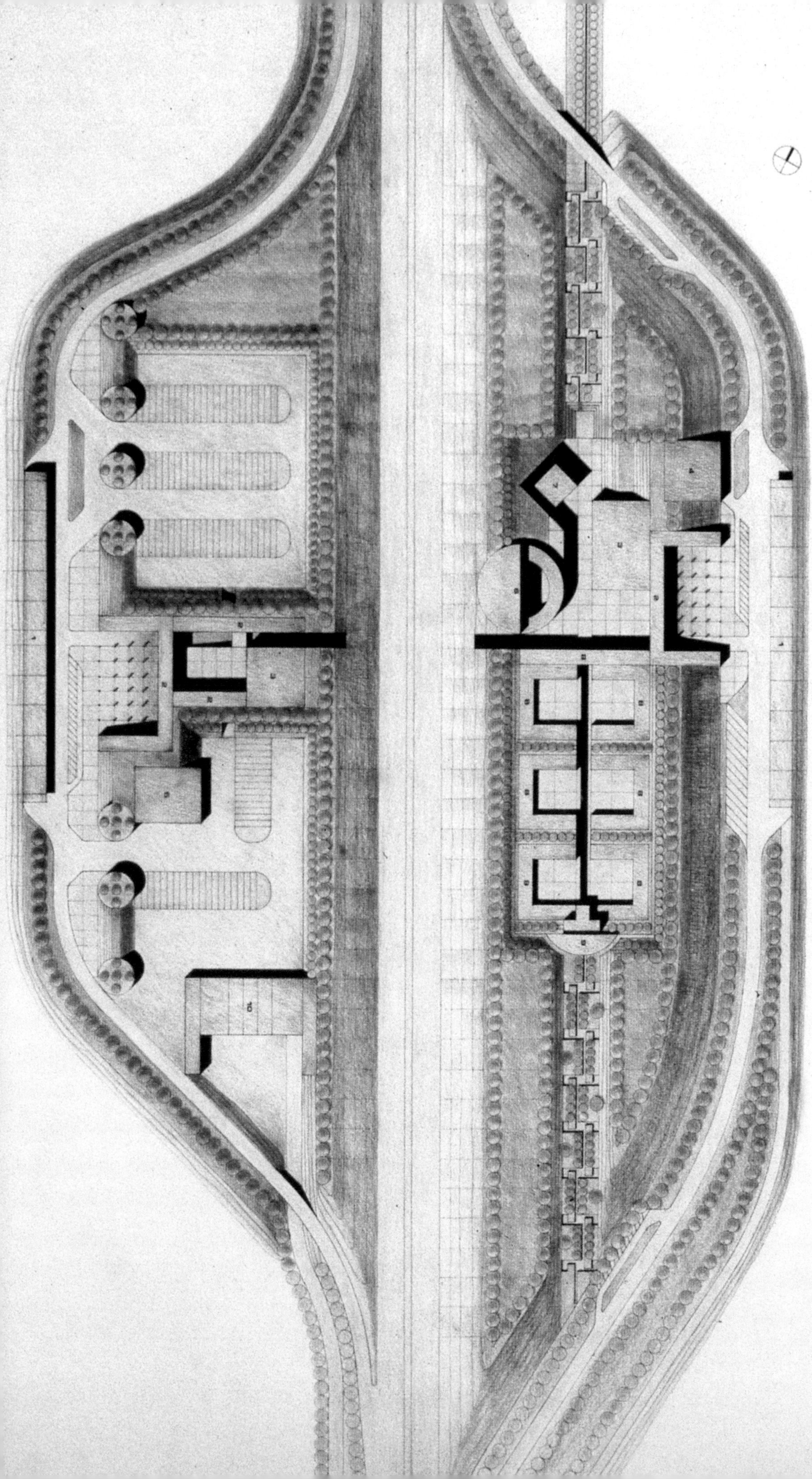

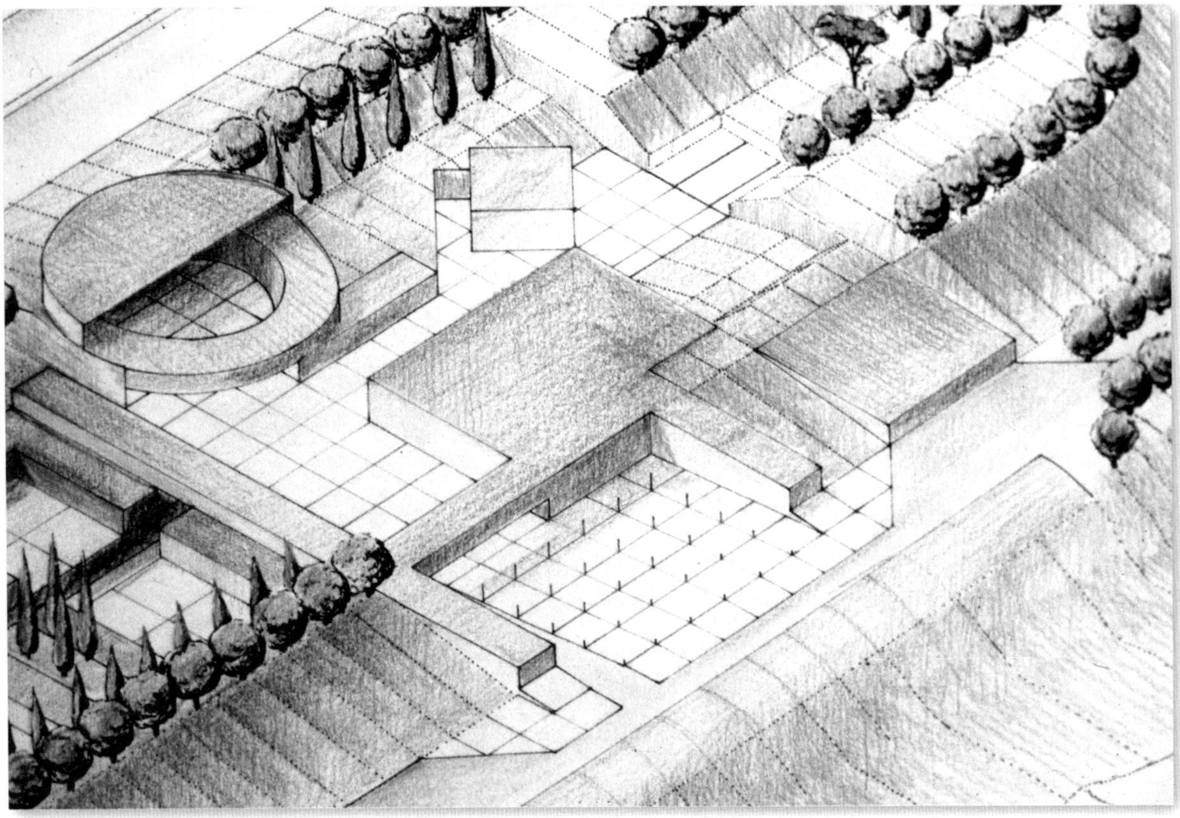

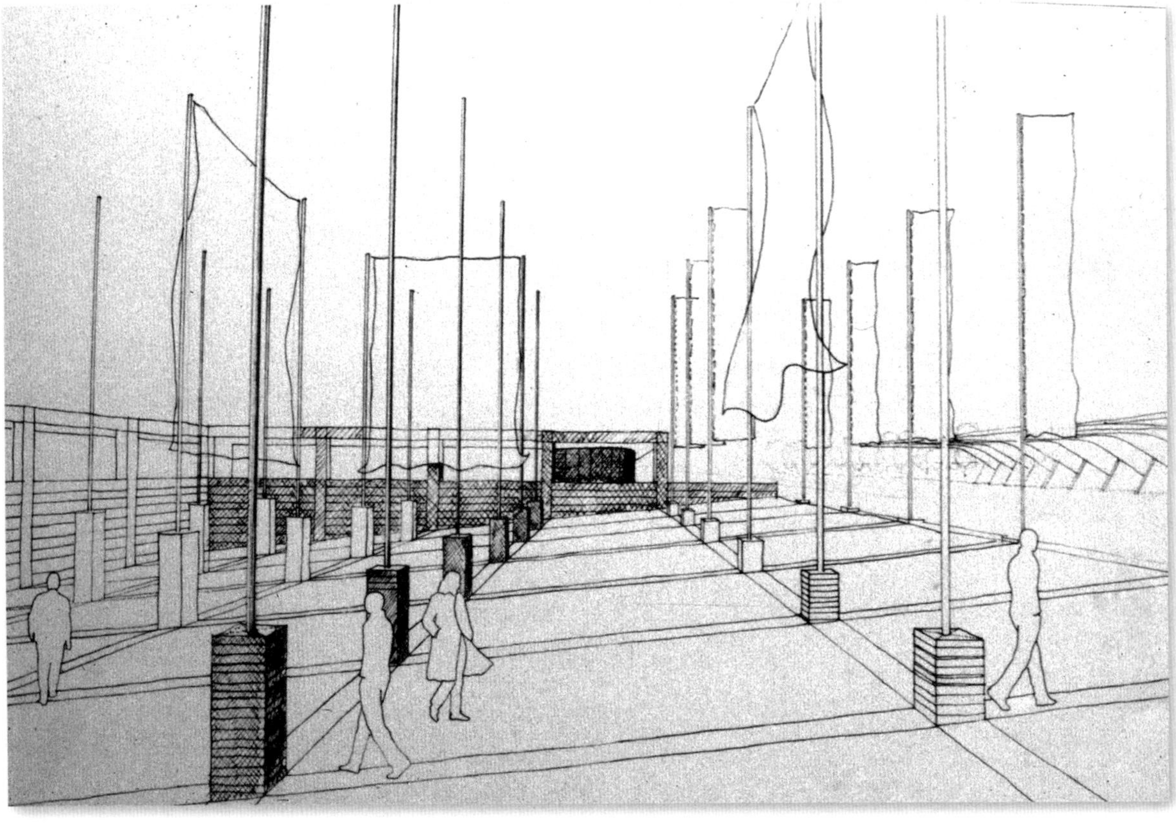

(B) North side area
(C) One of the two tilted plazas

(D) Birdseye view of the project zone
(E) Rest stop seen from the motorway

5.2 STANDING ON THE ROOFTOP FOR AN EXTRAORDINARY VIEW OF THE SEA
New regional council office building, Bari, 2003

The decision to locate the new headquarters of the Puglia Regional Council in a vast area east of Bari was seen by our project team as an opportunity to establish a relationship with the landscape and the open spaces, rather than with the features and structures of the city.

The offices of the institutions governing the region will communicate directly with the land and its natural features.

The shoreline along the Adriatic coast, the densely cultivated farmland, the skyline of the city-region, the infrastructures and geographic elements that connect the various parts of the region, are the elements considered in drawing up the project for the new headquarters.

The entire project honours the region's commitment to environmental sustainability and redevelopment. In particular, the functional solution of "plate" construction inserts it into the environment without creating strong elements of discontinuity while at the same time ensuring full utilization of the space.

In place of a single building, or of a complex of buildings as might be laid out in the city, the project opts for an "esplanade", rising gently from via Gentile toward the sea and presenting, at its edge, a terrace 200 meters long and 10 meters above the ground.

An open, passable public space designed preserving the nature of the site and the view of the horizon: not an addition to the city, or a bridgehead for future expansion, but an architectural organism generated by an elevation of the ground level.

The variation in height from the ground visually encompasses the existing building (thereby reducing its environmental impact) and supports the two buildings intended for the main functions of the Regional Council (the council hall and the office of the Presidency) connected to via Gentile through the pedestrian arcade and roadway.

(A) View from above of the model

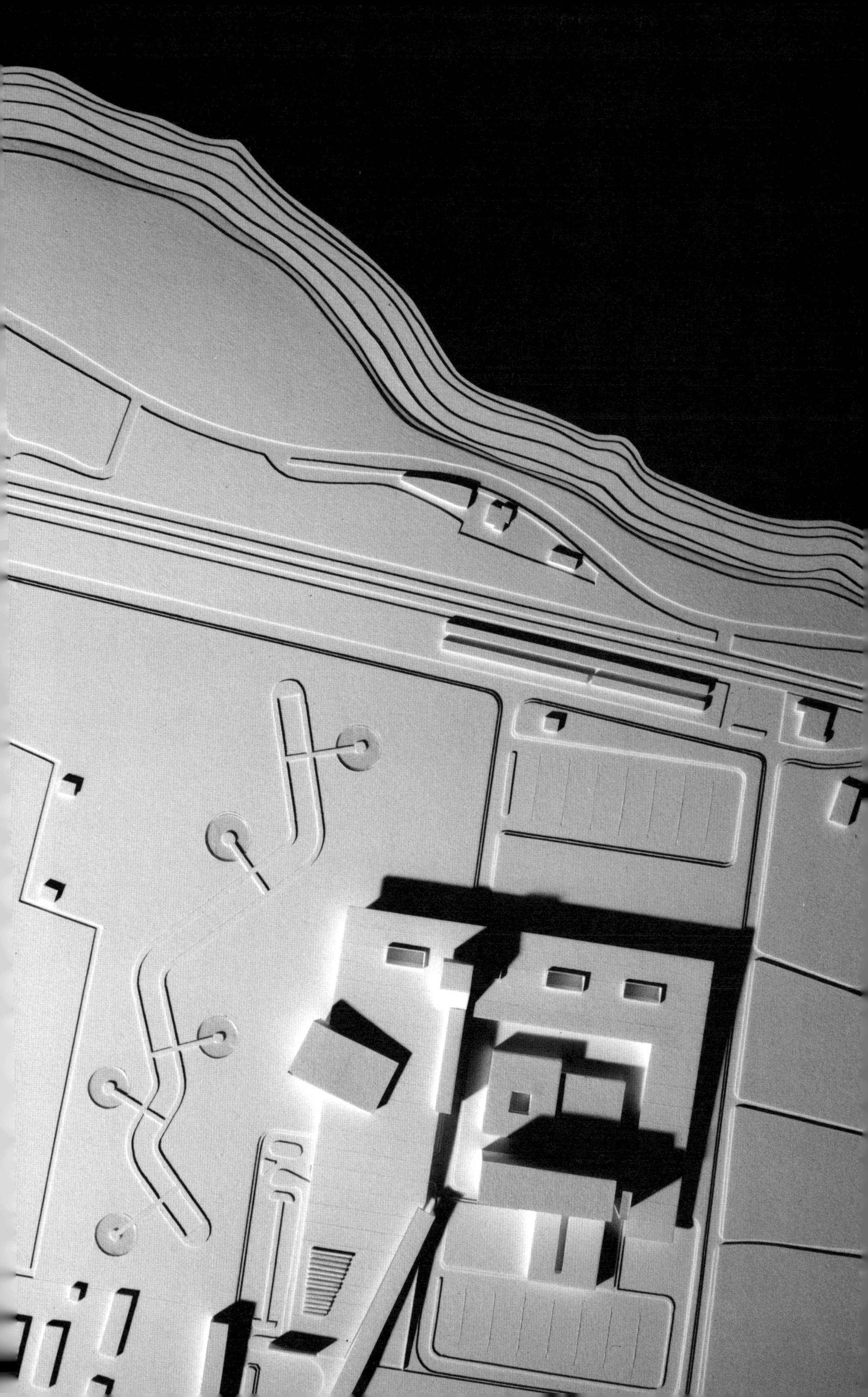

(B) Detail of the model, with the council hall in the foreground
(C) View of the model from northeast

 (D) View of the model from northwest

5.3 ENTERING FROM THE TOP TO DESCEND AND UNEXPECTEDLY DECIDE THAT YOU ARE HOME

University housing, Perugia, 2007

To anyone who observes an aerial view of the city of Perugia, the Monteluce site will be seen as a true natural fortress, rising between the broad valley of Santa Margherita and that of the Favarone, and extending beyond the ancient circle of medieval walls, to stand guard over the Tiber valley as the last urban outpost, protecting the farmlands and built settlements. Although on the outer limits of the central portion of the city, the Monteluce site is set in one of those environmental contexts that could be seen almost as a cliché version of the Umbrian landscape (to the extent that it is characterised by alternating terraces and winding ridges with their roots in its use as a necropolis favoured by the Etruscans), and enjoying a splendid scenic view toward the Apennine profile.

The project proposes a solution in which the protection of the landscape and environment is based on the balanced inclusion of the new university housing in a location strongly characterized by the presence of structures and historical settlements and by the view afforded by its panoramic position.

Based on these principles, the choice to work on a building that would adapt itself, through the staggering of the apartments and the ample rotundity of the roofing elements, the geometry of the surface curves suggests a sinuous unified volume repeatedly marked by voids and transparencies.

While, in the end, the levels of the structure can be imagined from the side that faces downstream, the height that is perceptible proceeding alongside the building on via Dal Pozzo is extremely limited, such that the presence of the new structure does not interfere in any way with the view of the wonderful scenery and of the front of the church of Bevignate. On the contrary, the roof – which effectively becomes an integral part of the façade – is a vast scenic terrace cantilevered over the valley.

Descending along via Dal Pozzo, the profile of the building emerges gradually with respect to ground level, revealing, through the large circular courtyards, the development of the communal spaces on the two levels below.

From the sidewalk, much like a quay to which the body of the building seems to be docked, a brief walkway accesses the roof-terrace where the volumes of the reception desk and cafeteria stand. All the rest is open space, furnished with seating and scenic observation points.

(A) View of the side overlooking the valley

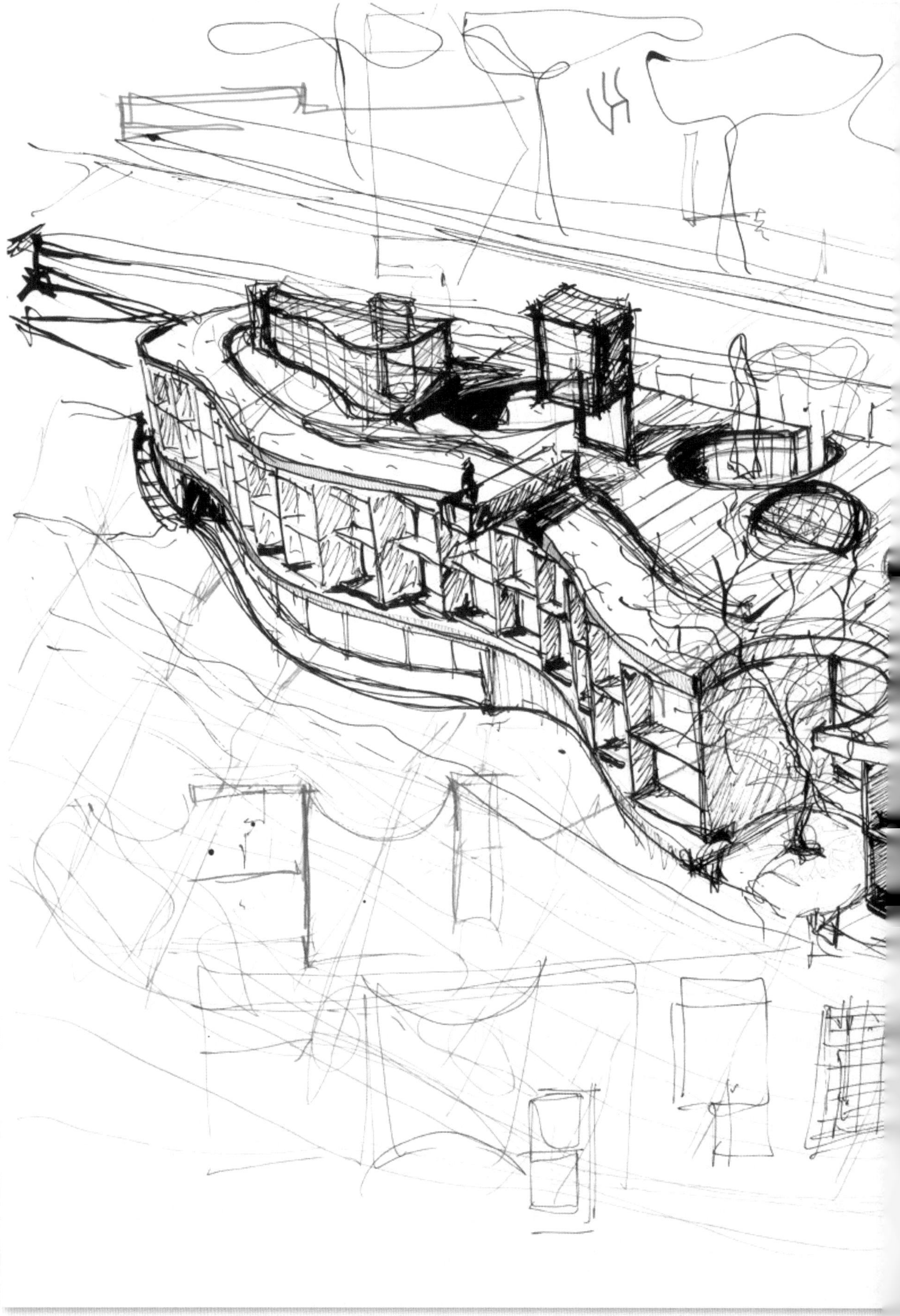

(B) Freehand drawing of the complex in its entirety

 (C) View from the large scenic terrace projecting over the valley

(D) One of the circular courts
(E) View of the walkway accessing the courts

5.4 IN THE BACKGROUND, INEXORABLY, THE GREAT MAIELLA
Office Centre, Atessa, 2007

Studying the area of Piazzano involved in the project, we found it to have the characteristics of a linear city, built along the roads linking the town to the valley below. This tended to create a sort of scattered urban system consisting of a backdrop of heterogeneous, random structures, lacking any element of identification.

With regard to the functions, the area lacks spaces for public and institutional services, service and retail businesses and offices.

The choice to concentrate all the functions in a single, centrally located district with respect to the flows of this vast area, and give it the characteristics of centrality necessary, appeared ideal to make the civic centre the axis of this part of the area.

The "linear city" needs what Kevin Lynch calls "a public image", that is, the common mental framework that large swaths of the citizens carry with them. The project developed out of this absence of legibility of the urban landscape and the need to identify reference points.

Everything develops along the Sangro valley, leading from the sea to the Maiella: the Grand Mother who dominates this part of the Abruzzo landscape and forms the natural background for the new structure.

(A) View of the north front

(B) View of the office centre toward the Maiella
(C) Office centre, seen from the south

 (D) View toward the towers

 (E) 3D overview of layout

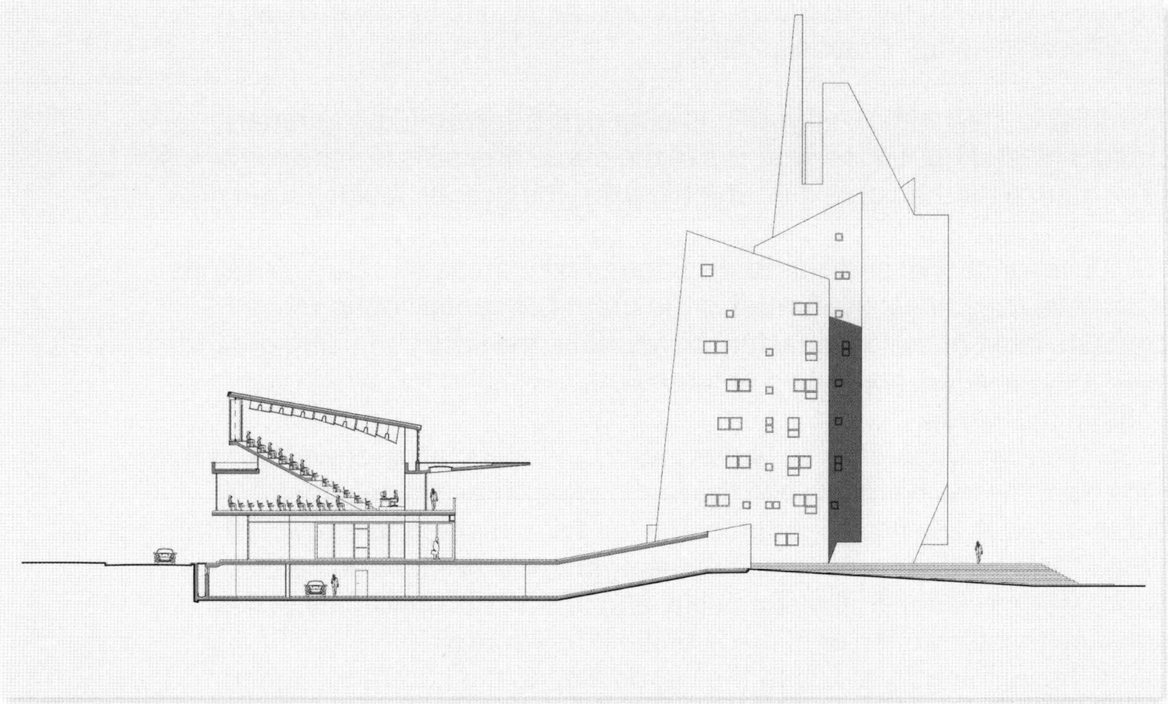

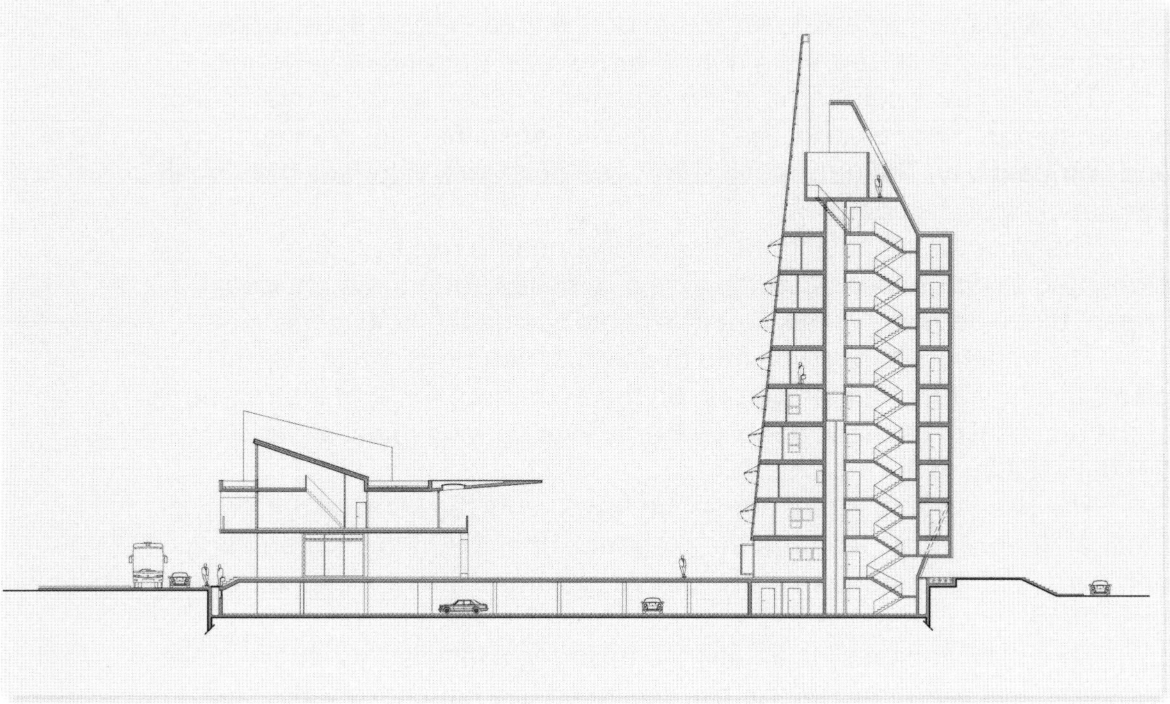

(F) Cross section of the auditorium
(G) Cross section view on one of the towers

5.5 A GARDEN ON THE ROOF, WITH ETNA IN THE BACKGROUND
New Hospital, Siracusa, 2020

The relationship with the layout of the land, the surrounding agrarian landscape and the dense patterns of the citrus orchards are the elements of reference for the context in which to plan the overall design of the new hospital structure.

The functional and distributive complexity of the structure develops along two main lines: the former is the great horizontal section that contains most of the hospital functions, while the latter, on rising ground, is slightly elevated, consisting of four two-story buildings, which will contain the wards.

The lower section, also two-story, is built along an east-west axis that runs from the main entrance to the to the west side. It is positioned in continuity with the natural slope of the land and marked by a row of three broad patio-gardens around which the aggregate services and areas converge, in relation to the specificity and functional uniformity of the services that they offer, or of the activities they contain.

The buildings that house the wards are, on the contrary, aligned diagonally next to one another and oriented on the north-south axis. This position opposite the service structure below means that all the rooms have a view of the surrounding natural landscape through large windows.

The altimetric solution and arrangements based on the simplification of architectural shapes exalt the principles of sustainability, permeability and compatibility. The qualitative sequence of spaces valorises the visual permeability of the complex.

The structures housing the patients appear to rise from the elongated structure below, which acts as a base to attenuate the visual impact that a complex of this size inevitably has on the landscape.

This function of insertion into the natural setting is exalted by the planting of a Mediterranean garden on the entire roof, without interruption, at the disposal of all those people who, in their various roles, experience the daily reality of the hospital.

The base is characterised, on the lower level, by courtyard-gardens. Each of them, in turn, features the presence of a singularity – a building or a particular arrangement of the plantings – that differentiates it from the others.

These “landscapes”, in addition to fostering a familiarity with the place depending on elements not exclusively linked to a hospital environment, also facilitate orientation and the recognisability of different areas.

(A) View of a patio-garden

(B) Main entrance to the hospital and office tower

(C) View of the wards section from the Mediterranean garden on the roof
(D) Detail of an inner court with the volume of the cafeteria

(E) Birdseye view of the completed structure

5.6 AN AQUEDUCT IN THE EMILIA COUNTRYSIDE
Office Centre, Parma, 2009

From the standpoint of the essential volumetric arrangement, the building consists of two parts, configured individually and distinctly so as to be clearly legible: a low trapezoid and a high linear structure, overlapping on the eastern edge.

These form two large volumes, respectively characterised by absolute horizontality and absolute verticality. On the formal and functional plane, however, these volumes are conjoined and complementary parts of a single interacting architectural organism.

The horizontal portion is formed by a large trapezoid plate, the sides of which are aligned, respectively, with the orientation of the axes of territorial centuriation and with the north-south axis of the building. From the distributive standpoint, the plate has a typical spatial organization, which allows for a high degree of internal flexibility.

The roof is covered "in green" achieved with plantings that, through the variation of tones and textures produced using different grassy species, reflect the architectural design of the surface cladding on the façade of the vertical block.

On the segmented profile of the east side of the plate stands the compact, regular linear block, positioned in a discontinuous manner and characterized by a sequence of broad doorways "generated" by the geometry of solids and voids that distinguish the edge of the plate.

The connections to the ground of these openings are the attestations of the functional zones of the plate, while their wide apertures (with the height that goes from six to eight floors) indicate the open sides of the different themed courtyards that penetrate deeply into the plate.

The composition of the volumes is design to make each bay correspond to the unit in line, an open court that penetrates into the plate, thus marking the different points of access to the various parts of the structure, depending on the specific activities and purposes.

The new complex seems to resemble, by analogy, a typical feature, strongly identifying it with Parma's urban history. We are alluding here, though of course acknowledging the differences, to the 18th century Palace of the Pilotta, the great Farnesian project of urban and environmental redevelopment on a vast scale, that gave a unique imprint to the city, according to a conception of urban architecture based on principles of spatial and functional integration.

(A) View of the usable roof toward the highest volume

 (B) General view of the project

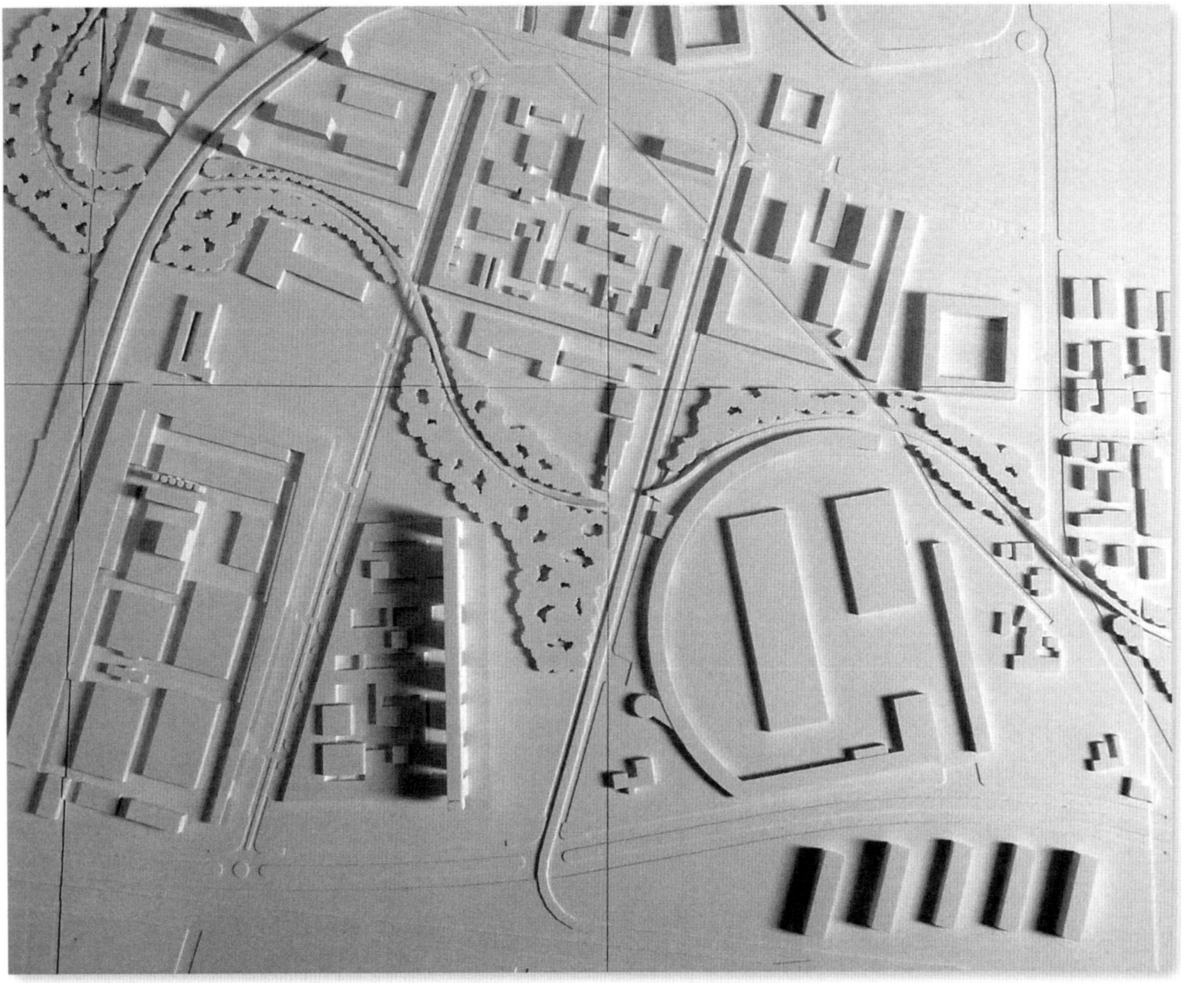

 (C) Aerial view of the model

(D) View of the model
(E) Floor plan of the fourth level

5.7 A HILL IN THE MIDDLE OF THE PLAIN
New Hospital, Cesena, 2019

The footprint created by the insertion of the hospital complex in the structure of an already densely populated landscape characterized by the network of Roman centuriation creates a sort of "fracture" along the north-south axis parallel to the network, interrupting the continuity of geometrical texture of the crops.

The choices made relative to the insertion of this project in the local context were based on this consideration. The "fracture" became a theme of the project's actual impact on the landscape: "elevating" the margins of the land, so to speak, and creating an artificial hill that would fit into the landscape, redesigning the flow of the area without altering the right-angled design of the Roman centuriation that so sharply defines the areas of the surrounding countryside.

The "elevation" of two surfaces creates a "gallery" on the north-south axis that becomes the *Hospital Street*.

The project suggests a volumetric layout characterised by two elements - *the tilted green surfaces and the hospital street* – which, while each maintains a relationship with the architectural scale and with that of the landscape, indicate a reinterpretation of the hospital's configuration as "as plate with lateral blocks".

The *tilted green surfaces*, the slopes of the artificial hill, converge without touching, up to a height above the highest level of the buildings. The dimensions – both the height and the length of the complex – establish a relationship with the landscape (the subdivisions and roads, the layout of the residential zones), which scales back their impact significantly.

The *hospital street* controls the accesses to the hospital complex with a gradual passage that restores the perception of the spaces first to the urban scale and then to that of the functional portions, and finally to the "domestic" dimension of the wards.

From the patients' rooms, all scrupulously ensured of a view of the surrounding landscape, the "hypernatural" element represented by the "vegetable" surfaces that climb up the façade takes on a screening role that protects from direct sunlight, from the east and west. As in the case of the *hospital street*, this is another decisive element for the balance between the different scales of interpretation and use of the hospital complex.

(A) Aerial view of photomontage insertion

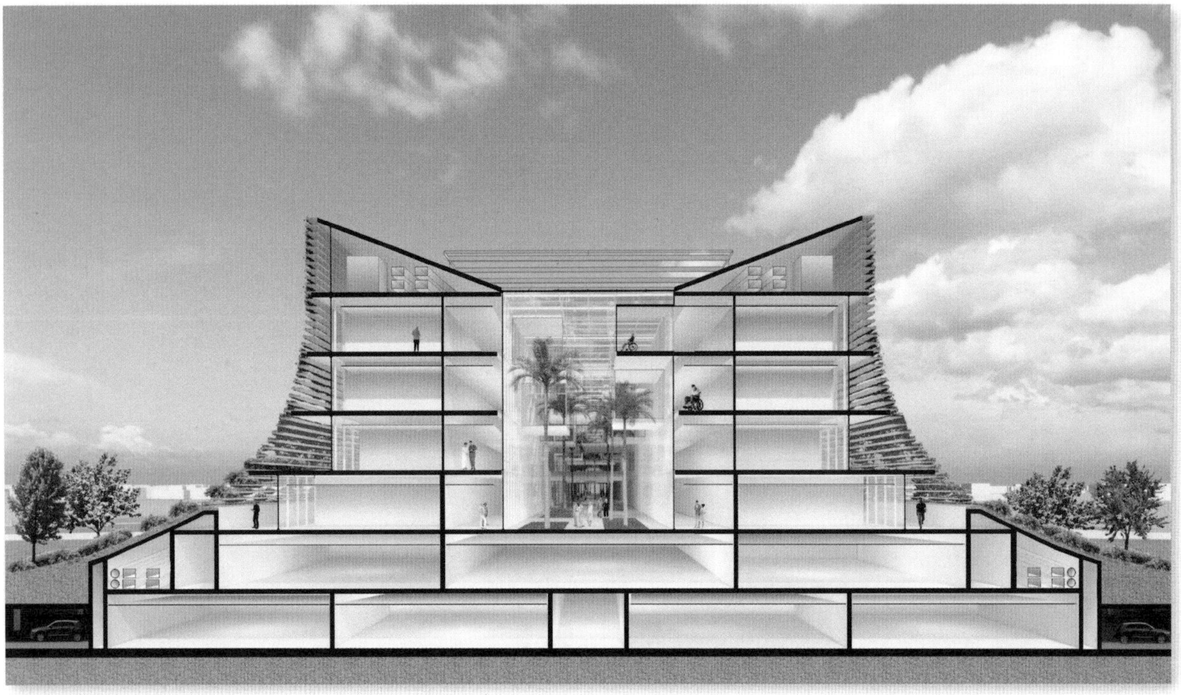

(B) Perspective section

 (C) Internal view of the *hospital street*

(D) External view of the building

5.8 INSIDE THE HILL, DEEP IN THE SOIL
Stadium, Siena, 2003

The project for the new stadium in Siena has to deal, in the first place, with the morphological characteristics of the site chosen: an empty area at a considerable distance from the city and largely intact within the foothill district, characterized by natural slopes and valleys that connect to a narrow central valley along which runs the Bandita canal.

Within the area selected, the choice of a site for the new stadium focused on a zone that was considered more suitable than others in that it did not obstruct the valley with its volume – which because of its size could block the natural convexity – and afforded optimum visibility inside the stadium because of its north-south orientation.

The structure was positioned on the highest point over the Bandita bed so that it would be possible to use the valley below for parking. It thus found itself naturally placed in a frontal and barycentric position with respect to the stadium and was less visible from the surrounding hills.

The stadium is partially buried in the hillside; the excavation follows the curves of the slope, and the natural orography with its cupped shape. The wall, like a giant dam, closes the side overlooking the valley, and is the element that gives the project its recognizability.

The decision of how to cover the stadium was resolved in the same way, resorting to the idea of "scarring": it is the surrounding land itself, randomly cut, which partially covers the bleachers. The retaining trusses, produced using reticular beams, contain the cabins for the television crews and equipment, and the service spaces. The lighting systems, electronic boards and loudspeakers are built along the walls.

The type of structure required is a stadium with three grandstands; the three sides stand on the hillsides while the fourth consists of a built structure facing toward the valley, like a dam in front of a field. The playing field thus acquires the character of a reference to the Campo, as the people of Siena refer to their main plaza which also has the appearance of a "sink" and, following the morphology of the site, functions like a dam to contain the built portion.

(A) View of the bleachers

PNEU EGGER
PNEU EGGER
PNEU EGGER
SF

(B) Aerial view of the nocturnal configuration
(C) View of roofing over the bleachers

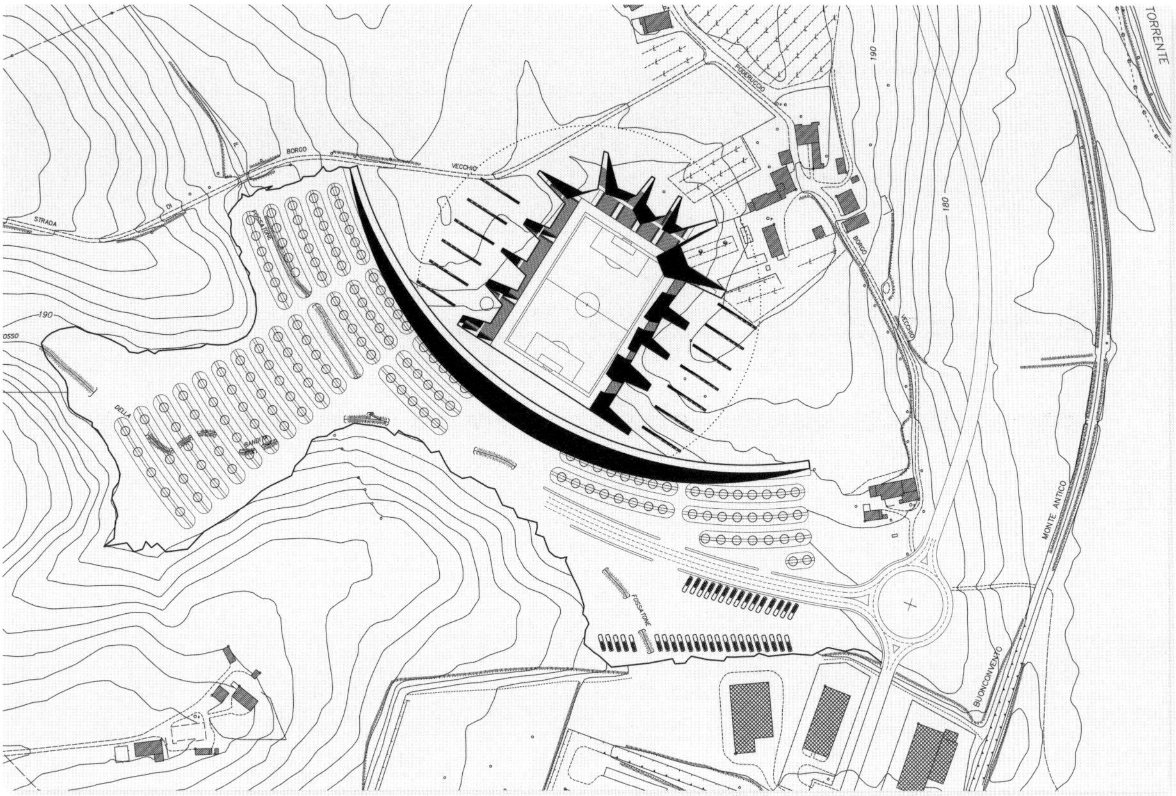

(D) Topography of layout

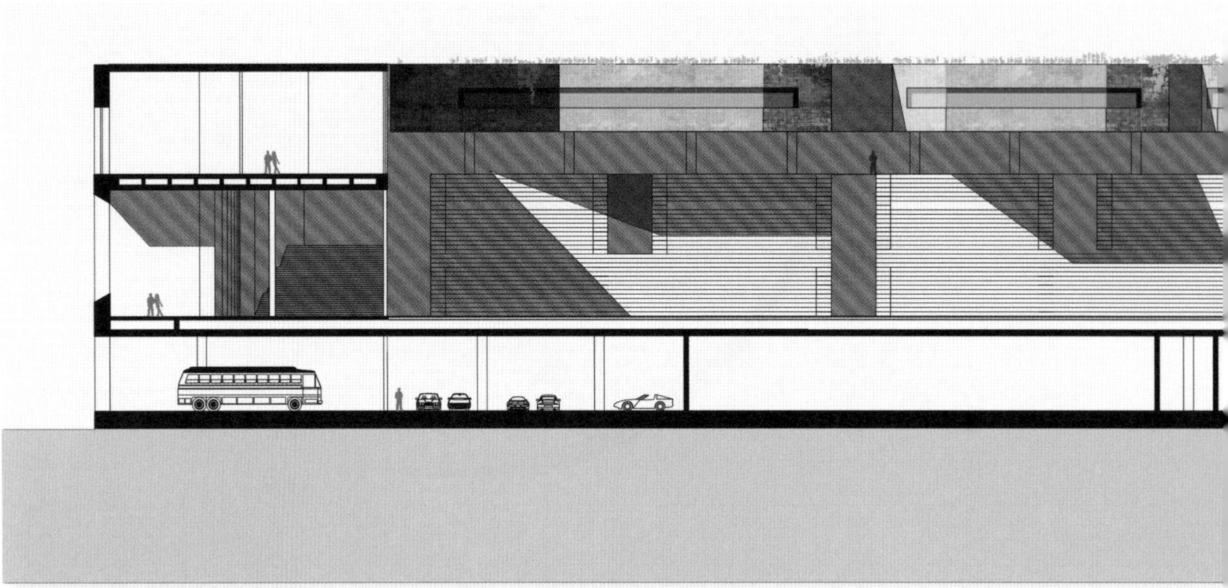

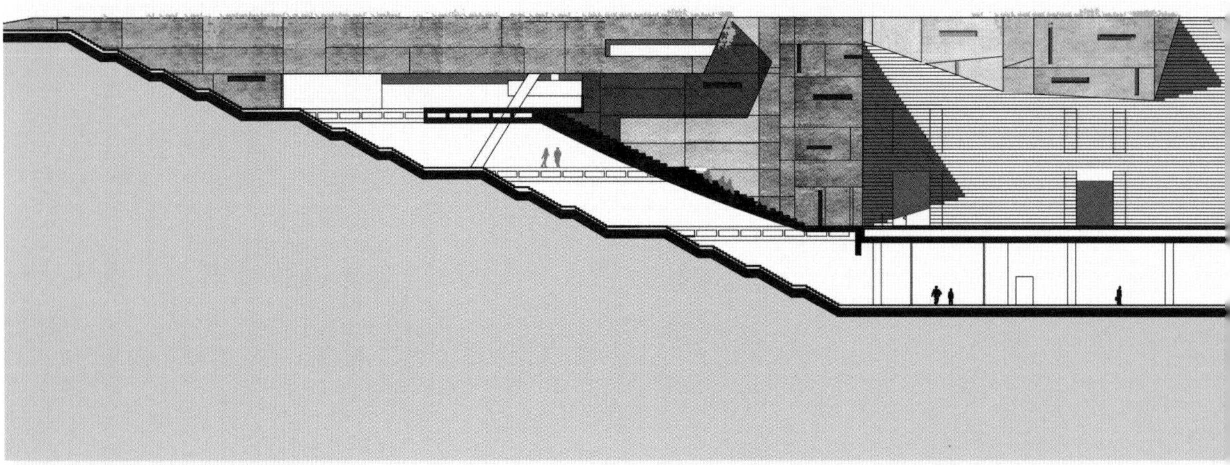

(E) Longitudinal section
(F) Cross section

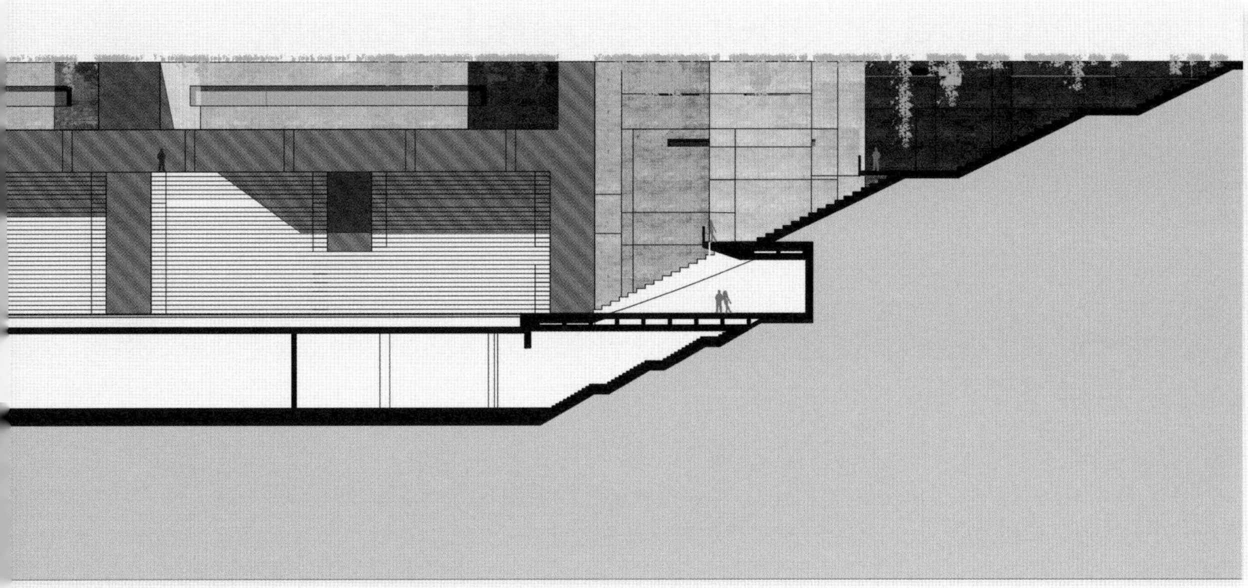

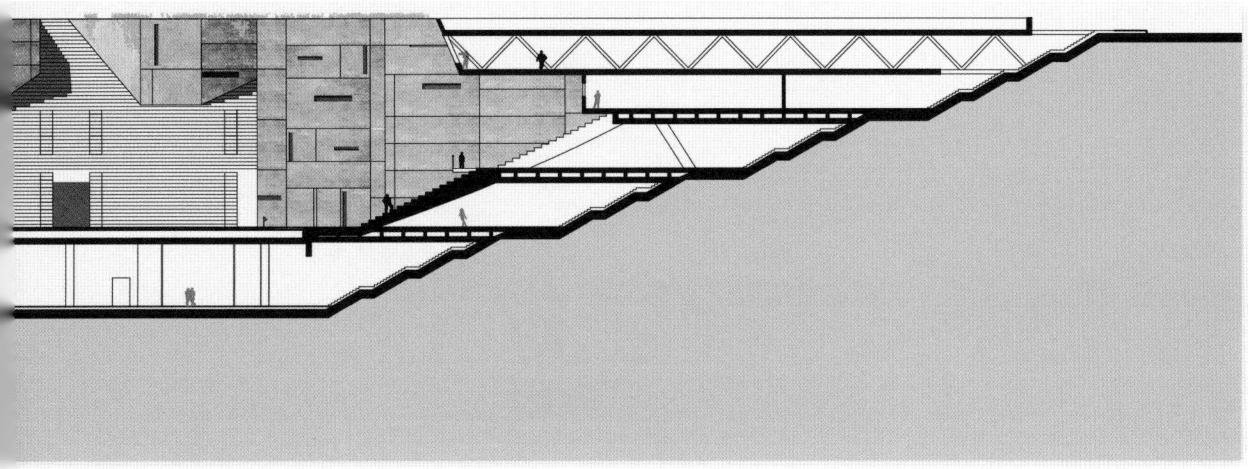

6. Everything happens around a court, whether open or closed.

The courtyard, circumscribed space, has always been central to the idea of construction, the perfect example of the distinction between a protected interior – where domestic life unfolds – and the exterior, a place of insecurity and otherness. The courtyard, patio or cloister has formed the basis for the spatial organization typical of many architectural styles, both public and private, throughout history. As a matrix, generating the architectural structure, the courtyard can take many forms, in order to fulfil different requirements. Around the void, a world of relationships is formed: it is the place of the community, of the communal life of the family, of the school, of the building, of the convent, in contrast with the private, more intimate spaces. In the three-part structuring of space, that of the courtyard is the mediation, the conjunction between public and private.

Even the language changes: in place of the rigid, closed, opaque exterior, we can have a light structure like that of the loggia and the arcade. Central space becomes simultaneously a distributor and an attraction, centrifugal and centripetal: the place of distribution from the centre toward the margins and, on the contrary, from the margins toward the centre. Traditionally, the courtyard is meant to be open, bare to rain and sun, but in light of its new uses and new needs, with time this space has been covered. The solutions are sometimes closed, sometimes transparent, but always attempting to exalt their centrality. From the covered solutions, which were the product of later additions, we evolved to architecture designed specifically with this premise incorporated into the plan: no longer a covered space transformed, but a central zone around which different uses revolved.

It was not just buildings that benefited from this concept, since the void is also a basic element of the city: the town square, the community meeting place for both organized and random encounters. Forum, agora, green: different names to designate, with various nuances, the same thing.

6.1 NEITHER INSIDE NOR OUT
Headquarters of the professional associations of engineers and architects, Bari, 1992

Overcoming the contrast between civilian and monumental architecture is the concept underlying an attitude that tends to deal with problems "case by case". The project we developed on this theme, balancing the monumental overtones with the rigours of the standards for use, and attempting, within the rules for the type of structure it was meant to be, to achieve the proper measure of this balance.

The coherence between type model and functional criteria led to the determination to build the structure around a court, based on the dynamic progression of four separate building units joined at the top level. The courtyard type of construction also gave us the opportunity to apply different languages to the outer public space and the private interior space – "In" and "Out" – differences that we read with analogous rigour in the design of the façades.

Compact construction, plasticity of volumes and continuity in the surfaces toward the exterior-public space; lightness and fragmentation, with metal shutters that veil the glassed surfaces, on the façades of the inner court, toward the private space.

The theme of dynamic progression in the layout returns in the extension, in the water tower that, in its ideal conception, coils upward in a spiral elevated well above the surrounding buildings.

(A) View in perspective on the main front

 (B) General view from the street

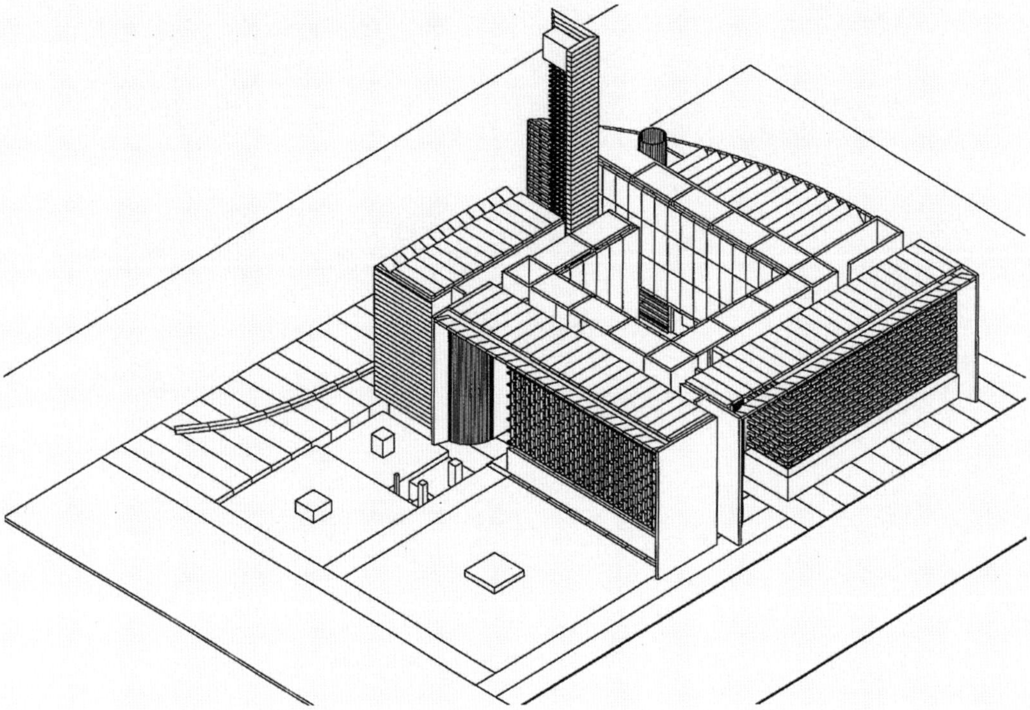

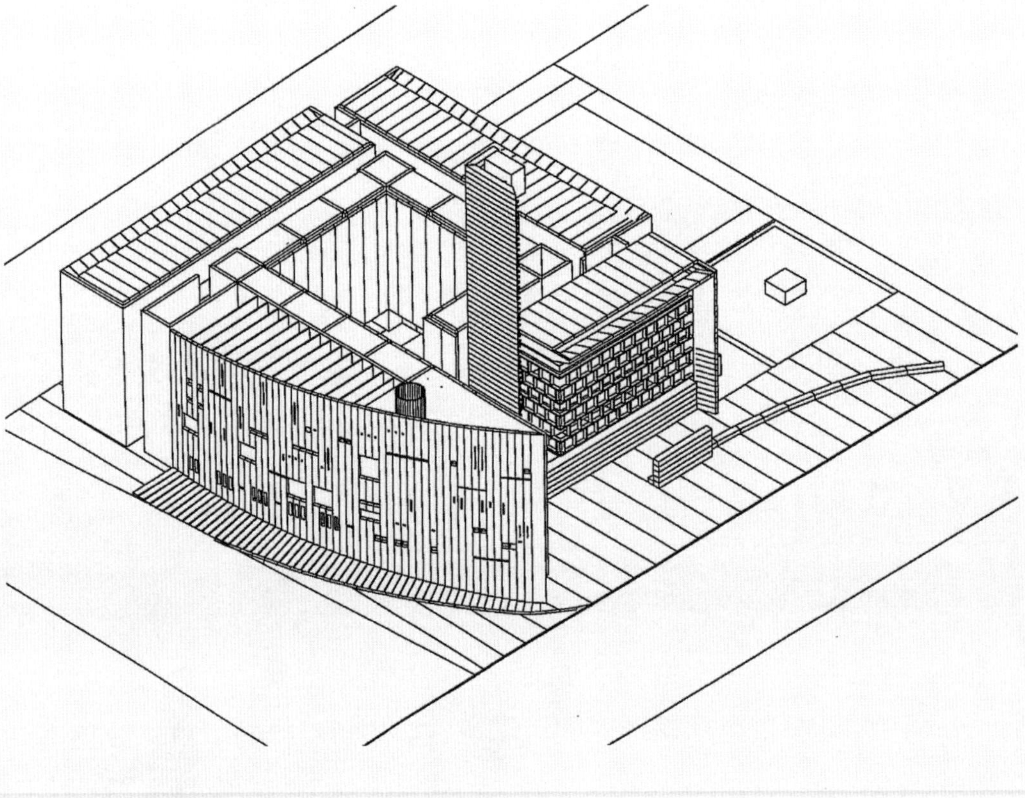

(C) Axonometric view from southeast
(D) Axonometric view from northwest

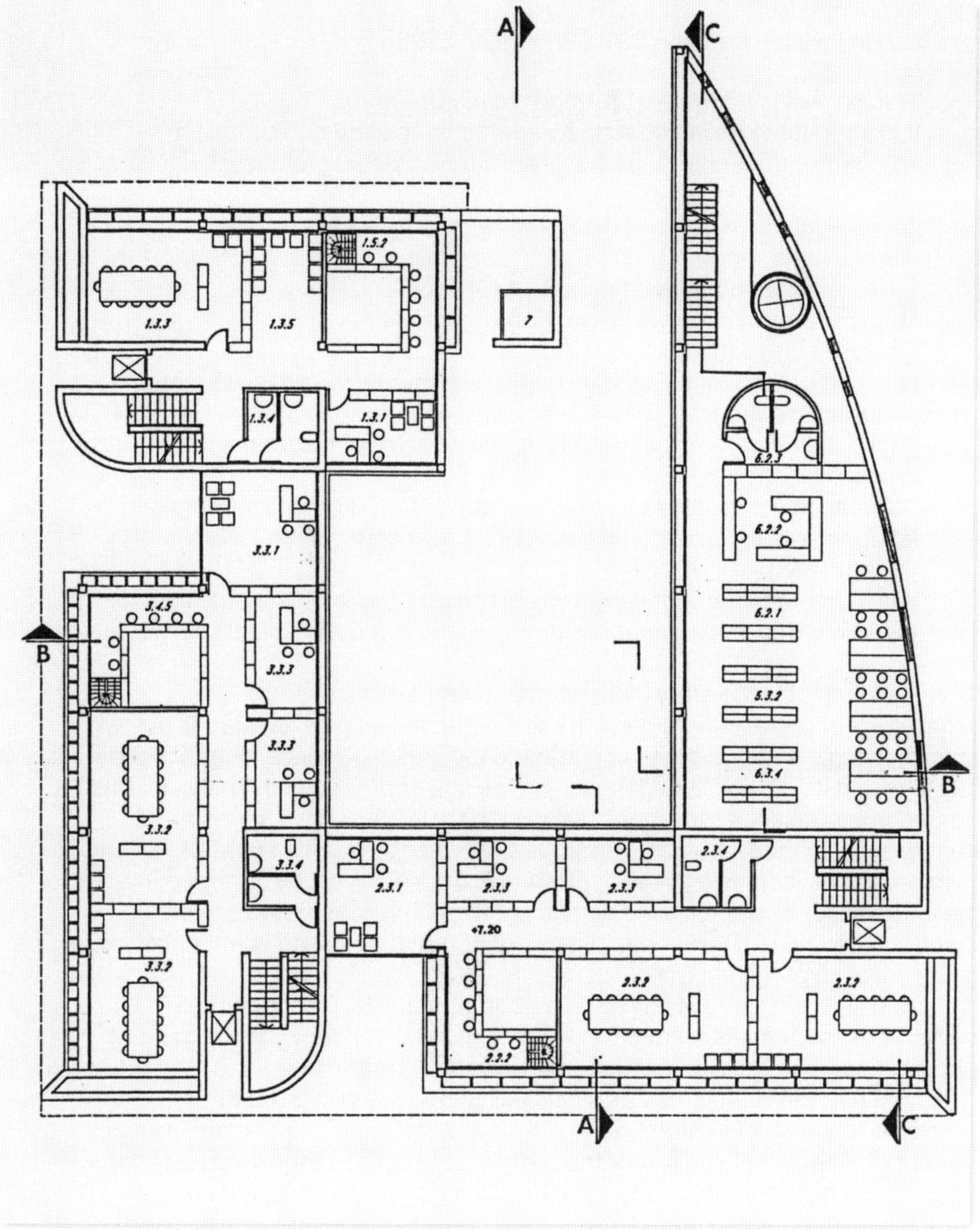

263 (E) Floor plan of the second level

6.2 NOW YOU SEE IT, NOW YOU DON'T
Italian Pavilion for Expo 2010, Shanghai, 2008

This project is a tribute to Terragni; to his Danteum.
It is a tribute to Italian culture, its stratifications and contaminations.
To our "hundred cities". To the city of Rome that was medieval, Baroque and again Renaissance.
To our cuisine, with the virtuosity of its hundreds of variations on an elementary theme.
To the relationship between East and West.
To the assonance between the Roman domus and the Chinese siheyuan.
It is a tribute to Venice, the city on the water, gateway to the Orient, unsurpassed model.
To the Italian gardens, to the Marittime Theatre of Hadrian's Villa, to the ideal city.
A tribute to the greatness of Italian cinema, La Dolce Vita, Mastroianni.
To opera and to Pavarotti and, why not?! To the Ferrari and the National Soccer Team.
It is a tribute to thought, to the world of ideas, to vision and intelligence, the only works that can make our cities, and our future, a better place.

The project is the story of an approach and a deep dive. From afar – from the other side of the river – the Italian pavilion stands out sharply, simple and rigorous, in contrast to the inevitable visual chaos of the city. By night it will look like a lantern. But as one approaches the pavilion, this compactness dissolves in a nuanced design that will reveal a series of images in which the ideal city, Pavarotti, the Ferrari, the Italian garden, Italian fashion, will be increasingly recognizable. A simple structural arrangement based on solids and voids – the seriality of the piling – disguises any image displayed behind it. It is an optical game of compactness and scattering: that is the essence of the pavilion.

The style structure is based on a geometrical matrix represented by two intersecting offset squares: another game that interrupts the general apparent compactness and allows access to the structure.

The pavilion is imagined as a narrative work, in which structure functions like a set of nested boxes; a simple stereometric space enclosing a system of other simple stereometric spaces in a play of effects and hints that accompany the visitor in discovery of the content: Italian style and culture.

Upon entering the open space of the courtyard, it is possible to glimpse some of the complex subdivision of the interior and exterior spaces, between walkways, ramps and staircases. It is an intimate, calm space, in contrast with the inevitable chaos of life outside the pavilion.

The route of the visit allows the visitor to discover the courtyard – characterized by the presence of the water – gradually, as they tour the exhibition rooms around it. These latter are small, enclosed spaces, illuminated from above, aligned along and connected by walkways that, like islands, appear randomly from the semi-submerged network of the traces left by the ruins of the house of the Faun.

(A) Entrance to the expo pavilion and inner court

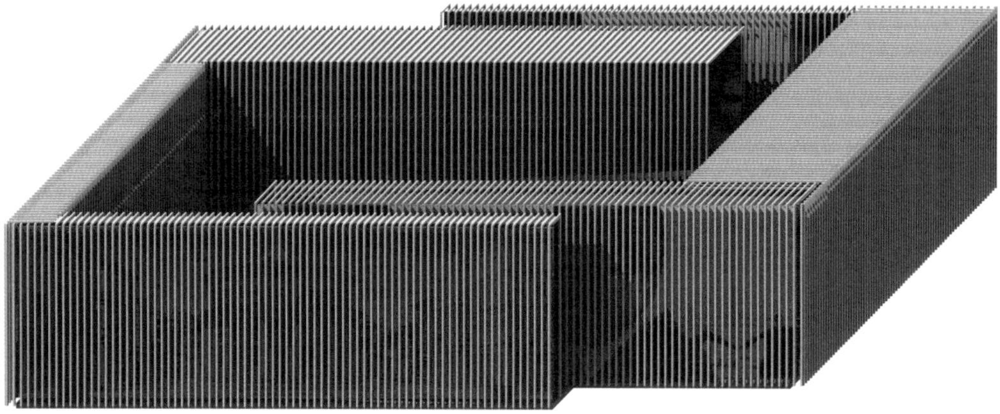

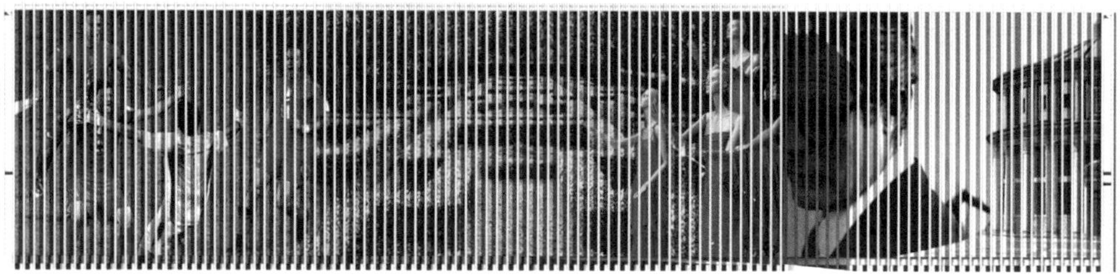

(B) Axonometric view
(C) Elevation

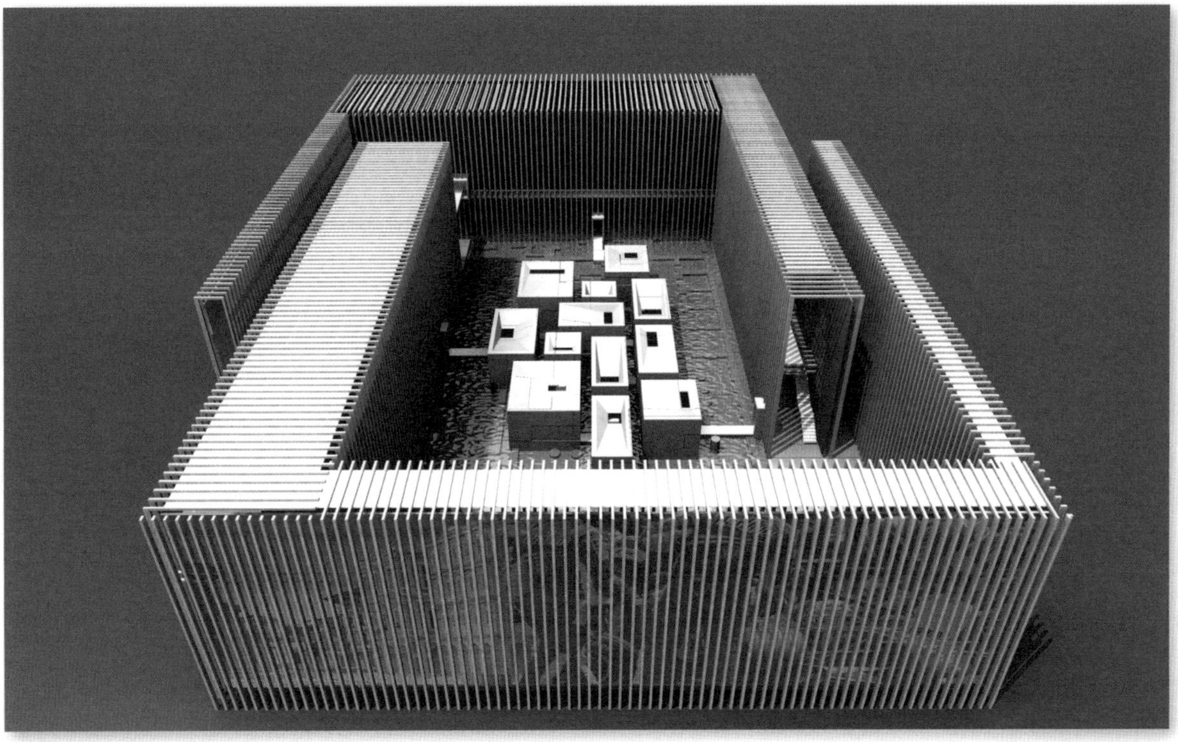

(D) Aerial view of the project
(E) View of the court and rooms on the water

6.3 IT STARTED FROM A COPY, WITH A DIFFERENT INTENT
University Library at "La Sapienza", Rome, 2021

This project not only never saw the light but, due to an error, was not even taken into consideration during the contract tender phase. For this reason, it is particularly dear to us, perhaps more than one might think, because it has taken on the character of a testimony, thus surpassing its simple value as a project.

The Library of Humanistic Subjects of the Sapienza University in Rome is unquestionably and stylistically an academic library. The new Unified Library of the Humanistic Area which, as such, has to be recognizable, is a building with a powerful morphological impact within the sphere of the urban system of Sapienza University.

With these considerations in mind on both the urban scale and the structural scale, we imagined the building.

The basic principle is rooted in a determination that the building should have a compact structure, erected on the remains of early buildings demolished in the past. Everything revolves around the central hall, a space that runs the full height of the building and is the generator of the library.

To the eyes of an informed observer, the similarity of this project to the library designed by Louis Kahn for Phillips Exeter Academy will be obvious. We are all indebted to him. The façade, however, is not just the site of morphological characterisation of the study rooms, but also of the emancipation from the model: its ransom.

(A) Detail of the façade from the garden

(B) View of the entrance to the library

 (C) Perspective section

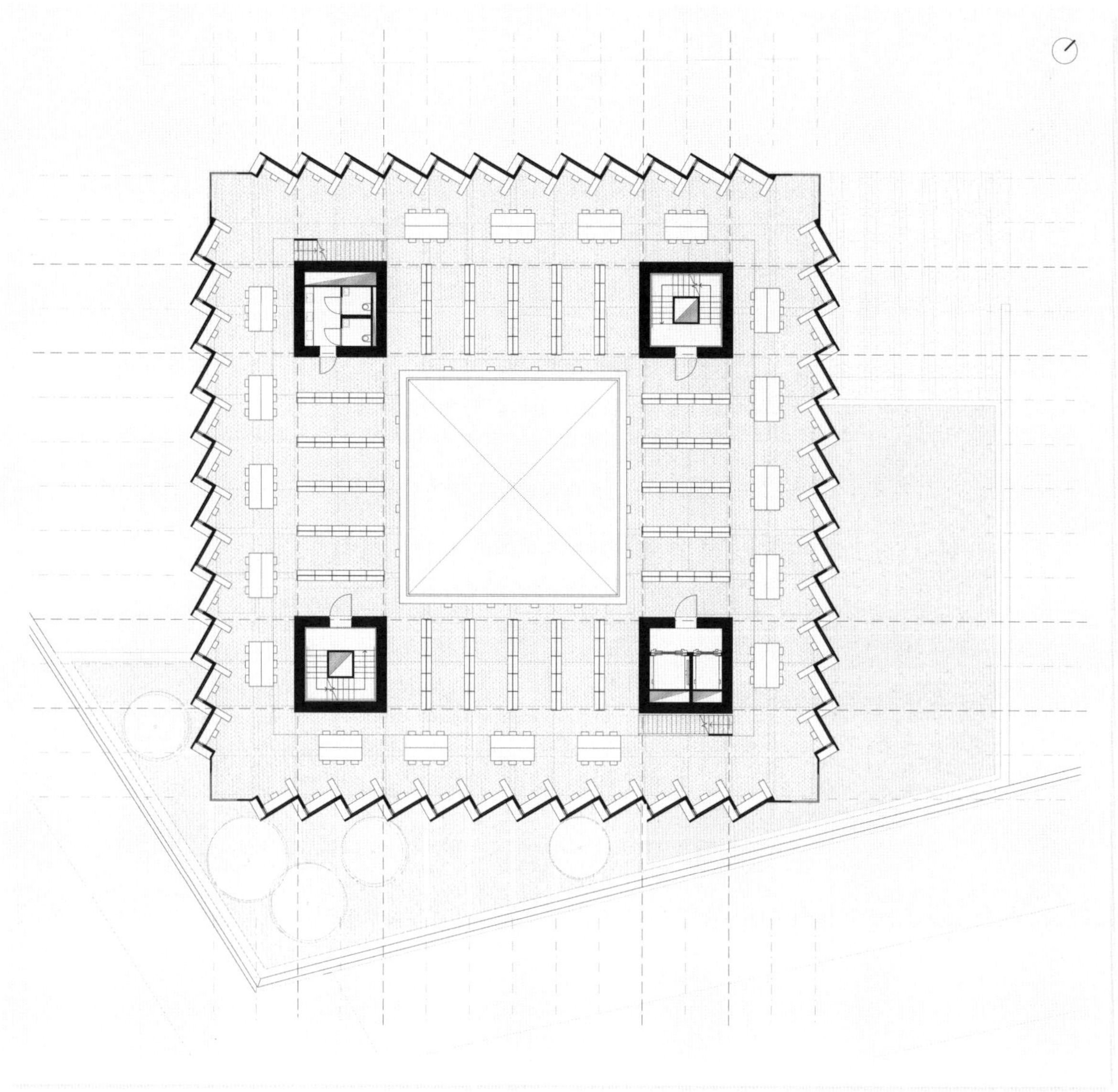

(D) Floor plan of the second level

(E) Main hall to full height
(F) Reading room and computer workstations

6.4 SOMETHING OF A CHALLENGE TO FLORENCE'S GRAND PALACES
Office building at Novoli, Florence, 2008

Three buildings in a unified system to produce the headquarters of Findomestic in Florence was the project assigned to three studios of architecture: Ipostudio, Mauro Galantino, Werner Tscholl. It was a unique, extraordinary event and experience for three groups of architects to work together, each brings different backgrounds and vocabularies, which could have generated conflict: a wager. As it turned out, the project for Findomestic imagined in that way – three parts in one – was able to achieve completion with a unified identity; with hindsight, we can say that it was a project that challenged and pitted itself against the great tradition Florence's noblest palaces.

The project completes the new square left by the former Fiat plant in Novoli, carrying on the heritage of the plan for which the area would have three independent buildings with varied uses.

The new block thus aggregates the three original lots, completing the western front of the future plaza, and is an element of transition between the new district and the two critical borders to the north and west.

An important element of the project was assigned to the construction of a dual-purpose area between institutional and urban, a fundamental principle above all in a city like Florence where the historical memory and value of public spaces is enormous.

In Florence, there is no architecture that is not urban.

The elevated body is a necessity dictated by the two glassed halls facing one another, at a distance, across a new urban space that runs through the palazzo at the centre.

After crossing the two threshold systems, two great halls open, expressing two similar principles with different materials: the north-facing one opens onto a pool which augments, with its reflection, the luminous quality of the glassed surfaces; the south-facing one, instead, overlooks a garden, densely planted like a vast, open-air greenhouse. The first, to the north, is a more enclosed space, containing the offices, the special conference rooms and classrooms for training on the ground floor. The second, on the south side, benefits from the "impossible" size of the factory building.

(A) Entrance hall and stairway to offices

 (B) View from northeast

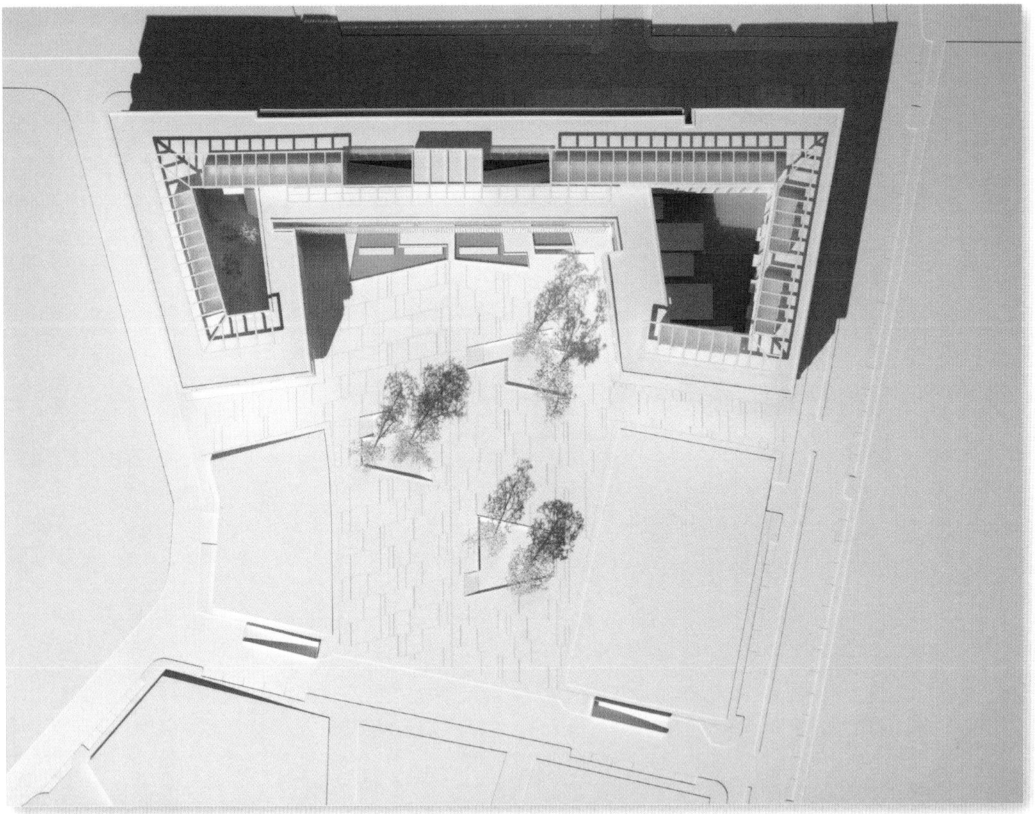

(C) Aerial view of model
(D) View of model from north

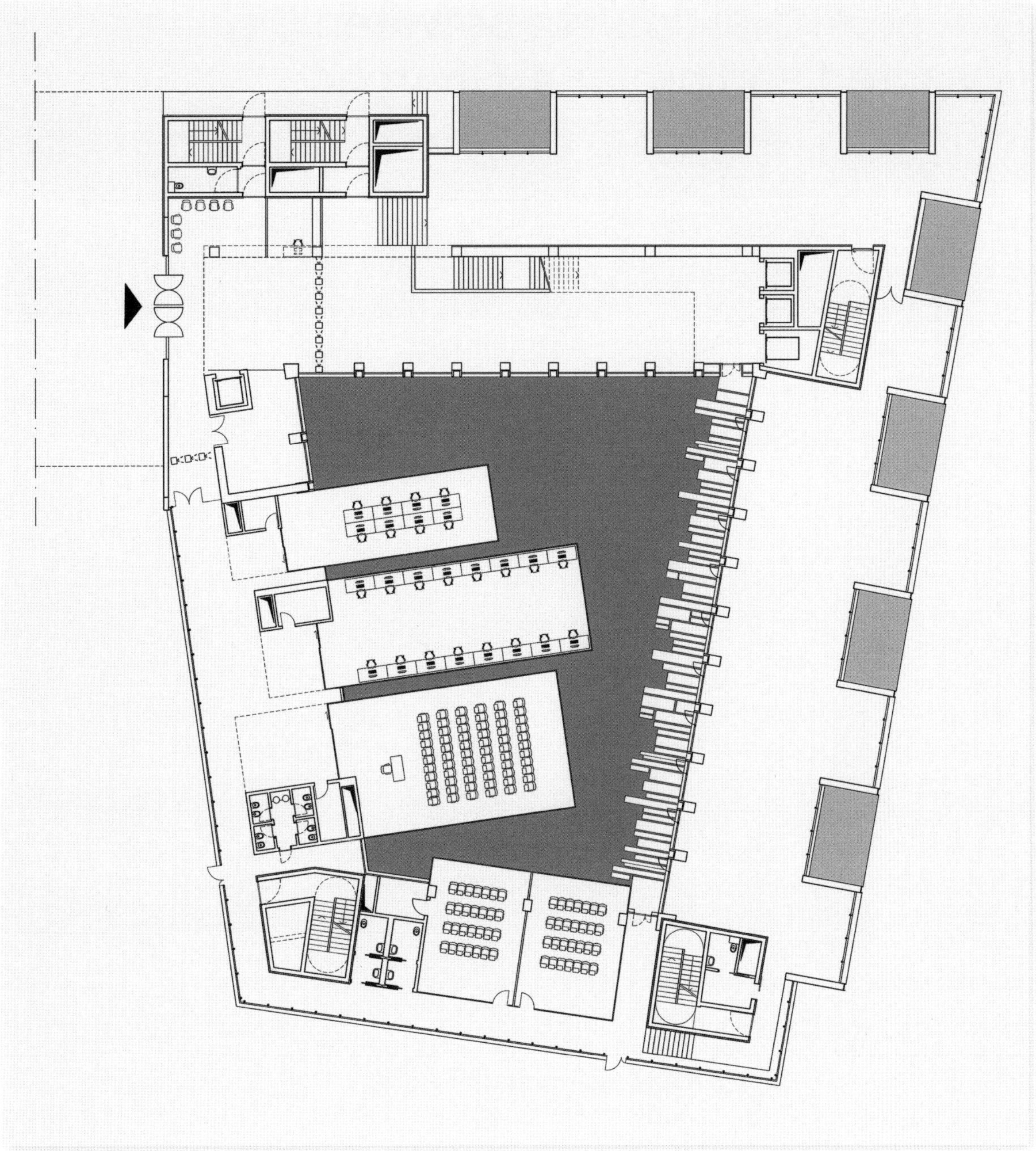

 (E) Floor plan of second level

7. A perennial conflict between sacred and profane: Churches.

Why does every religious building, a church, for example, whether Catholic or Protestant, have to resemble a conference hall or a meeting room nowadays, rather than a special place?

Certainly, it is no longer possible in our time to generate the excitement that once surrounded the construction of churches or, even more, of cathedrals.

Still, it is difficult to think of these as places where events occur according to a precise ritual that does not admit of any deviations but only, at the most, interpretations. These rituals are performed with extremely precise timing and rhythms and only accept certain nuanced variations that coincide with the belief of the different cult, according to rules set over the centuries, altered by small changes only after long discussion and debate.

Paradoxically, the layperson – the non-religious architect to whom by chance, or by choice, a religious building is given to design – may use a linguistic repertoire attributed to the culture of the sacred more than might a professional who personally lives the daily reality of the religious community that is the client for the work.

Why is that? The answer is complicated and belongs to the personal dimension, to the relationship that, believer or not, each of us establishes with the religious theme: something that belongs to the sphere of the wordless. The sacred is a dimension that eludes rationality and, for that reason, is all the more fascinating to the eyes of someone who must give shape and substance to this elusive quality. Designing a building that apparently does not contain anything other than its commitment to the rites that are held there is, paradoxically, an action full of potential and symbolism. What other building offers the Author all this potential for freedom and suffering? None!

7.1 IT LOOKS LIKE ANYTHING COULD HAPPEN HERE
50 churches for Rome 2000, Tor Tre Teste, Rome, 1994

The reason and meaning of the project can be translated briefly into a few programming principles: the clear geometrical structure, the organic separation between inside and outside, the rejection of rhetoric and symbolism and explicit meanings.

The architectural choice is to contrast the outside with the inside dialectically. If, indeed, from outside the church is a solid structure characterised by two elevated sides forming the bell towers, inside the space alters and becomes a soul of wood, like a sound box that reacts to the light: reflected, dappled and changeable light that flows in from the sides, defining the walls.

The bell towers play a particular role in that they contain the mechanism of reflection of the light and of propagation of the sound of the bells, and at the same time represent the dualism between inside and outside.

(A) Detail of northern elevation

PROSPETTO NORD

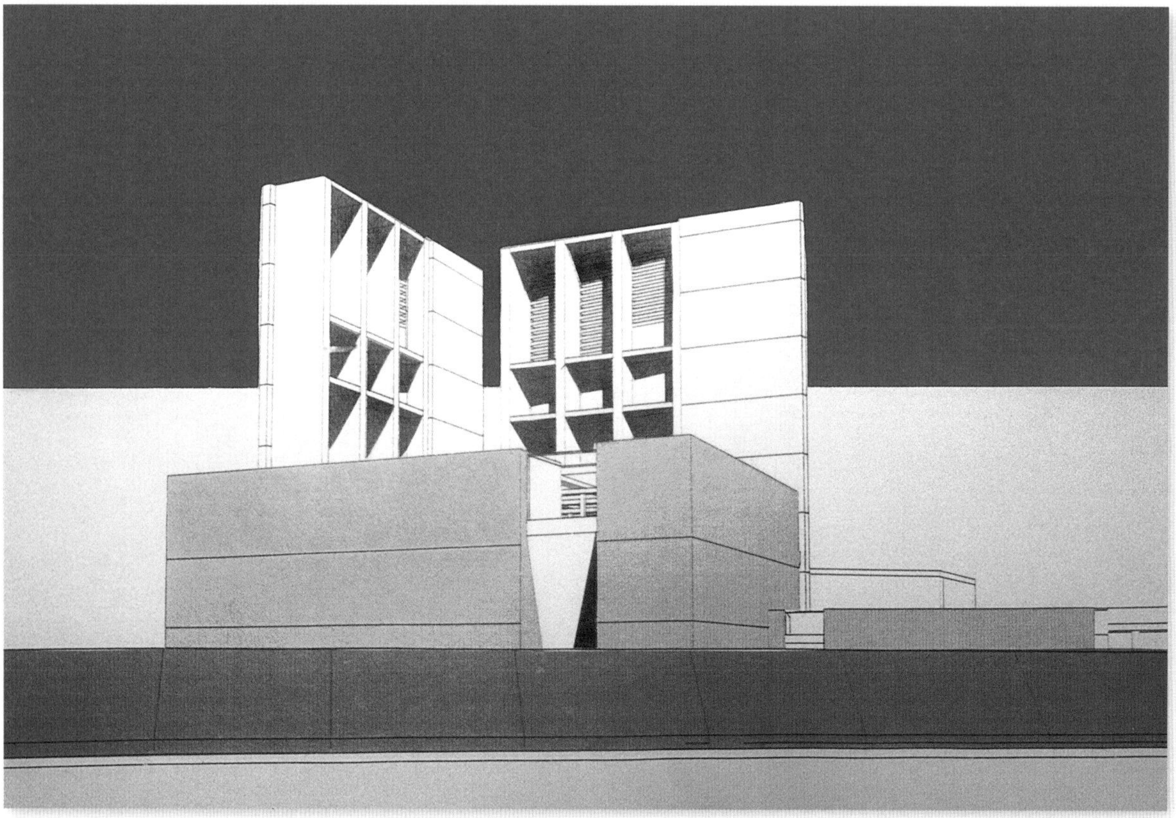

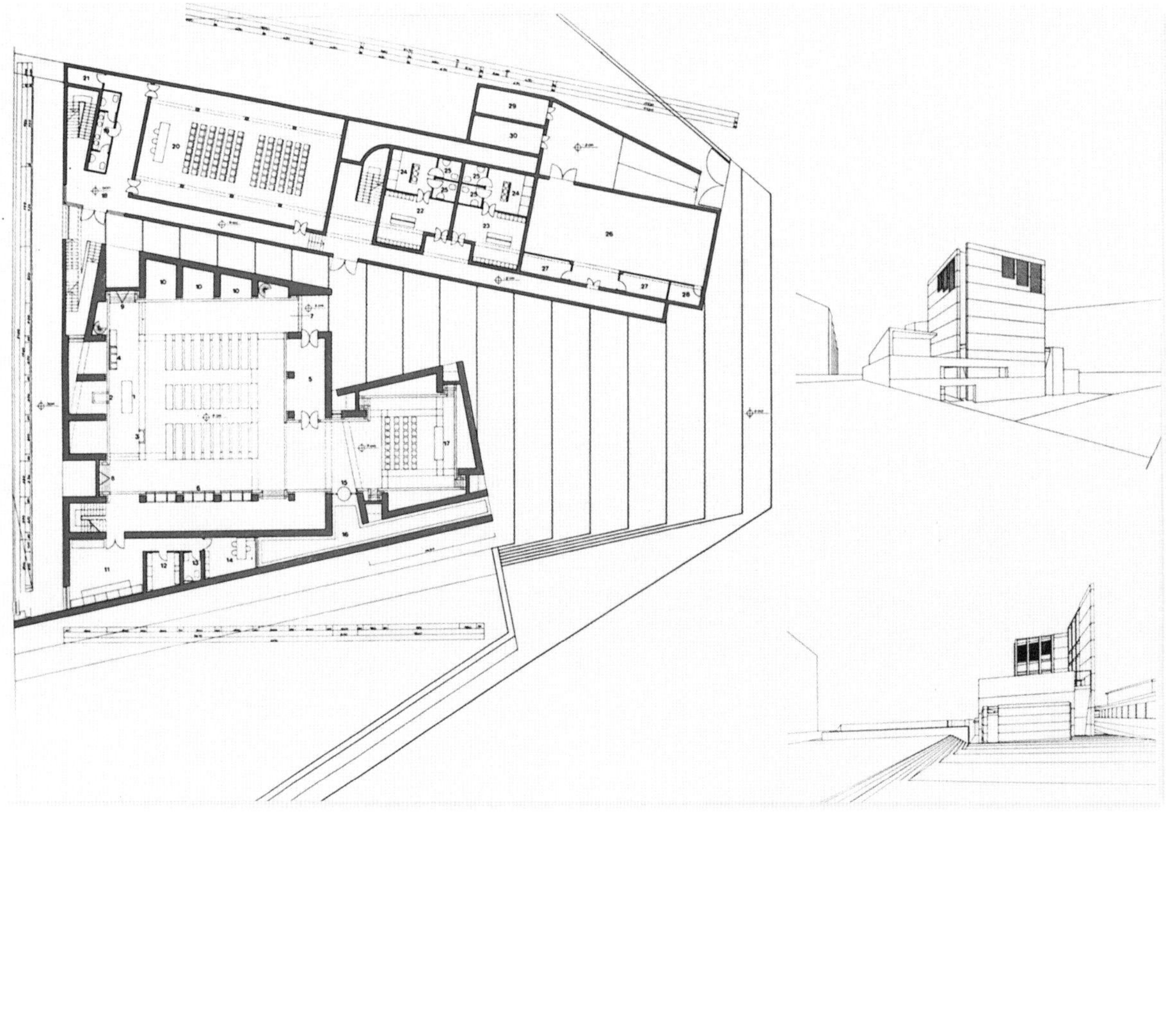

(B) View of elevation
(C) Floor plan of the ground level and views in perspective

 (D) Perspective section

7.2 LIKE A VIKING SHIP ABOUT TO SET SAIL
Church at Våler, Norway, 2012

This work is the only case in which a previous project, or rather, part of one, was recycled. We were so disappointed at the idea of abandoning a project developed for Copenhagen – which had originated in the same cultural environment of a Scandinavian country – that we decided to transfer one of the wings of the Danish library to the new Norwegian context.

The new church of Våler rises as a compact volume. On the path leading to it through the cemetery, the monolithic aspect of the church reveals, however, a more complex nature: through its shingled exterior cladding, the inside of the church can be glimpsed, and vice versa at night – so much so, not only for the constant change between day and night, but also between the summer and winter months, at these latitudes – that the light from the inside can filter out, turning the church into a great lantern.

The use of wood, a traditional material, permits the creation of a complex cladding in which the external shingles alternate with fixed sectors and portions that can be opened. Adjusting the latter and arranging the shingles, it is possible to regulate the penetration of the light inside the church and establish a visual relationship with the outside, through the thick woodland to the manicured smoothness of the cemetery.

The space of the church responds to the needs of a community that can assemble a large group; for the ceremonies where there is a smaller influx of worshippers it is possible to use only a portion of the church: the apse area consists, in fact, of a platform that, when rotated, limits and serves a reduced section of the floor area.

Both the church and the sacristy are positioned three meters above ground and are accessed by means of a linear structure. The choice to elevate the church off the ground and raise it responds to the need to make the building accessible at all times, even when snowdrifts could create a hindrance.

The site of the new church is on the edge of the forest, in a park zone that includes the old cemetery. At the centre of the park, the ruins of the old church will be filled with water: the traces of the foundations will convey a "living" memory of the building, destroyed by fire that, with the changing seasons, is transformed from a fountain to a frozen pond.

(A) Interior view of liturgical hall

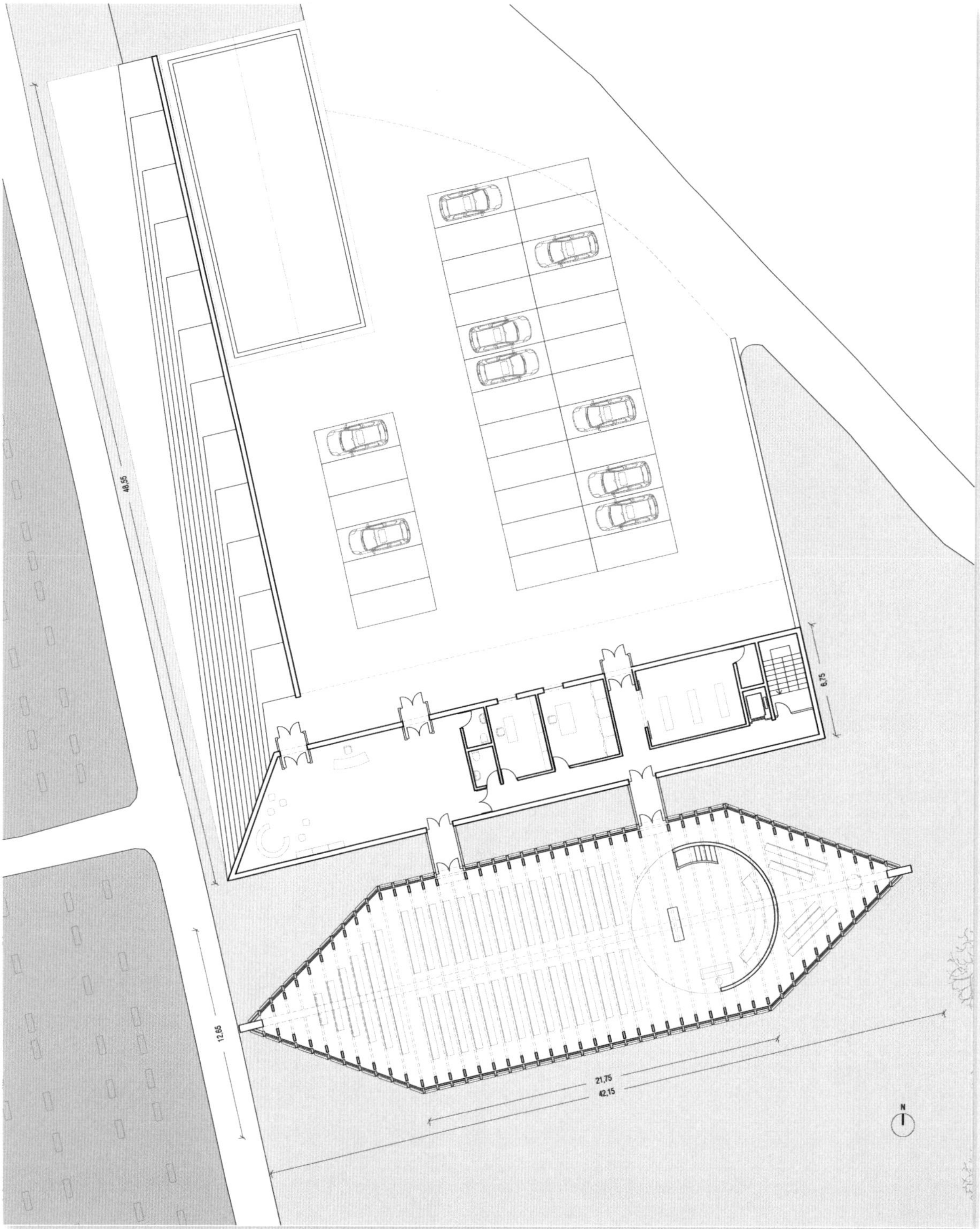

 (B) Floor plan of the first level

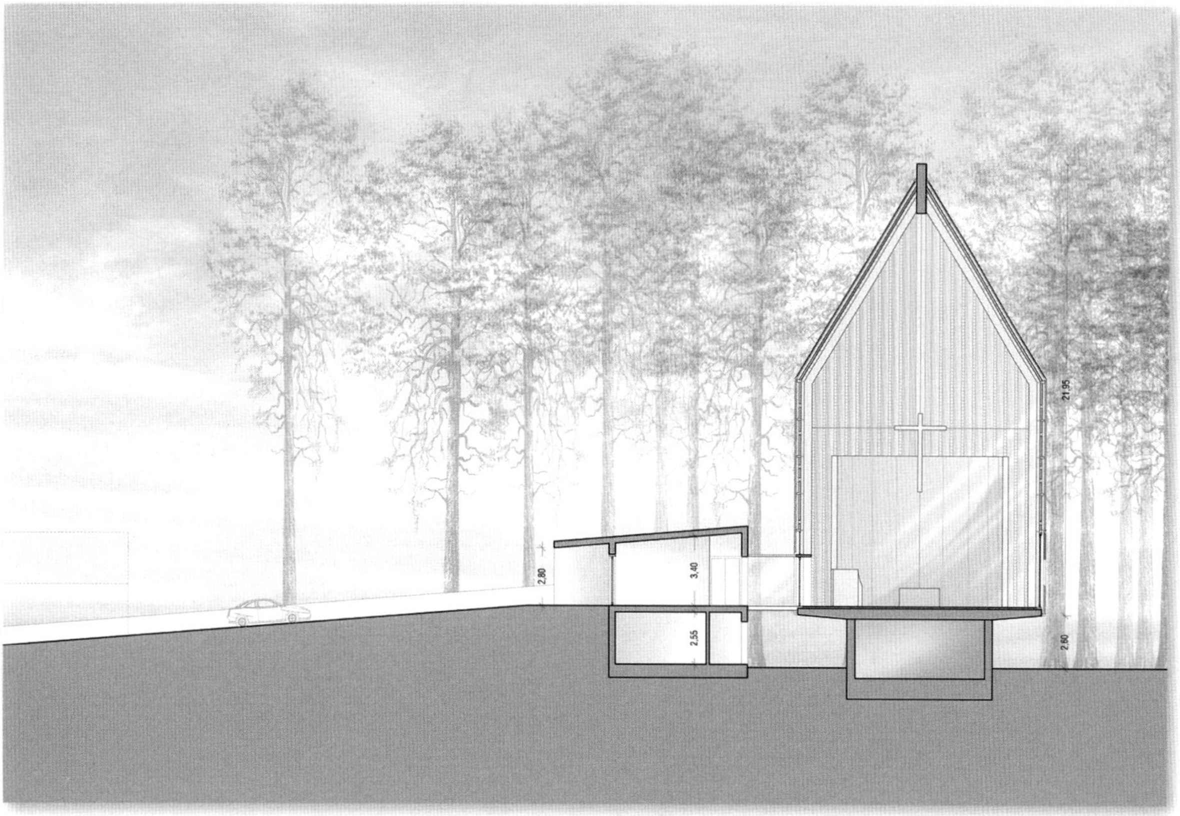

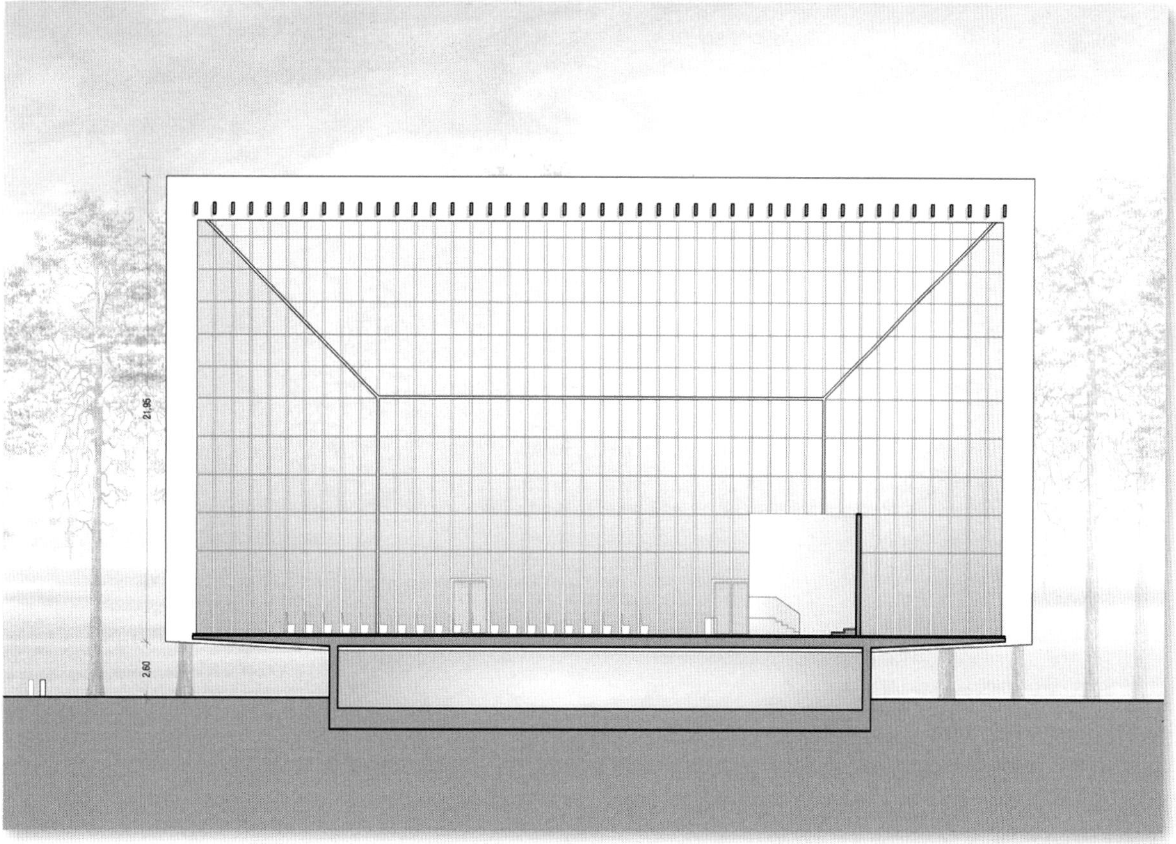

(C) Cross section
(D) Longitudinal section

 (E) Nocturnal view from the street

(F) Main front with entrance to linear structure
(G) Overview

7.3 LIFTING OFF ON A DOVE'S WINGS
New parochial church, Cibeno di Carpi, 2007

A particular urban periphery, just as the development of Carpi from the post-war period to the present has been particular: this is the site of the Church of Cibeno.

The primary intention was to transform the new church into a nodal point of a new spaciousness capable of bringing order and relaunching elements that until then had been scattered and separated in the area: the Church of St. Agatha, future main church, the rectory, the parish hall, the former cemetery enclosure, now Don Berni Park.

The new church, built alongside the old cemetery wall, generated a series of old and new open spaces. This play of ancient and modern walls is the simple answer that the project gave to the theme of the reorganization. Every built portion, whether open or closed, played a role.

The shape of the roof is the synthetic re-elaboration of two iconic elements: the open wings of a bird in flight – a dove, symbol of peace – and the vaulted roof of the nave, a Christian tradition.

The two asymmetrical wings of the roof create a differentiated and hierarchical space, as if they were two naves of different heights characterising the interior of the church, differentiating the zone of the vestibule from the main body of the assembly, while maintaining the uniformity of the space.

A subtle gold laminate covers the inside of the two naves, creating a precious effect of shaded light which increases in intensity directly over the presbytery.

The vaults, considered as a unitary and homogenous element, act like a single structure which, simply resting on the two tilted outer walls, in its gentle dip toward the ground almost touches the earth. A narrow shaft of light in the connecting point between the roof vaults and the supporting walls creates the sensation that the vault barely touches it and almost takes flight.

(A) External view of main front

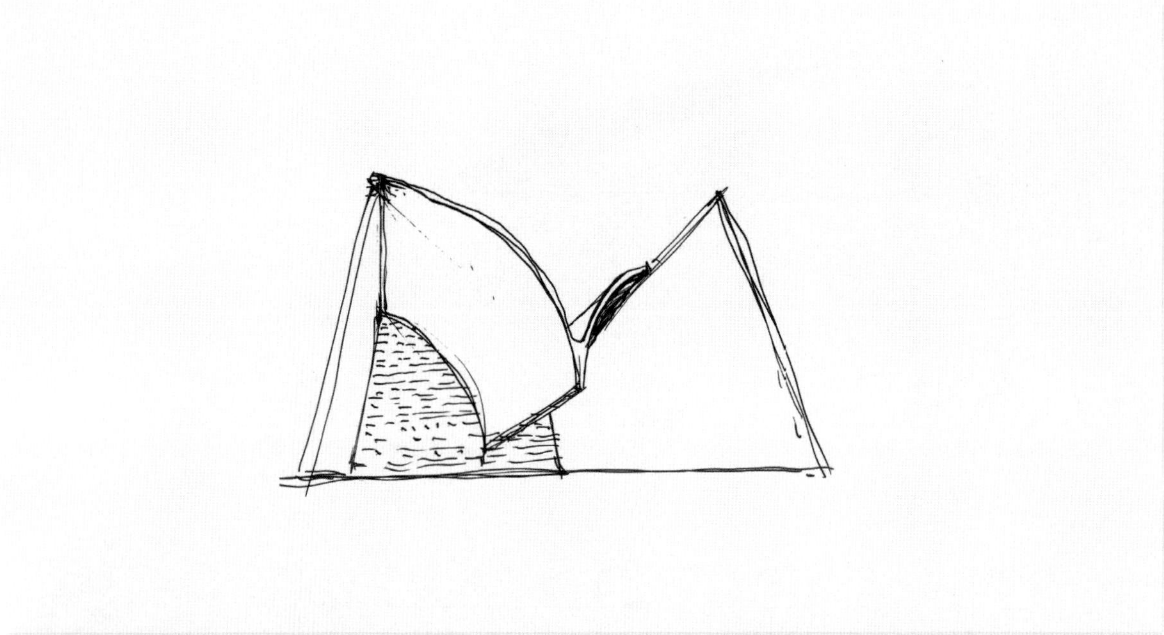

(B) Sketch of the project
(C) Internal view of liturgical hall

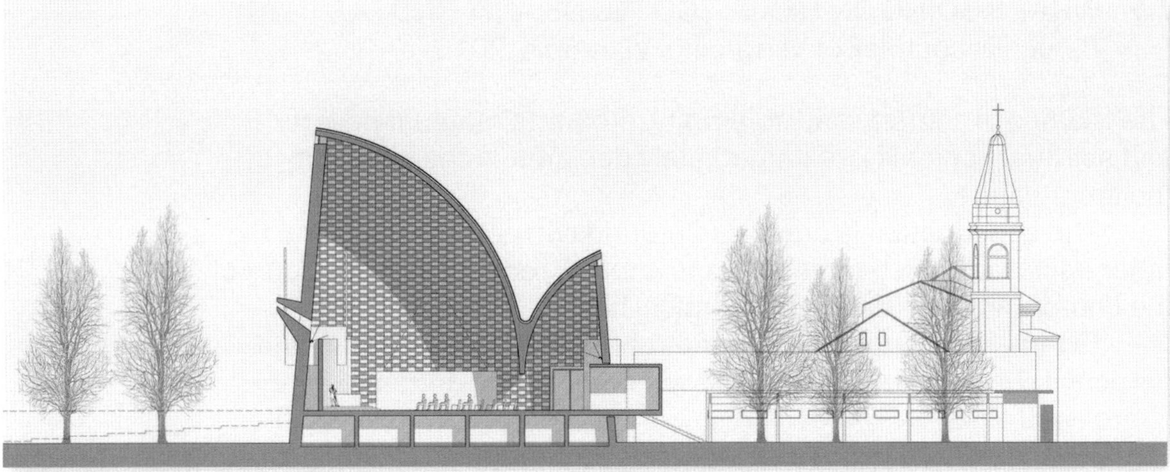

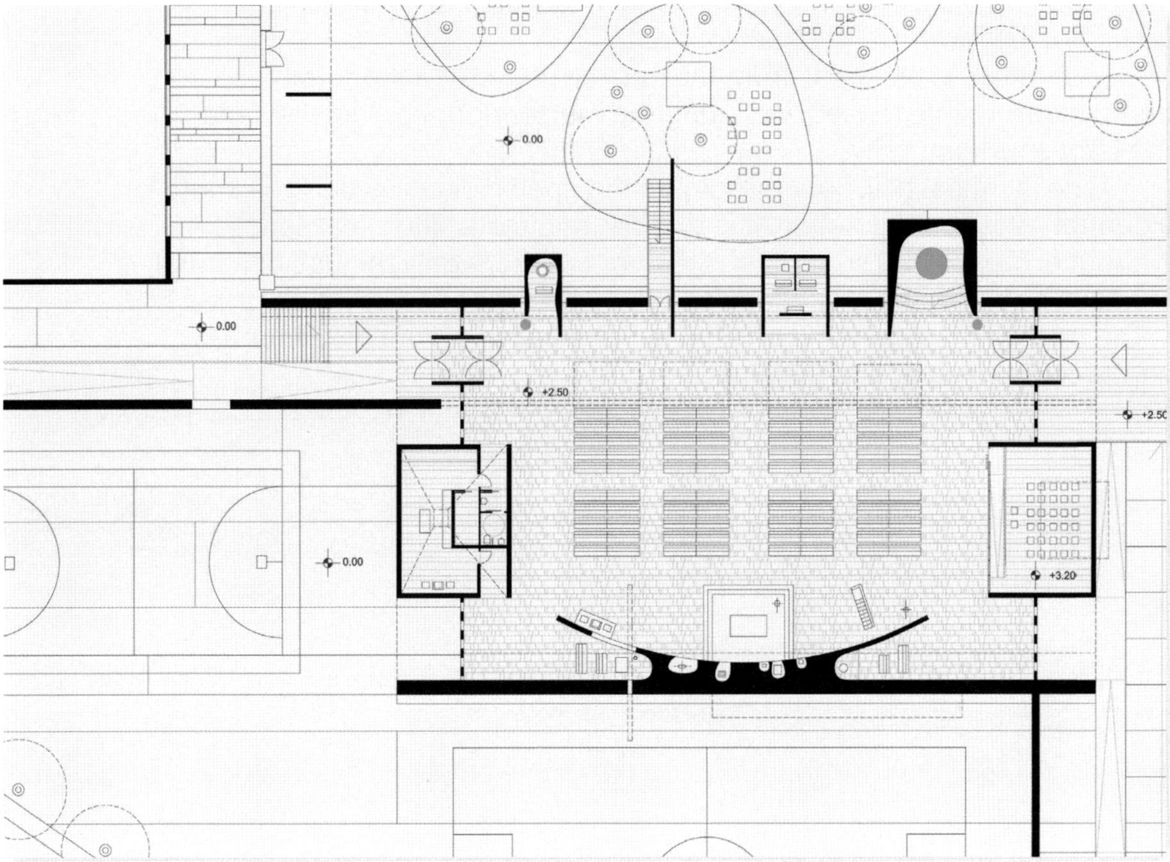

(D) Cross section
(E) Floor plan of the ground level

7.4 WHAT'S GOING ON HERE?... GO INSIDE AND FIND OUT!
Parochial complex of Varignano, Viareggio, 2015

The themes of sobriety and solemnity, proper to material poverty and spiritual richness, are immediately declared in the simplicity of the architecture.

The construction is organized around two courts, one open, the other enclosed, which penetrate one another reciprocally: the court of the churchyard and that of the liturgical hall.

Externally, the point of co-penetration between the urban and parochial space is identified by the wide arch at the entrance on the churchyard side.

The complex occupies its lot almost entirely, with a clearly horizontal structure about 6 meters high, from which only the bell tower emerges vertically, the tower of light and sound.

A number of elements from the current church – scheduled for demolition – will be reused, including the marble flooring, the altar, and the baptismal font.

The liturgical hall, counterpoint to the open cloister, is designed with a central layout configuration. It is a sober, minimalist liturgical space without excesses and superfluous elements, where only the use of natural light can be said to be redundant, and that expresses its maximum power in the presbytery, where the bell tower – the tower of light and sound – captures it to convey it to the altar.

(A) Birdseye view of the parochial complex

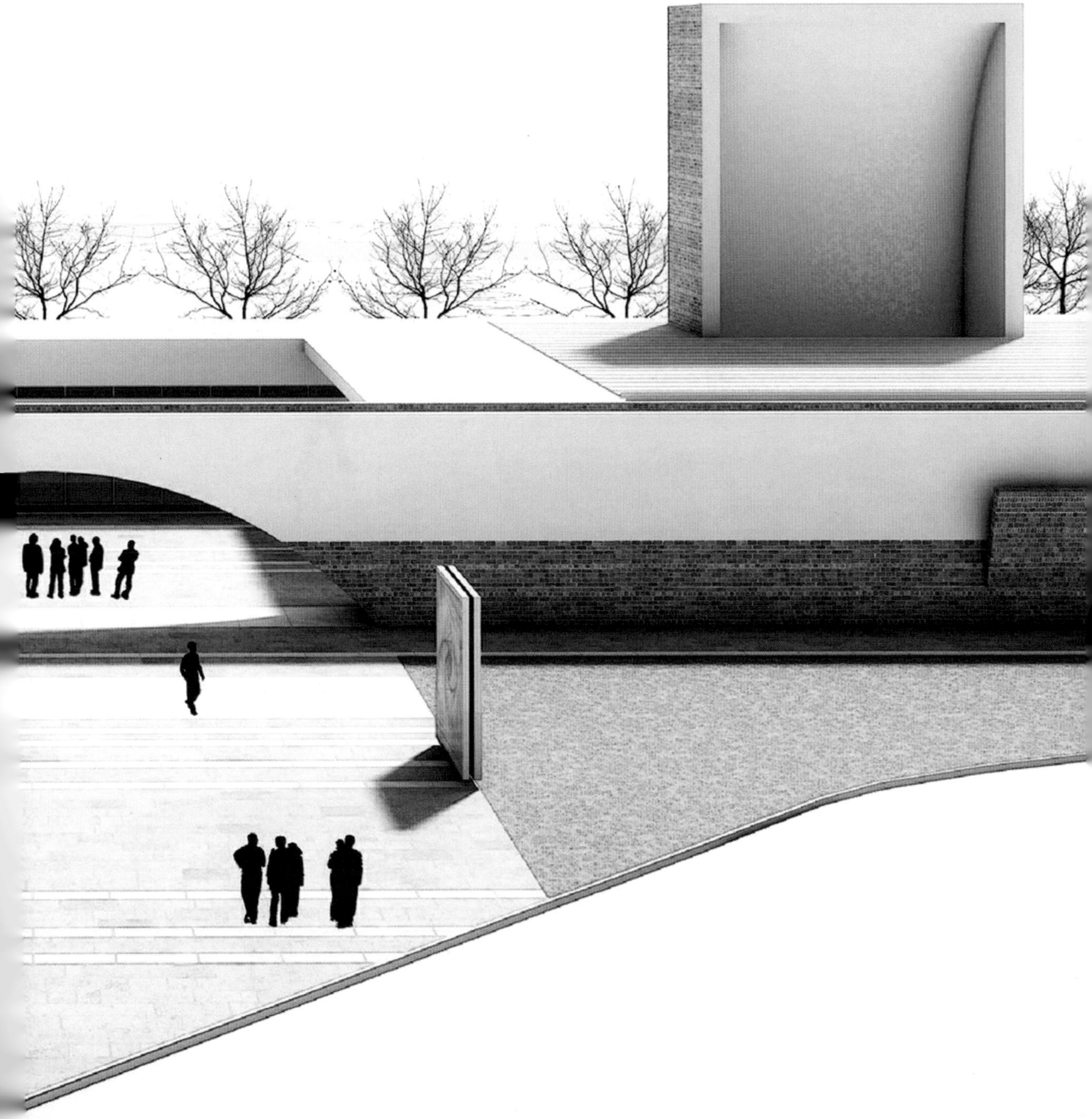

(B) View from the street, showing the arch over the entrance to the churchyard in the corner

(C) Arched entrance to the cloister

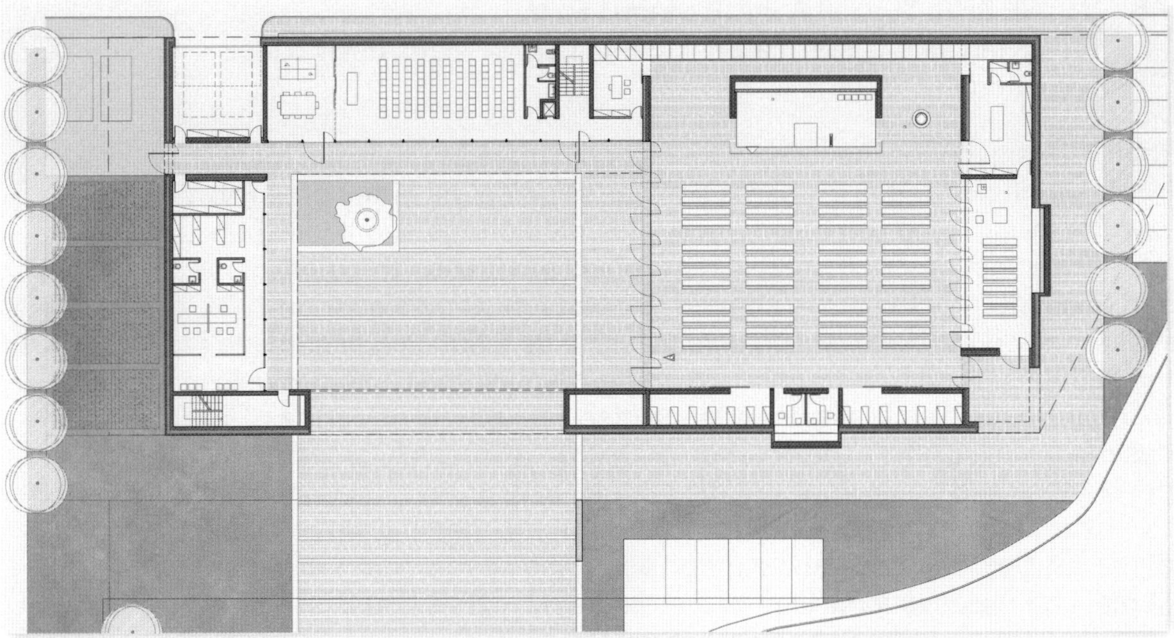

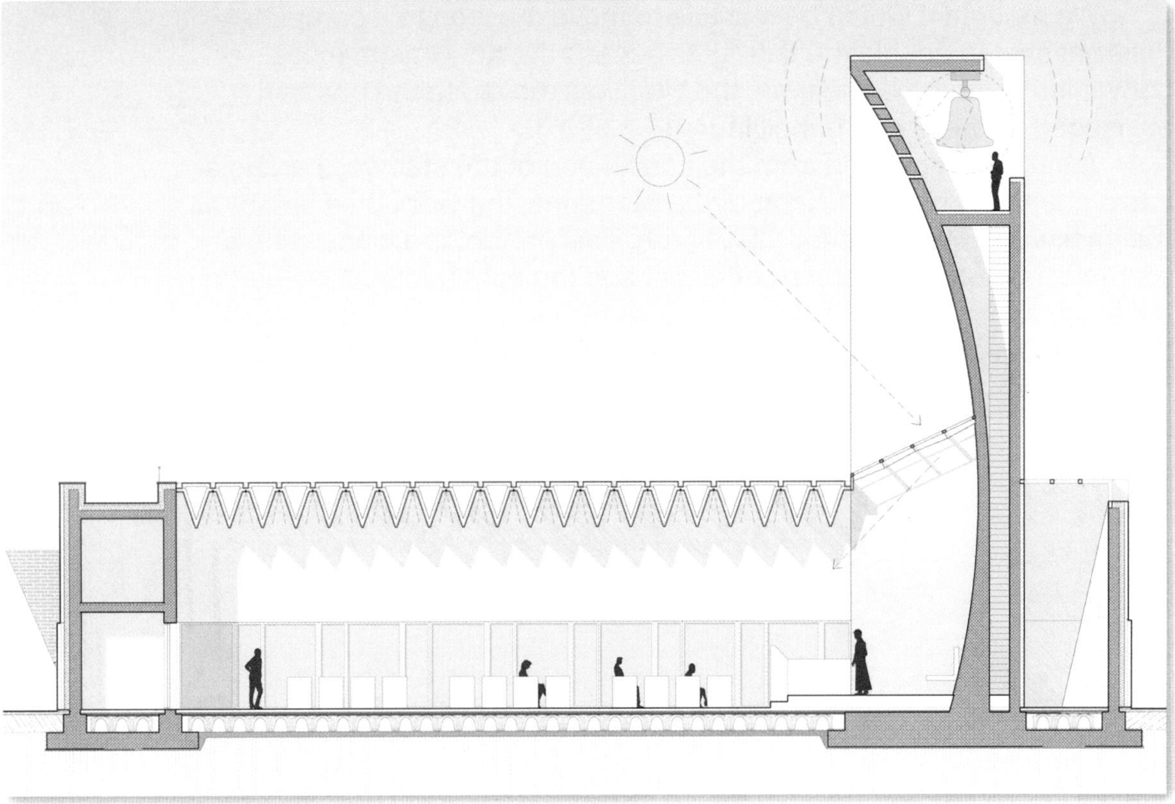

(D) Layout of the complex
(E) Longitudinal section

7.5 IN THE SHELTER OF A BLUE MANTLE
Presbytery of the Basilica-Sanctuary of Santa Maria dei Miracoli, Casalbordino, 2014

Totally reconsidering the location of the icon of the Madonna of Miracles in her sanctuary, and at the same time redesigning the entire presbytery, was like laying hands on the memory of our childhood and adolescence.

The sanctuary as it now exists – rebuilt in 1962 on the ruins of the earlier chapel erected at the end of 1500 and rebuilt previously in 1824 – was intended to be a basilica to receive the devotion and pilgrimage of the faithful from all over the Abruzzo region. None other than Gabriele d'Annunzio testified to the importance of the sanctuary as early as 1550, describing in his novel *The Triumph of Death* the intensity of the desperation and tragic power of the masses of pilgrims who visited it.

The idea of the new presbytery came after a meeting with the prior of the Basilica, disturbed and worried about the conditions of the altar containing the devotional icon of the Madonna, which could only be accessed from a narrow stairway around the altar.

We thought it would be feasible to move the icon to a completely different spot to enable the faithful to access the holy image more conveniently. At the same time, the altar was moved to the position envisaged by the post-Council liturgy.

A blue veil, resulting from the conversion of the stairway parabola into a starry sky, holds the icon of the Madonna; the work thus becomes the backdrop of the nave for the church. This project too, consisting of a simple, immediate gesture, will never see the light because, aside from the fascination with which it was received, change very often appears dangerous and strange. Actually, that is rather odd because the place has been through many far more radical changes than one might imagine... and yet!

(A) View of the presbytery with the new location of the devotional icon

(B) Lateral view of the blue veil

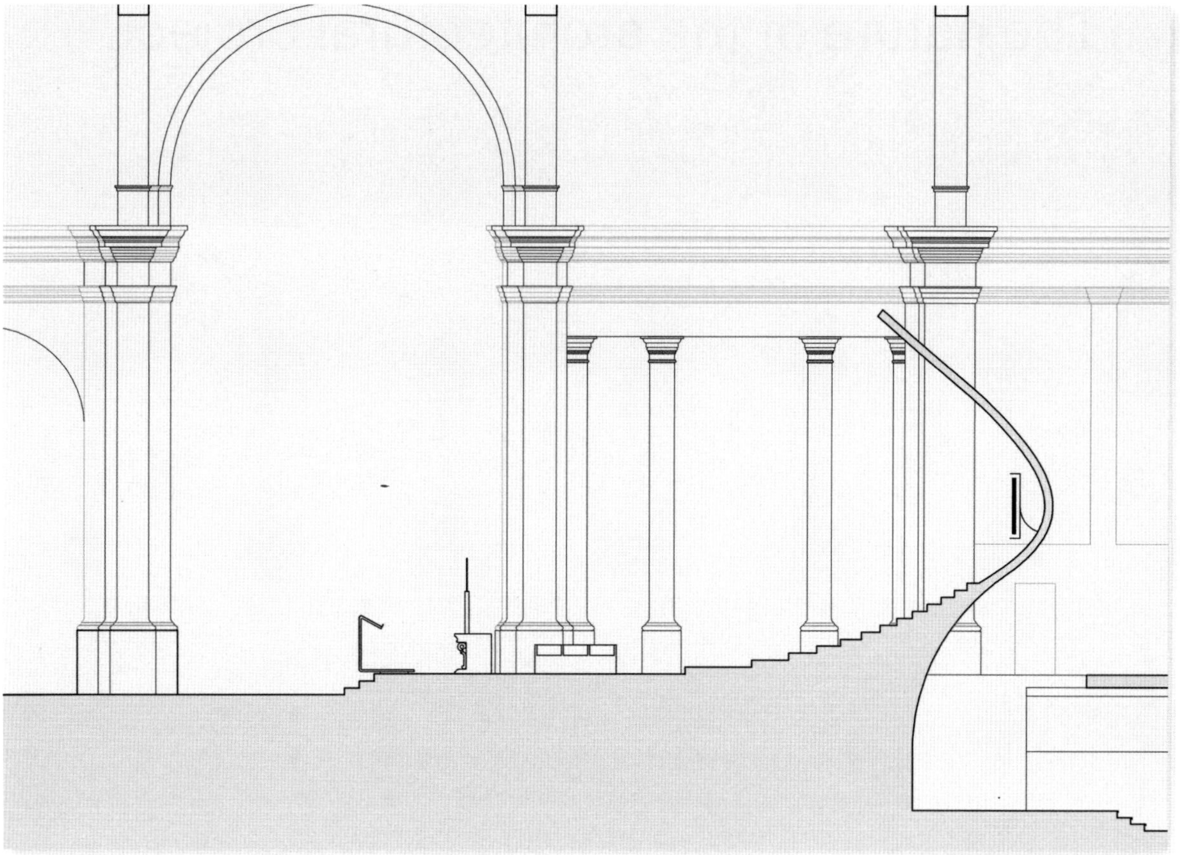

(C) Longitudinal section

The nature of the architectural project.

A great deal of contemporary architecture appears outsized and unrelated to any historical context. If it can validly be described in terms of a category of person, it appears often supercilious and arrogant. We live in a time in which changes to the global power structure of the world, the loss of many of our certainties and illusions cause anxiety, fear of doing or saying the wrong thing and a general sense of imminent tragedy.

The "hope" that is such an integral part of architectural and urban planning has to be accompanied by the awareness of the limits of our own development; only through the acknowledgment of this can we face the often contradictory and paradoxical issues that crowd our drafting table.

We need to take a responsible attitude toward our projects, based on the awareness of our own shortcomings. Awareness is essential because we always have to remind ourselves that our actions can damage the land, altering its geomorphological balance but, at the same time, our "hope" suggests that we have the ability to repair that damage with our architecture. It doesn't always work out that way, however. That is why we have to try to develop a new attitude in our architectural practice – one that will lead us to take new directions or perhaps to rediscover others abandoned in the past, while always having a clear understanding of the goal we are trying to achieve.

We have to pick up from the limits, from the crises, from this awareness of the possible end of everything, if we want to re-appropriate the future and the profound sense of what it means to create architecture. We know that architecture does not only alter the conditions achieved by an anthropic organism – landscape or city – but that it is also an original way of interpreting the world, explaining phenomena of organization, structuring and developing the land.

Architecture produces "artifacts", that is, works that derive from an intentional process of change enacted by human beings and is, for this reason, the only discipline that can give an "explanation" to the intimate structure of those changes.

The architectural project is a method of study and at the same time a tool with which to act: it is only through new projects that architecture can establish and innovate its normative theoretical body, its disciplinary rules. Moreover, when we "design buildings" we are also saying something about the purpose and sense of the work.

Architectural research is thus the necessary and sufficient method whereby we reveal what emerges from the interaction between man and his environment and from the evolution of artifacts. The result of this action, the work of architecture, at that point becomes an event, an epiphany.

Architecture is not a science, but the design process, on the contrary, has the characteristics of a scientific procedure. It is just by virtue of its ability to investigate predictively that the design process should be removed from this arbitrary condition, without rules, inclined to disregard theoretic reflection and thus not instructive, not transferable. Designing should and must have a sense and a scope; unlike what we often see in daily use, it should have a cynicism that tends to preserve the importance of doing it, even in the absence of an end.

Architectural design is many things at once, each of which reveals a different active strategy; all converge on a single objective: to make what we imagine into something real. Our ability to imagine is the basis of the project action and, lacking this, it is impossible to think and act in architecture.

The ability to alter reality, even if only at the human and not at the divine level, contains, however, an ineffable visionary power capable of anticipating slightly that which will be.

To design a project is to predict, since it contains an idea of what came before the object, and the act of creating the project is an act of faith toward the future, an act of “hope”. Now we need to accompany that hope with a new sense, the sense of “tragedy” and essential “piety”.

Appendix

CARLO TERPOLILLI

Founder partner of Ipostudio Architects, Firenze-Lugano.

Carlo Terpolilli is Professor at the DIDA Department of Architecture and Design, University of Florence.

His work focuses on innovation in the design and construction process of architecture; he coordinates design activities within Ipostudio, with particular experience in urban design and the restoration of complex monumental buildings.

He has been invited to several universities, seminars and conferences and also been accorded special awards, in Italy and abroad. His projects received awards in several design contests at national and international level, have on several occasions been published in Italy and abroad, including Casabella, Area, Abitare, Ottagono, Monumental, Bauwelt, Arquitectura Viva, Future, A10, and displayed at exhibitions, including the Venice Biennale and the Triennale of Milan.

Since 2017 he has been Key Expert Architect for the design of the MICAS Malta International Contemporary Art Space in Malta, which is currently under construction.

Carlo Terpolilli is the author, among other texts, of:

A. Ulisse, A. Ghisetti Giavarina (curated by) *Confronti sul progetto, Testimonianze sull'architettura tra storie, idee, progetti, maestri e committenti*, Libria, Melfi 2022;

"La transformation du musée de l'Hopital des Innocents", in *Monumental, Dossier Musées et Monuments historiques,* semi-annual magazine no. 2, 2017;

A. Sgolastra (edited by), *Il governo del territorio: bellezza, sviluppo, tutela*, in: *Piano con Paesaggio. Visioni e Confronti. Un laboratorio sul piano territoriale di coordinamento della provincia di Firenze*, FrancoAngeli, Milan 2014;

"Oltre il restauro. La valorizzazione del patrimonio edilizio pubblico monumentale, l'Istituto degli Innocenti e il progetto MUDI", in *TECHNE – Valorizzare il patrimonio edilizio pubblico,* no. 3, Firenze University Press 2012;

Progettando edifici. Considerazioni sul progetto di architettura come arte della tecnica, Forma Edizioni, Florence 2012;

3 Città (im)possibili. Forma Edizioni, Poggibonsi, 2012;

"Terremoto e politica. Un silenzio assordante", in *Opere*, no. 33, 2012;

M. Balzani (edited by), *Restauro, recupero, riqualificazione. Il progetto contemporaneo nel contesto storico,* Skira, Milan 2011;

*Emergenza del Progetto, Progetto dell'Emergenza. Architetture Con-Temporaneit*à, Federico Motta, Milan 2005.

IPOSTUDIO

Ipostudio Architects is a working group founded in 1983 in Florence, engaged in the business of architectural design and civil architecture, in the sectors of culture, museums, health care and social welfare facilities, special residences and, in general, large projects for urban complexes.

The work of the studio, with offices in Florence and Lugano, is based on vast experience in public and private works, ranging from international competitions to architectural and urban project design, with specific expertise in the field of restoration and urban redevelopment.

The works of Ipostudio have won recognition in national and international competitions and have been published many times in Italy and abroad, and exhibited at events like the Venice Biennale and the Milan Triennale.

The studio has won numerous national and international awards: Ipostudio was the winner of the National and Tuscan Regional Award IN/ARCH 2020; the FAF Award for Tuscan Architecture 2017 and the XIX International Competition "Sistema d'Autore", 2011. It was also a finalist in the BigMat International Architecture Award 2019 and the Gold Medal award for Italian architecture 2006 of the Milan Triennale; it was mentioned for the XIX Gold Compass award ADI 2001, and received honourable mention at the Florentine Architecture Award 2014.

Many of its works are published in the monograph *Ipostudio, the concreteness of modernity* by Marco Mulazzani, with a preface by Franco Purini, published by Electa in 2008, for the series "Documents of Architecture".

The founding parners are Lucia Celle, Roberto Di Giulio, Carlo Terpolilli and Elisabetta Zanasi Gabrielli; from 1983 to 1988, Emilio Bria and Mario Manfroni were also partners; in 2014, Luca Belatti, Mariagiulia Bennicelli Pasqualis, Panfilo Cionci and Beatrice Turillazzi were associated with the studio. Currently, the active partners, responsible for project design, are: Lucia Celle, Carlo Terpolilli, Elisabetta Zanasi Gabrielli and Panfilo Cionci.

The partners are frequently invited to present their work by Universities, as well as Italian and foreign institution, including the major Polytechnical schools and Italian architecture departments, as well as at the Festival of Architecture in Parma, the Mantovarchitettura Review, the Piaggio Museum in Pontedera, the Florentine campus of Kent State University - KSU Florence, the Annals of Architecture Foundation and of the City of Naples, the Milan Triennale; abroad, they have been guest speakers at the Polytechnic Institute of Lisbon, the Italian Institute of Culture in Malta and in Prague, the

TU-Polytechnic Institute of Braunschweig and the BAUHAUS foundation of Dessau.

The work of Ipostudio has always focused on its interest in civil architecture, qualified by a social and collective character, in particular seeking out frequent new opportunities through participation in competitions: this is an approach that remains a distinctive feature of the studio still to this day.

The studio has obtained excellent results in many of the competitions in which it has competed, often succeeding in winning the relative contracts to build its projects; among the most recent were the 1st prize in the competition to restore the former convent of the Discalced Carmelites in Lecce and conversion to university housing, one for the Charity Hospital of Locarno and one for the urban restoration of via Grande in Livorno, all assigned in 2022. In addition to these, in recent years the studio won the competition and contract to build the Angelina Lauro nursery school in Longarone in 2021 and the contract to build the City Hospital of Lugano in 2017: in this latter case, the project stage continued until 2021, when the executive project was finally approved and contracted.

The studio also built the Innocenti Museum in Florence, a work that was extensively publicised and awarded, also at the international level, and inaugurated in 2016. The project had won the first prize in the international competition announced by the Innocenti Institute in 2008, and the same year the studio also won the international competition for an Internaat in Lommel, Belgium, which was eventually built in 2014.

Before that, we should mention the construction in 2002 of a bank building in Chianti, at Sambuca in Florence province, a contract that was obtained after winning the competition announced by the Banca del Chianti Fiorentino, a banking institution of Credito Cooperativo, dating back to 1996. The competition for the "City of Education" – a scholastic complex meant to consist of three high schools as well as cafeteria service, library, gymnasium and auditorium, announced by the Province of Salerno following the tragedy of the Sarno mudslide in 1998, and won in 2000: in the years that followed, Ipostudio continued through the design stage all the way to the executive project.

Among the most recent successes are: the 1st prize in the competition for redevelopment of the façade of the Le Scotte Hospital in Siena in 2021, while the most recent, in 2023, is the 1st prize won in the competition for the Third Tower of the Tuscan Region, for expansion of the Tuscan Regional Office Centre in Florence. In 2021 Ipostudio was also selected by the Cassa di Risparmio di Firenze Foundation to design the Swimming Pool Centre at S. Bartolo a Cintoia, as part of the European Program "Next Generation EU" for the City of Florence, a project that was completed in 2023 and is now in the contracting stage.

Among the other recognitions awarded to Ipostudio were, in 2022, the 3rd prize at the international competition for the restoration of the P.L. Nervi stadium in Florence, and in 2009, in the competition for the Library and Municipal Offices in Brescia and at the competition for the Area Northwest of Parma. In 2010 the studio obtained the same placement in the competition for the Citadel of Assisted Living in Riva del Garda; it won the 2nd prize in the three competitions for the design of new churches to which Ipostudio was invited by the CEI and the dioceses of Lucca and Prato: the former for the parish centre of Cibeno di Carpi in 2007, the second for the parochial complex of Varignano in Viareggio in 2015 and the last for the Church of St. Pius X in Prato in 2020. Finally, the studio received mention in the important international competition for the MEIS National Museum of Italian Jews and the Shoah in Ferrara.

Also noteworthy was the selection of Ipostudio in a number of international competitions, including, in Belgium, "Open Oproep" – literally an open call for quality architectural design – for the Vlaams Bouwmeester of the Belgian government of Flanders, where the studio was invited to participate in the competitions for the Mercator University Library at the Gent Campus in 2010, for a technical school in Brasschaat in 2007 and for the Internaat of Lommel in 2008 (which it also built); while in Switzerland, after taking second place in the competition for the OBV Hospital in Mendrisio, in 2015, Ipostudio was invited by the EOC Cantonal Hospital Organization, which manages public health for Ticino Canton – to participate in the competitions for Expansion of the Charity Hospital of Locarno and the City Hospital of Lugano, winning 1st prize in both, in 2022 and 2017. Other restricted procedures were the Competition for redevelopment of the Complex of Sant'Agostino in Modena, by invitation from the Cassa di Risparmio di Modena Foundation (third place); for the new Campus of Social and Economic Sciences "Piave Futura" in Padua, at the invitation of the University of Padua; for redevelopment of the university complex of S. Chiara in Piazza dei Miracoli, for the City of Pisa; for "Campidoglio 2", the new office centre for the city of Rome; for the Area of first access and consultation hall of the Library at the Higher Normal School of Pisa.

PRINCIPALI OPERE REALIZZATE

Innocenti Museum, Florence
Client: Innocenti Institute, Florence
Project design 2008–2011, construction 2012–2016

Campus Firenze, residence for university students on viale Morgagni, Florence
Client: Birillo 2007 scarl, for the University of Florence
Project design 2016, construction 2016–2019

Internaat, protected residence for disabled and non-self-sufficient boys, Lommel, Belgium
Client: Gemeenschapsonderwijs (Ministry of Education of the Flemish Community)
Project design 2009–2010, construction 2011–2014

Student housing Villa Val di Rose, Sesto Fiorentino (Florence)
with Paolo Felli, Massimo Gennari
Client: University of Florence, "P. Spadolini" Department of Architectural and Design Technologies

Project design 2002, construction 2008–2013
Assisted Housing Facility, Montemurlo (Prato)
RSA with 40 beds + 10 at day care centre
Client: National Health Service Agency 4, Prato
Progect design 2006–2007, construction 2008–2011

Expansion of the Argenta Hospital (Ferrara)
Client: National Health Service Agency, Ferrara
Project design 2004–2005, construction 2008–2011

New Entrance to Careggi - Office Centre of the University Hospital of Careggi, Florence
with CSPE and Elio Di Franco
Client: University Hospital Company of Careggi, Florence
Project design 1999–2005, construction 2006–2010

Bank of Chianti Fiorentino, Sambuca Val di Pesa (Florence)
Client: Bank of Chianti Fiorentino, Sambuca Val di Pesa (Florence)
Project design 1996–1998, construction 1999–2002

Assisted Housing Facility, Poggibonsi (Siena)
RSA with 60 beds + 15 at day care centre
Client: National Health Service Agency 7, Siena
Project design 1999, construction 2001–2005

MAIN WORKS CURRENTLY IN PROGRESS

MICAS - Malta International Contemporary Art Space, Floriana, Malta
with EMDP Ltd
Client: The Central Government Authority, for the Restoration directorate, Floriana, Malta
Project design 2017–2020, construction 2020–in progress

Region of Tuscany Institutional Office Center, the "Third Tower", Florence
1st prize in the competition for redevelopment of the area of the institutional office center of the Region of Tuscany
Client: Region of Tuscany
Project design 2023

Restoration of the former convent of the Discalced Carmelites, and conversion to university housing, Lecce
Client: ADISU Puglia, Bari
Technical and economic feasibility project, 2022–in progress

Expansion of the Regional Charity Hospital in Locarno, Switzerland
Client: EOC Cantonal Hospital Agency, Bellinzona, Switzerland
Preliminary project design 2022, definitive in progress

New urban development in Outapi, Namibia
Client: Camelthorn Business Ventures
Project design 2015–2018, construction 2020–in progress
Urban restoration of via Grande, Livorno
Client: city of Livorno
Technical and economic feasibility project 2022, definitive project 2023

R. Fucini Elementary School, Albinia (Grosseto)
Client: City of Orbetello (Grosseto)
Project design 2012–2018, construction 2020–in progress

Restoration of the Grand Hotel Milano, Brunate (Como)
Client: Tresorel srl
Project design 2013–2017, construction in progress

"The City of Education", Sarno (Salerno)
Scholastic complex, three high schools, cafeteria, library, gymnasium, auditorium
Project design 2001–2009; construction in progress

Swimming Pool Centre at San Bartolo a Cintoia, Florence
Client: Cassa di Risparmio di Firenze Foundation for the city of Florence
Project Design 2021–2023

Expansion of City Hospital, Lugano, Switzerland
Client: Cantonal Hospital Agency, Bellinzona, Switzerland
Preliminary project, definitive, executive 2017–2021

Reorganisation and New Entrance to the Library of the EUI European University Institute
Client: European University Institute EUI, Fiesole
Project Design 2017–2020

Expansion of the IH Italiana Hotel Florence, Florence
Client: Mediterranea srl
Project Design 2019

New Library of the Architecture Department in the former Murate prison, Florence
with Mariagrazia Eccheli
Client: University of Florence
Project Design 2004–2006

Luigi Andelini, Amir Asgari Daryan, Francesco Balducci, Vincenzo Balì, Silke Barth, Anna Bartolaccio, Alfonso Basilico, Roberto Basilico, Alberto Birindelli, Egle Borgia, Ilaria Brogi, Agnese Cacciamani, Valeria Cagnetta, Paolo Calimici, Marco Cannata, Arianna Carbone, Jacopo Carli, Aurora Cavaliere, Benedetta Cavaliere, Gianni Cinali, Maddalena Coccagna, Stefano Combet, Maria Antonietta Corrias, Sheyla Cosentino, Piero D'Agostino, Jan De Clercq, Félicia De La Tullaye, Germana De Michelis, Elisabetta Dini, Francesco Fanfani, Giuseppina Fantozzi, Elena Fei, Sofia Fondelli, Giovanni Galanti, Daniele Galliani, Gilda Giacchi, Vanessa Giandonati, Daniele Grieco, Debora Guerini, Alessandra Guerreschi, Kine Haugen, Fabio Iocco, Serena Jaff, Azin Khaleghi, Alba Lamacchia, Ferruccio Loni, Marina Mancini, Valentina Mansi, Francesco Martella, Mara Marton, Dania Marzo, Elena Mastrangelo, Francesco Matucci, Francesco Messina, Sandra Meštrović, Pino Mincolelli, Fabrizio Monaci, Giuseppe Monterisi, Maurizio Muraglia, Roberta Paganucci, Laura Panichi, Sebastiana Patania, Giulia Pellegrini, Maria Letizia Pennetta, Stefano Piluso, Massimo Quadri, Costanza Quentin, Ramona Ribolini, Sara Riggi, Felix Rodriguez, Mirko Romagnoli, Arianna Sardone, Silvia Scarponi, Mario Sturma, Franca Tartaglia, J. Miguel Ternero Gil, Patrizia Toscano, Roberto Trebo, Livio Valente, Juan Carlos Van Den Hende, Andrea Vanni, Barbara Vanni, Anouk van Oordt, Stefania Verdigi, Luigi Vessella, Julia Voormann, Lennart Wiechell, Leonardo Zaffi

Barbara Antonelli, Rita Baldini, Maximiliano Basso Benelli , Oscar Benaim, Giulia Berti, Dalton Bertini Ruas, Sofia Maria Bluthgen, Stefania Cangini, Paolo Capacciola, Francesco Cerri, Alessio Cosentino, Giacomo De Biasio, Fabrizio Dei, Filippo Dozzi, Martino Duni, Marco Fabri, Ekaterina Foutaki, Roberta Germano, Alida Ghiandoni, Maximiliano Luis Giusti, Maire Kiely, Anna Kuljis, Massimo Le Pera, Michele Longo, Sofia Lorenzini, Andrea Magrini, Miliça Maras, Juan Patricio Marenco, Giulio Margheri, Matteo Mastrandrea, Federico Mazzoli, Diego Manuel Novo Menéndez, Philippos Michael, Vincenzo Moschetti, Keiko Nakamura, Giovina Natale, Serena Nenciarini, Giovanni Neri Serneri, George Oranye, Antonio Panetta, Marcella Panetta, Thiresia Papakonstatinou, Annarita Papeschi, Cesare Pergola, Antonia Placanica, Alessia Plini, Michelangelo Poli, Eleonora Righetto, Sissi Roselli, Roberta Russi, Maria Sanchez Guerrero, Saverio Simoncini, Alessandra Sirianni, Corrado Sortino, Eleonora Stella, Marta Stojani, Luca Tedeschi, Elena Terzi, Antonio Teti, Alessandro Travascio, Marcel Verda, Victoria Veselovskaya, Dante Vinciguerra, Enrico Viviani, Leo von Caprivi, Giovanni Voto, Anka Vujanovic, Francesco Woudenberg, Katia Zizzi

MAIN PUBLICATIONS ABOUT IPOSTUDIO

V.P. Mosco, "Viaggio in Italia. Architetture e città", in *The Plan*, 2021.

M. Mulazzani, *Campus Firenze. Un progetto di Ipostudio*, Electa architettura, Milan 2020.

M. Costanzo, *Viaggio nell'architettura italiana del 3° millennio*, Edizioni Efesto, Rome 2019.

"Identità dell'architettura italiana" 3rd to 17th National Convention, Edizioni Diabasis, Parma 2005-2022.

S. Redecke, "Brunelleschi und Stradivari, Golden Tore fur das Findelhaus", in *Bauwelt*, Germany 2017.

K. de Barañano, "Elogio del palimpsesto. Dos museos en Florencia, [Two Exemplary Rehabs in Florence]" in *Arquitectura Viva*, no. 196, Spain 2017.

M. Mulazzani, *L'Ospedale degli Innocenti di Firenze. La fabbrica brunelleschiana, gli Innocenti dal quattrocento al novecento, il nuovo museo*, Electa architettura, Milan 2016.

F. Dal Co, M. Mulazzani, "Firenze, il museo degli Innocenti di Carlo Terpolilli, Ipostudio", in *Casabella*, no. 865, 2016.

A. Natalini, "24 giugno, giorno di san Giovanni patrono di Firenze: una visita al Museo degli Innocenti", in *Casabella* no. 865, 2016.

J. Stammer, *Dentro Firenze*, Maschietto Editore, Florence 2014.

M. Biraghi, S. Micheli, *Storia dell'architettura italiana, 1985-2015*, Einaudi, Turin 2013.

M. Mulazzani, *Ipostudio, la concretezza della modernità*, Documenti di architettura (174), Electa architettura, Milan 2008.

Ipostudio, M. Galantino e W. Tscholl, in *Novoli da periferia a città. Le trasformazioni urbane di Firenze*, edited by M. Biagi, Electa architettura, Milano 2008.

F. Fabbrizzi, *Opere e progetti di scuola fiorentina, 1968-2008*, Hoepli Editore, Milan 2008.

F. Purini, *La misura italiana dell'architettura*, Editori Laterza, Bari 2008.

F. Fabbrizzi, *Topografie. Linguaggi di architettura ambientale*, Alinea, Florence 2008.

Ospedali di Comunità: Montalcino, in B. Turillazzi, *Edilizia sanitaria territoriale: il progetto e la realizzazione di strutture sanitarie destinate all'assistenza, la cura palliativa e la lungodegenza: residenze sanitarie assistenziali, hospice e ospedali di comunità*, Maggioli editore, Santarcangelo di Romagna 2007.

IPOSTUDIO architetture, Libria, Melfi 1997.

LIST OF WORKS

1.1 EXTENDING THE CITY ALL THE WAY TO THE WATERFRONT
Redevelopment of the waterfront, Messina
With V. Melluso/Mellusoarchitettura, Benno Albrecht, Bodàr Bottega d'Architettura
International Competition
Competition commission: City of Messina
Hydraulic Infrastructures: HydroSoil srl
Energy: Alberto Bizzarri
Structures: AEI Progetti srl
Systems: Consilium srl
Landscape: MMAA Studio Manfroni&Associati
2011

1.2 NORTH-SOUTH, EAST-WEST... BRINGING ORDER TO WHAT WAS BROKEN, DIVIDED, FRAGMENTED
Recovery of the Spreebogen area, Berlin
International Competition
Competition commission: Federal Republic of German and Land Berlin

1.3 A NEW DISTRICT, RISING ON NEW GROUND
Residential complex on the site of the former "Tuscan Wolves" barracks, Florence
Competition of ideas
Competition Commission: City of Florence, Area of Urban Development Coordination
2016

1.4 TO EACH HIS OWN HOME, LIKE A CHARM BRACELET
Living at Milano/2, Milan
International Design Competition Living at Milano/2
Area of via Civitavecchia: shortlisted project
Competition Commission: Municipal Administration of Milan
2005

1.5 SMALL TOWERS RISE ABOVE THE GUTTER LINE
Flaminio Project, District of the City of Science, Rome
With Francesco Messina
Design Competition
Competition Commission: Municipal Administration of Rome, CDP Investimenti Sgr
2015

1.6 EXCAVATING ROOMS IN THE OPEN AIR
Urban park on the former Boschetti area, Padua
With Francesco Messina
Design Competition
Competition Commission: City of Padua
2015

2.1 ATTEMPTING TO DETACH THE SHADOW FROM THE GROUND!
New provincial headquarters, Arezzo
With Jan De Clercq, Camilla Curzio, Michele Dota, Francesco Matucci
European Design Competition, 2nd prize
Competition Commission: Provincial Administration of Arezzo
2005

2.2 FLOATING ABOVE A PARK
"La Romanina" school complex, Rome
With Massimiliano Rendina
International Competition "Three schools in Rome", selection to the second stage
Competition Commission: Municipal Administration of Rome
2004

2.3 IN PLACE OF THE WALLS AROUND THE ROOMS, OPEN SPACE
Daegu Gosan Public Library, Daegu, South Korea
Design Competition
Competition Commission: Daegu Metropolitan City Suseong-gu Office
2012

2.4 A CASTLE APPEARS, SUDDENLY, ADMIST THE MULTITUDE OF HOUSES
Region of Sicily Office Centre, Palermo
With João Nunes PROAP and V. Melluso/Mellusoarchitettura
Design Competition
Competition Commission: Region of Sicily
2020

2.5 SKATING AMONGST THE ICICLES ABOVE GROUND LEVEL
National Museum at Vestbanen, Oslo
Design Competition
Competition Commission: Ministry of Culture of the Norwegian Government
2009

2.6 SHELTER AND PROTECTION FOR BOOKS, TREES, PEOPLE
BEIC European Library of Information and Culture, Milan
With Eutropia Architettura, Bodàr Bottega d'Architettura, João Nunes PROAP
Design Competition
Competition Commission: City of Milan and B.E.I.C. Foundation
Renderings: Slim Studio

Structures: AEI Progetti srl
Systems: Aicom spa
2022

3.1 INSIDE THE MURATE... BOOKS INSTEAD OF FELONS
New library of Architecture, Florence
With Maria Grazia Eccheli
Client: University of Florence
Structures: Andrea Vignoli
Systems: Enzo Giusti
Economic Analyses: Michele Dota
2006

3.2 THE DESIRE TO LEAVE EVERYTHING AS IT IS AND THE DESIRE TO CHANGE
Citadel of assisted living, Riva del Garda
Day Centre, Service Centre and Assisted Living Facility
With Manuela Baldracchi
Competition in two stages, 3rd prize
Competition Commission: Public Agency for Personal Services, City of Riva
Structures: AEI Progetti srl
Systems: Consilium srl
2010

3.3 NEVER TO BE FORGOTTEN!
MEIS, Italian National Jewish and Shoah Museum, Ferrara
With André Benaim, Eugenio Vassallo, Michele Dota
Design Competition, first project mentioned
Competition Commission: MiBAC Emilia Romagna Region
Structures: AEI Progetti srl
Systems: Consilium srl
2010

3.4 LIKE A MATRYOSHKA
P.L. Nervi Stadium and Campo di Marte, Florence
With Eutropia Architettura
Competition in two stages, 3rd prize
Competition Commission: City of Florence
Structures: Pini Group Italia, srl
Systems: Consilium srl
Renderings: QuattroTerzi Lab
2022

3.5 NOTHING BUT A DIAPHRAGM SEPARATES US
Aluartforum, Zagreb, Croazia
Academy of Fine Arts Gallery
With Sandra Meštrović, Vlatka Rajčić
Design Competition
Competition Commission: Udruženju hrvatskih arhitekata (UHA)
2014

3.6 HOPING, WAITING FOR THE SOLUTION, AND MEANWHILE THIS PLACE RECEIVES ME
Expansion of S.M.A. Hospital, Bagno a Ripoli
With Riccardo Bartoloni, RED architetti associati
Competition Commission: National Health Service Agency 10, Florence
Client: Cooperativa Edil-Strade Imolese
Structures: AEI Progetti srl
Systems: Tecnoengineering srl, Sergio Giuseppini
2012

3.7 TRYING TO MEASURE UP
Pedestrian bridge over the Valley of the Temples, Agrigento
With Bodàr Bottega d'Architettura
Competition of ideas, selection for the second stage
Competition Commission: Region of Sicily, Regional Council of Cultural and Environmental Legacies and of the Sicilian Identity, Archeological and Scenic Park of the Valley of the Temples of Agrigento
2013

3.8 OVER A BRIDGE
Expansion of the OBV Hospital, Mendrisio, Switzerland
Competition in two stages, 2nd prize
Competition Commission: EOC Cantonal Hospital Agency
Structures: AEI Progetti srl
Systems: Visani Rusconi Talleri, Erisel, Ufficio Consulenza Energia
2015

3.9 AN EXHIBITION SPACE IN THE SQUARE
Library and municipal services, Brescia
Competition of ideas, 3rd prize
Competition Commission: City of Brescia
2009

4.1 REFLECTING IN THE LAGOON
Cà' Venier dei Leoni, Venice
With Emilio Bria, Mario Manfroni
International competition "Venice Project", project selected and exhibited at the "Third International Architecture Exhibition" of the Venice Biennale
Competition Commission: The Venice Biennale
1985

4.2 UNDER FULL SAIL IN SEARCH OF THE SUN RATHER THAN THE WIND
Science Centre, Naples
With Francesco Messina
Design Competition
Competition Commission: IDIS City of Science

Foundation, Federation of Association of Architects and Engineers
2015

4.3 WHEN THE SHIPS REMAINED AT ANCHOR IN THE HARBOUR, AWAITING THE TIDE
Royal Library, Copenhagen
International Competition
Competition Commission: Danish Culture Ministry, City of Copenhagen, Federation of Danish Architects
1993

4.4 MEASURING OURSELVES AGAINST THE VAST HORIZONS OF VENETIAN TERRITORY
Office Complex, Porto Marghera
International Competition, second stage, 5th prize
Competition Commission: APV Holding, Port Authority of Venice
Structures: AEI Progetti srl
Systems: Consilium srl
Economic and Security Analyses: Michele Dota
2003

4.5 RISING FROM THE SEA, SHE TURNS TO STONE
New IUAV campus headquarters, Venice
International Competition, second stage, 5th prize
Competition Commission: IUAV University of Venice Institute of Architecture
1998

4.6 A FOREST OF MASTS AND RIGGINGS
Tourist port, Piombino
Client: Tourist Port of the Archipelago srl
Investment advisor: Marte Marine srl
Engineering and sea works: HydroSoil srl
2012

4.7 TOUCHING THE SKY WITH MUSIC IN OUR EARS
Landmark Tower/U2 Studio, Dublin
Design Competition
Competition Commission: Dublin City Council, Dublin Docklands
2003

4.8 UNEXPECTED COUNTERPOINT ACROSS THE RIVER
Ponte della Musica, Rome
International competition "Two pedestrian bridges on the Tiber", project selection
Competition Commission: Municipal Administration of Rome
Structures: Gipieffe Architettura, AEI Progetti srl
Systems: Consilium srl
2000

4.9 TURNING POETRY INTO BARCODE
Guggenheim Museum, Helsinki
Design Competition
Competition Commission: Solomon R. Guggenheim Foundation, State of Finland, City of Helsinki
2014

5.1 PAUSING TO STROLL AMONG THE RUINS...
Prenestina zone on the A1 Milan/Naples motorway
National Competition, 1st prize
Competition Commission: Società Autostrade spa
1988

5.2 STANDING ON THE ROOFTOP FOR AN EXTRAORDINARY VIEW OF THE SEA
New Regional Council headquarters, Bari
With Politecnica, Netti Architetti, Stefano Serpenti
International Competition
Competition Commission: Region of Puglia.
2003

5.3 ENTERING FROM THE TOP TO DESCEND AND UNEXPECTEDLY DECIDE THAT YOU ARE HOME
University Housing, Monteluce, Perugia
With Paolo Belardi, Alessio Burini
Design Competition
Competition Commission: A.DI.S.U., University Agency for the Right to Study, Region of Umbria
Structures: AEI Progetti srl
Systems: Setingegneria srl
Economic and Security Analyses: Michele Dota
2007

5.4 IN THE BACKGROUND, INEXORABLY, THE GREAT MAIELLA
Office Centre, Atessa
Client: Europiemme srl
Structures: AEI Progetti srl
Economic Analyses: Michele Dota
2007

5.5 A GARDEN ON THE ROOF, WITH ETNA IN THE BACKGROUND
New Hospital, Siracusa
With Emanuele Fidone, Bruno Messina, Tommaso Bartoloni
Competition of ideas
Competition Commission: Region of Sicily, ASP Siracusa
Structures: AEI Progetti srl

Systems: MAIN Management e Ingegneria srl
2020

5.6 AN AQUEDUCT IN THE EMILIA COUNTRYSIDE
Office Centre, Parma
With Politecnica, STS, Celestino Porrino
Competition in two stages, 3rd prize
Competition Commission: City of Parma
2009

5.7 A HILL IN THE MIDDLE OF THE PLAIN
New Hospital, Cesena
With AEI Progetti, CSPE
Open tendering procedure
Competition Commission: National Health Service Agency of Romagna
Structures: AEI Progetti srl
Systems: Studio TI Ingegneria & Architettura srl
2019

5.8 INSIDE THE HILL, DEEP IN THE SOIL
Stadium, Siena
International Competition
Competition Commission: City of Siena
Structures: AEI Progetti srl
Systems: Politecnica scrl
2003

6.1 NEITHER INSIDE NOR OUT
Headquarters of the professional associations of engineers and architects, Bari
National Competition
Competition Commission: Regional Association of Engineers and Architects of Puglia
1992

6.2 NOW YOU SEE IT, NOW YOU DON'T
Italian Pavilion EXPO 2010, Shanghai
Design Competition, project mentioned
Competition Commission: General Government Commission for the Universal Exposition of Shanghai 2010
2008

6.3 IT STARTED FROM A COPY, WITH A DIFFERENT INTENT
University Library at "La Sapienza", Rome
Design Competition
Competition Commission: Ministry of Infrastructures and Transportation, University of Rome, "La Sapienza" campus
Structures: AEI Progetti srl
Systems: MAIN Management e Ingegneria srl
2021

6.4 SOMETHING OF A CHALLENGE TO FLORENCE'S GRAND PALACES
Office building at Novoli, Florence
Former Fiat Plan site recovery plan for the western area
Client: Immobiliare Novoli srl
Structures: Massimo Vivoli
Systems: Raul Tassinelli
2008

7.1 IT LOOKS LIKE ANYTHING COULD HAPPEN HERE
50 churches for Rome 2000, Tor Tre Teste, Rome
European Competition, project mentioned
Competition Commission: Vicariate of Rome
Structures: Carlo Blasi
1994

7.2 LIKE A VIKING SHIP ABOUT TO SET SAIL
Church at Våler, Norway
With André Benaim
Design Competition
Competition Commission: Parish church of Våler
2012

7.3 LIFTING OFF ON A DOVE'S WINGS
New parochial church, Cibeno di Carpi
Competition by invitation, 2nd prize
Competition Commission: Dioceses of Carpi
Liturgist: Mons. Giuseppe Busani
Economic Analyses: Michele Dota
2007

7.4 WHAT'S GOING ON HERE?... GO INSIDE AND FIND OUT!
Parochial Complex of Varignano, Viareggio
International Competition in two stages, 2nd prize
Competition Commission: Archdiocese of Lucca
Artistic Mosaic: Roberto Giovannelli
Liturgist: Don Luca Bongini
Structures: AEI Progetti srl
Systems: M&E Impianti srl
2015

7.5 IN THE SHELTER OF A BLUE MANTLE
Presbytery of the Basilica-Sanctuary of Santa Maria dei Miracoli, Casalbordino
Client: Benedictine Brothers of the Basilica-Santa Maria dei Miracoli Sanctuary
2014

THANKS

To Lucia, my partner in life and in my work,
to my companions at Ipostudio, with whom I've shared 40 years of life and work,
to those who are still there and those who have gone

To Anna Bartolaccio, with whom I started this adventure,
and to Ilaria Brogi, who concluded it with me,
and also,
to Alessia Plini, Marta Stojani and Sofia Lorenzini,
who gathered and selected the material that went into this book

To Paolo Terpolilli and his suggestions for the introduction to the book

To the long-time secretary of Ipostudio, Elisabetta Dini,
and to young Aurora Cavaliere

To Vincenzo Balì, Agnese Cacciamani, Arianna Carbone, Stefano Combet, Alessandra Guerreschi, Azin Khaleghi, Francesco Martella, Laura Panichi, the current staff of Ipostudio

And finally,
to Alice... my cat

Forma Edizioni Srl
Firenze, Italia
redazione@formaedizioni.it
www.formaedizioni.it

Editorial director
Laura Andreini

Editorial staff
Maria Giulia Caliri
Monica Giannini
Giulia Turini

Graphic design
Deepa Parapatt

Translations
Katherine Fay

Photolitography
Forma Edizioni

Paper
Fedrigoni Arena White Smooth 120 grs

Texts
© Carlo Terpolilli

Iconography
© Ipostudio architetti

Photographic credits
Savorelli e associati: pp. 61, 98, 99, 278
Studio Rendina: pp. 68, 69
Davide Virdis: pp. 167, 168, 169, 200, 201, 217, 218, 219

First edition: May 2023
ISBN 9 788855 211550

This volume was printed in May 2023
by Lito Terrazzi, Prato, Italy